The Septuagint Translation of Jeremiah and Baruch

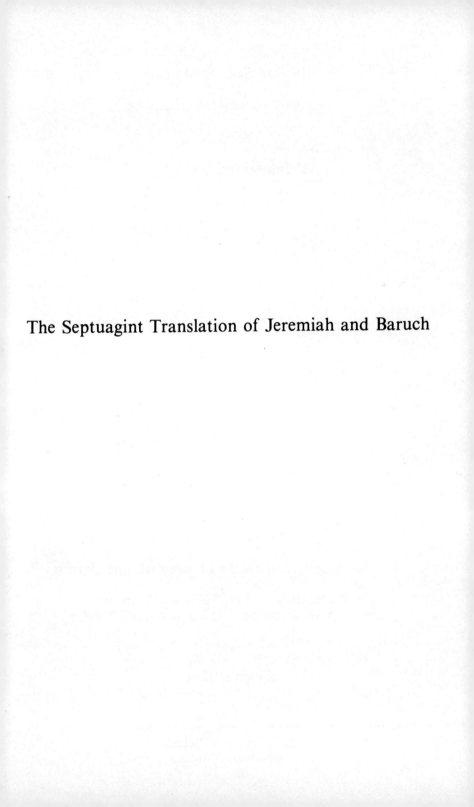

Harvard Semitic Museum

Harvard Semitic Monographs

Edited by

Frank Moore Cross, Jr.

Number 8

The Septuagint Translation of Jeremiah and Baruch

A Discussion of an Early Revision of
the LXX of Jeremiah 29-52 and Baruch 1:1-3:8

by

Emanuel Tov

SCHOLARS PRESS
Missoula, Montana

The Septuagint Translation of Jeremiah and Baruch

A Discussion of an Early Revision of
the LXX of Jeremiah 29-52 and Baruch 1:1-3:8

by

Emanuel Tov

Published by

SCHOLARS PRESS

for

Harvard Semitic Museum

Distributed by

SCHOLARS PRESS
University of Montana
Missoula, Montana 59801

The Septuagint Translation of Jeremiah and Baruch

A Discussion of an Early Revision of
the LXX of Jeremiah 29-52 and Baruch 1:1-3:8

by

Emanuel Tov

Library of Congress Cataloging in Publication Data

Tov, Emanuel
　The Septuagint translation of Jeremiah and Baruch.

　(Harvard Semitic monographs ; no. 8)
　A revision of the author's thesis, Hebrew University,
1973.
　Bibliography: p.
　Includes indexes.
　1. Bible. O.T. Jeremiah. Greek. Septuagint—
Criticism, Textual. 2. Bible. O.T. Apocrypha. Baruch.
Greek. Septuagint—Criticism, Textual. I. Title.
II. Series.
BS1524.G7S45　1975　　224'.2'06　　75-43872
ISBN 0-89130-070-8

Printed in United States of America
1 2 3 4 5
EDWARDS BROTHERS, INC.
ANN ARBOR, MICHIGAN 48104

To Lika

To Ophirah, Ariel and Amitay

PREFACE

Old Testament textual criticism has become a highly spe-
cialized branch of research. Therefore I need not apologize
for presenting this study which illuminates, hopefully, merely
a corner of Septuagint research.

The present monograph grew out of my doctoral dissertation
of the same title. Some sections of the dissertation were
omitted, others rewritten, while little new material was added
in its revised form.

The bulk of the research for my dissertation was performed
during the years 1967-69 at Harvard University. The dissertation was submitted to the Hebrew University in January 1973 and
accepted in July of the same year. The manuscript of this book
was completed in the summer of 1973, while some alterations
were inserted in the summer of 1975. At that time I also added
some bibliographical references.

It is a very pleasant duty to express my thanks to all
those who guided my research, criticized my work and helped me
in other ways. First of all, the two mentors of my thesis,
Prof. S. Talmon of the Hebrew University and Prof. F. M. Cross,
Jr., of Harvard University criticized my argumentation and for-
mulations and in this way helped me to crystallize my thoughts
in a better way. Some scholars were kind enough to read earlier drafts of this book and to comment on matters of detail. I
am grateful to Prof. J. Strugnell of Harvard University, Prof.
I. Soisalon-Soininen of Helsinki, Dr. M. Stone of the Hebrew
University and Mrs. S. Ory of the Hebrew University Bible Pro-
ject.

I should like to thank Prof. I. L. Seeligmann and Prof. M.
Goshen-Gottstein of the Hebrew University for the many methodological insights I learned from them in the course of the years.

Prof. F. M. Cross, Jr. was kind enough to suggest this
monograph for publication to the Scholars Press. I am grateful
to the director, Prof. R. W. Funk, to the production manager,
and to the manuscript typist, Joann Burnich, for their efforts
and fine work.

I dedicate this book to my dear wife and children. They made it easier for me to perform the research and to write this book by creating an atmosphere in which it was pleasant to live and work.

September 1975
Jerusalem, Sukkot 5736

C O N T E N T S

CHAPTER I

INTRODUCTION

1. *A Review of the History of Research*
into the LXX of Jer

—— The Septuagint translation of Jeremiah (Jer-LXX) is best
known for its many differences from the Masoretic Text (MT),
both in length and in arrangement of the text. In fact, it is
the classical example for differences of this kind, and the
problem of its relationship to MT has therefore been much discussed by scholars. It is our understanding that the majority
of the LXX's differences from MT in length and arrangement reflect a Hebrew *Vorlage* different from MT. Recently this view
was defended by J. G. Janzen as well as by the present writer.[1]
The present study, however, will not deal with the mentioned
discrepancies between MT and the LXX.

—— In addition to the problem of the relationship between
Jer-LXX and MT, the Greek translation offers the scholar a certain amount of *inner*-Greek problems, i.e., problems which have
no direct bearing on the question of which Hebrew text the
translator used. The most important inner-Greek problem is
that of the relationship between the different sections of the
book. For it has been recognized that lexical differences between chapters 1-28 and 29-52 exist, and, as a result, it has
been assumed practically unanimously that two different translators participated in the Greek translation of Jer. The aim
of the present study is to question the scholarly consensus on
this matter and at the same time to propose a new way of understanding the relationship between the two parts of the book.
Firstly, however, it is necessary to summarize the various
opinions which have been expressed on the problem at issue:

—— The two-translator theory of the Septuagint version of
Jeremiah is connected with the name of H. St. J. Thackeray,
who, at the beginning of this century, was the first scholar to
develop an elaborate theory on the problem in question. He had,
however, not started *ex nihilo*. The literature preceding him
contained various statements on the special character of this

translation. In fact, all the scholars who had seriously investigated Jer-LXX, with the exception of Kühl,[2] noted its pe-
culiarities. Spohn, for example, realized as early as 1794
that several Hebrew words were "inconsistently" reproduced in
Greek;[3]/e.g., both the recurring phrase כה אמר ה' and נוה are
represented in Jer-LXX by various translations. The first
phrase, for example, was rendered 61 times by τάδε λέγει κύριος
and 72 times by οὕτως εἶπε κύριος (for precise details concerning כה אמר ה', see chapter III, example 18 and for נוה, see
III 48). Spohn mentioned the possibility that the lexical variation resulted from the occasional insertion in the manuscripts of Jer-LXX of readings culled from "another translation."[4] Although he did not elaborate on this assumption, he
probably referred to Aquila, Symmachus or Theodotion.

——Frankl[5] appears to have been the first scholar to hypothe-
size seriously multiple authorship for Jer-LXX./ His assumption
was based on the various renditions of מגור מסביב (III 16) and
of דמן (III 13). Workman,[6] Streane[7] and Kneucker[8] later expressed the same theory.

——Even though some scattered remarks on multiple authorship
had been made, no one had attempted to analyze the situation in
depth. Thackeray was the first scholar to do so. In 1903 he
found that a substantial number of Hebrew words were rendered
in the first part of Jer differently from their regular equivalent in the second part.[9] This discovery led him to assume
that two different translators (named by him Jer. α' and Jer. β')
were responsible for Jer 1-28 and 29-51 (following the LXX sequence of chapters) and also to suggest that chapter 52 was
rendered by yet a third translator (Jer. γ'). Only few data
could justify the assumption of a third translator, but Thackeray was able to draw up a rather impressive list of differences between the first and second translators. Thackeray recognized that Jer. α' and β' did not work in complete isolation,
since he found a certain amount of agreement between them.
Thackeray made two additional suggestions: He proposed that
Jer. α', the Minor Prophets and Ezekiel (or part of that book)
were translated by one translator. Furthermore, he discovered
that the second translator of Jer was also responsible for the

translation of the first part of the apocryphal book of Baruch
(1:1-3:8).[10]

In his subsequent publications,[11] Thackeray elaborated upon his own views on Jer-LXX and introduced various major and
minor changes. He also developed similar theories of multiple
authorship for the Septuagint versions of Ezekiel and 1-4
Reigns.[12] Indeed, Thackeray is the "father" of theories of
multiple authorship for the individual books of the LXX since
he was the first scholar to demarcate precisely the boundaries
of each translation unit in a given book. For each book Thackeray provided lists of lexical differences between its individual sections and he also discussed the relationship between
each section and other books of the LXX. It is natural that a
theory such as Thackeray's would be applied by scholars to other books as well. Indeed, the bibliography on this topic is
extensive, so that it may suffice merely to indicate the books
for which a theory of multiple authorship has been suggested:
the Pentateuch as a whole as well as Genesis and Numbers, Josh-
ua, 1-4 Reigns, Psalms, the Minor Prophets as a whole as well
as Amos, Isaiah, Jeremiah, Baruch, Ezekiel and Daniel.

Since the days of Thackeray, it has been taken for granted
that differences in vocabulary between two or more sections of
a book suffice to prove multiple authorship. However, the ra-
tionale behind the theories of multiple authorship has never
been proven. Epiphanius' testimony about the thirty-six pairs
of translators translating the whole Bible into Greek[13] at best
supports a theory that books were rendered by pairs or small
groups of translators who cooperated. Certainly it cannot be
taken to support a theory of the bisection of books for purposes of translation; it should, in fact, be stressed that we
lack any external evidence supporting theories of multiple authorship. Therefore, opponents of such theories naturally
turned to the very data on which these were based. Discussion
has especially centered on the books of the Prophets and 1-4
Reigns, which make the best "case" for multiple authorship.

While Thackeray's theory on 1-4 Reigns has been strongly
questioned and his views on Ezekiel have been undermined,[14] the
LXX of Jeremiah has not been restudied. The reason the problem
of the multiple authorship of Jeremiah has never been

reinvestigated is the fact that, of all the books for which theories of multiple authorship have been suggested, the case is probably strongest for Jeremiah.[15] But although the problem has not been studied as a whole, important contributions have been made by several scholars who studied some of Thackeray's criteria for the distinction between Jer α' and Jer β' and deduced new ones. Such work was done by Redpath,[16] Köhler,[17] Baudissin,[18] Ziegler,[19], Martin,[20], Soisalon-Soininen,[21] and Walters.[22] Other scholars merely expressed their agreement with Thackeray's views without studying the evidence independently.[23] Only Baudissin[24] and Soisalon-Soininen[25] raised doubts about the correctness of Thackeray's views, but both were aware of the very limited scope of the investigations leading to their criticism.

2. *The Purpose and Content of the Present Study*

Thackeray's main contribution to the research on Jer-LXX was the discovery of a pattern which accounted for the distribution of differing renditions of the same Hebrew word within Jer-LXX. Furthermore, his list of examples is impressive, and in recent decades some evidence has been published (see notes 16-22) which seems to corroborate his views. Only one hesitantly dissident remark of Ziegler, well concealed in a footnote, questions the validity of Thackeray's thesis as a whole:

> "Mann muss Thack. zustimmen; nur müsste noch
> genauer untersucht werden, ob wirklich zwei Über-
> setzer beteiligt waren oder bloss ein Redaktor
> am Werk war, der den einen Teil nur überarbeitete.
> Es kann nämlich beobachtet werden, dass sich in
> der ganzen Ier.-LXX einheitliche Züge finden, die
> sie von anderen Büchern abheben" (Ziegler, "Ein-
> leitung," 128, n. 1).

While not agreeing with the details of Ziegler's proposal, the present writer concurs with Ziegler in the observation that similarities between the two parts of Jer considerably weaken Thackeray's thesis. Thackeray recognized only a few of these important similarities, and it was probably because of this fact that he attributed them to secondary factors. At different times he provided different explanations:

1.   Jer. β' imitated Jer. α' ("Gr.Tr.Jer.", 253-4).

2.   Later redactors or scribes were responsible for "a certain amount of mixture of the two styles" (*ib*., 254).

3.   The similarities resulted from "imperfect collaboration of two workers, the second of whom only partially followed the lead of the first" (*Septuagint*, 35).

In chapter II we shall discuss these suggestions in deatil. It seems to us that Thackeray's explanations of the agreements cannot be sustained. Moreover, it is very questionable methodology to assign important agreements between two sections of one and the same book to a secondary factor. Rather, they bear witness to a first translation of Jer. After all, the most obvious explanation of idiosyncracies common to two parts of the same book is that they stem from the original translator. Furthermore, the nature of many of the similarities is such that they cannot have arisen secondarily. If we succeed in demonstrating the incorrectness of Thackeray's explanations, it seems to us that the following alternative view should be considered correct by implication:

    Since there exist important similarities between the two sections of Jer which distinguish them from the remainder of the LXX, it may be suggested that these renditions point to the first translation, to be called the Old Greek (OG) translation of Jer. If this assumption be correct, the present differences between the two sections of the book can only be accounted for by postulating a revision of the OG, now preserved only in part. The revisional character of many renditions in the second part of Jer (chapters 29-52) suggests that it is this section which has been retouched. The assumed revision aimed at a more precise and consistent rendering of the Hebrew.

    A working hypothesis designed to account for the special character of Jer-LXX is outlined in the next paragraphs. This hypothesis will be substantiated, step by step, in chapters II-VI:

One translator was responsible for the Old Greek translation of the book of Jer and apparently also of Bar 1:1-3:8.
This OG translation is preserved in its original form in Jer
1-28 (Jer a'), but it has been lost in chapters 29-52 (Jer b').
At a later time, the OG of Jer[26] was reworked by an unknown reviser to be designated Jer-R.[27] This revision probably
included the whole of the OG version, but is now extant only
for Jer b'. Interestingly enough, the first part of the Greek
translation of the apocryphal book of Baruch (1:1-3:8) was submitted to the same revision.[28]

Important agreements between Jer a' and b' indicate some
of the elements of the lost OG of Jer b' which have not been
touched by the reviser. In other words, the present form of
Jer b' is composed of two strata: a substratum (the lost OG)
which may sometimes be recognized, and a second stratum con-
sisting of the revisional elements inserted by Jer-R.

In the process of proving the validity of the working hypothesis, a certain amount of circular reasoning cannot be
avoided. However, some of the assumptions utilized from the
very beginning will be substantiated further on in this study.[29]

The reader will note that the suggestions set forth in the
working hypothesis meet with some difficulties: (1) The question of what may be expected from a revision of the LXX; (2)
the inconsistency of Jer-R's revision; (3) the question of why
the revision of Jer-R has been preserved only in Jer b'. Questions (1) and (2) are discussed on pp. 21-22 and question (3)
on p. 23.

Our explanations of these difficulties may or may not be
correct. In any event, we prefer the uneasy assumption out-
lined above over the "easy" two-translator theory suggested by
Thackeray: It seems to us that the agreements between the two
sections of Jer (chapter II) are of such a nature that the two-
translator theory cannot be sustained.

We shall now outline the contents of chapters II-VII:
Several important similarities between Jer a' and b' distinguish both sections from the remainder of the LXX. These
similarities are listed in ch. II under two headings:
(1) unique and rare *renditions*, (2) rare Greek *words*. While

recognizing a few of the striking agreements between Jer a'
and b', Thackeray contended that they resulted from a secondary
factor, such as imperfect collaboration between the translators
Jer. α' and Jer. β'. However, owing to both methodological considerations and to unacceptable presuppositions by Thackeray,
this assumption cannot be sustained. The evidence can only be
accounted for by assuming that similarities between Jer a' and
b' point to the existence of a complete OG translation for Jer,
which is preserved in Jer a' in its pure form and is recognizable as the substratum of Jer b'.

   Differences between Jer a' and b' in the translation of
the same Hebrew word are the subject of chapters III and IV.
   Chapter III deals with different renditions of the same
Hebrew word, which relate to each other as an original (i.e.,
the rendition found in Jer a') to its revision (i.e., the rendition found in Jer b'). It is postulated that the renditions
in Jer b' replaced earlier renditions identical to those now
found in Jer a'. Jer-R and the underlying OG text in Jer b'
therefore probably related to each other as Jer b' to Jer a'.
   That Jer-R was related to Jer-OG as a reviser to the original translation is made probable by a discussion of the following tendencies of Jer-R:

1.   Jer-R replaced some renditions of Jer-OG with renditions
     which, in his opinion, better expressed the meaning of the
     Hebrew.

2.   Jer-R corrected some erroneous renditions of Jer-OG.

3.   Jer-R tended to prefer certain stereotyped (literal) ren-
     ditions rather than the non-stereotyped (free) ones of
     Jer-OG.

4.   Jer-R replaced some earlier renditions of Jer-OG with ren-
     ditions which were meant to reflect the Hebrew in a more
     consistent fashion.

5.   Jer-R revised Jer-OG in other ways.

   Appendix 1 to ch. III discusses the alternative hypothesis that Jer a', and not Jer b', embodies a revision, although
of a different character. Appendix 2 deals with Thackeray's

tentative proposal that ch. 52 incorporates a third translation unit (Jer. γ').

While chapter III deals with renditions of Jer a' and Jer b' which show a basically different treatment of the Hebrew *Vorlage*, chapter IV lists examples of different renditions in Jer a' and b' which do not differ in tendency. Since the listed renditions are also found concurrently in the LXX, without any discernible grammatical or contextual factor determining the occurrence of one rather than the other, we suggest calling them "synonymous renditions". From a translator's point of view, they are synonymous representations of the same Hebrew word.

While the examples of chapter III are supposed to demonstrate that Jer b' has been revised, the examples of chapter IV can also be taken as proof of a two-translator theory. However, since the revisers of the LXX are also known to have replaced earlier renditions with synonymous ones, the data provided in this chapter can be accommodated to our working hypothesis.

An appendix to this chapter uses the data collected in chapters III and IV in order to pinpoint the exact dividing line between Jer a' and b', between chapters 28 and 29 of the Greek.

Chapter V deals exclusively with one section of Jer b', viz. the Greek translation of the underlying Hebrew of Bar 1:1-3:8. This chapter is intended to prove one of the presuppositions on which some of the examples of chapters II-IV were partially based, namely, that Bar 1:1-3:8 was revised by Jer-R.

The classification of the relevant data is rather complicated since several facts and assumptions must be considered. For example, one notes immediately that Jer-LXX and Bar share many peculiar renditions which distinguish both from the remainder of the LXX. Explanation of this phenomenon is complicated by the fact that the Hebrew *Vorlage* of Bar very frequently quoted the Hebrew text of Jer, so that secondary influences of the text of Jer-LXX on Bar such as revisional harmonization and imitation cannot be precluded. But such assumptions must be rejected after a closer look at the similarities between

Jer-LXX (always Jer b'!) and Bar which are found both within
and outside quotations from Jer b'. Since the latter group is
the larger one, later revisional activity becomes highly improbable. It is further recognized that all the similarities
between Bar and Jer-LXX are confined to Jer b', both in isolated renderings in Jer b' and Bar and in recurring renditions
which distinguish Jer b' as a whole from Jer a' (and the remainder of the LXX). The possibility that Bar imitated only
Jer b' and not Jer a' cannot be justified nor can any form of
secondary influence emanating from Jer b' on Bar be substantiated.

As a result, there cannot remain much doubt that Jer-R also retouched Bar 1:1-3:8. This assumption is further corroborated by the fact that Bar, even when quoting from Jer a', concurs with Jer-R, whenever the latter's vocabulary differs from
Jer-OG (Jer a').

Chapter VI deals with peculiar renditions and rare words
which distinguish Jer a', Ez and the Minor Prophets (MP) from
the remainder of the LXX. The nature and number of the examples adduced leads to the assumption that Jer a', Ez and the MP
were translated by one individual or else by one group. Since
he (they) produced a translation which we describe as the OG,
it follows by implication that the extant translations of Ez
and the MP also exhibit the OG version.[30] One should be aware
of the tentative character of the conclusions drawn in ch. VI,
since they are based on similarities between Jer a', Ez and the
MP which were met in the course of the study of Jer-LXX only.[31]

That the similarities between Jer a', Ez and the MP, as a
rule, are not found in Jer b' must probably be attributed to
Jer-R's replacement or elimination of these renditions in Jer
b'. Indeed, in several instances we can successfully trace the
renditions with which Jer-R replaced earlier renditions which
were common to the OG of Jer, Ez and the MP. This conclusion,
in turn, provides some support for our hypothesis about the relationship between Jer a' and Jer b'. Since in these cases the
renditions in Jer b' are revisional, the evidence supplied by
Ez and the MP supports our hypothesis more than that of Thackeray.

Chapter VII contains some conclusions based on data, which admittedly are not very extensive.

Firstly, an attempt is made to characterize Jer-R's revision. Jer-R presumably had serious intentions of making Jer-OG conform to his idea of a more literal and consistent translation. However, several pieces of evidence show that he did not persist in carrying out his plans.

An excursus to this section touches on a few renditions common to Jer-R and the "Three".

The next problem is the question of the preservation of Jer-R's revision in Jer b' only. Our tentative solution is that the person responsible for the archetype of our MSS used two scrolls of a different text type (OG in Jer a' and Jer-R in Jer b').

Chapter VII also deals with the assumed date of Jer-R's revision, with some criteria for the reconstruction of the lost OG of Jer b' and with some implications of the present study for the understanding and use of the "LXX".

A bibliography, which at the same time serves as a list of abbreviations, is found at the end, as well as Greek and Hebrew indexes of the words and renditions discussed in chapters II-VII.

We shall attempt to prove the validity of our working hypothesis with evidence taken from the LXX of Jer only. However, since we question Thackeray's hypothesis of multiple authorship, it is of relevance to mention here the fate of similar theories of multiple authorship suggested for other books of the LXX:

Some of the theories of multiple authorship suggested by Thackeray and others have been strengthened by scholars, but more have been questioned strongly (a good example of the latter is Ziegler's fine study of the MP[32]). It seems to us that, except for Jer, the best cases for multiple authorship are 1-4 Reigns, Is, and Ez, but even these have been questioned recently.

Thackeray's theory for 1-4 Reigns has--in our opinion--convincingly been replaced by Barthélemy with a translator-

reviser theory.[33] Although much discussion is still going on
regarding many aspects of Barthélemy's views,[34] it seems that
his theory that certain parts of the "LXX" of 1-4 Reigns contain an early revision is gaining acceptance.

The problem of the character of the translations of Is and
Ez has not yet been solved. For Ez, both two-translator theories and translator-reviser theories have been suggested.[35]
The evidence in favor of multiple authorship of Is is less
clear, but nevertheless for this book also a two-translator
theory has been suggested by some scholars while others have
mentioned the possibility of a partial revision of the book.[36]

If theories of multiple authorship cannot be held for 1-4
Reigns and Jer, there remain only the ambiguous cases of Ez and
Is. In view of important agreements recognized between the
various assumed translation units,[37] the whole assumption of
multiple authorship of books of the LXX is in need of serious
reinvestigation. Probably this reinvestigation will result in
a trend towards translator-reviser theories.

3. *Some Introductory Remarks*

a. The text of Jer-LXX is quoted from Ziegler's edition.[38] The numbering of chapters and verses follows the LXX;
the corresponding numbers of MT are added in brackets.

Ziegler's eclectic text constitutes a deliberate attempt
to restore the archetype of Jer-LXX,[39] best represented by MSS
ABS.[40] Since we shall discuss only those renditions included
in the assumed archetype of all known MSS of Jer as well as
renditions belonging to a postulated earlier stage, variants
which developed after the time of the assumed archetype have
little bearing on the issue. It would not be correct, however,
to list in our discussion only one reading, while excluding
presumably later variants since any one of the variants may
have belonged to the assumed archetype. Thus we always indicate variants for the renditions listed in the course of our
discussion; but, in order not to burden the notation with mani-
fold details, only the variants of uncial MSS (including the
group C) are referred to, while the variants found in minus-
cules are listed only when they are the sole witness for a

significant reading.[41] In a few cases the apparatus of Ziegler
is quoted in full.

    b. The basic tools used in the preparation of chapters
II-VII were the concordances to the Hebrew[42] and Greek[43] Bible.
It should be kept in mind that HR lists only variants from
manuscripts A, B, S and the Sixtine edition (1587) and excludes,
among other things, words originating from emendations, such as
ἐπίχειρα in Jer 29:11 (49:10) (cf. III 4).[44] Thus the full
evidence relating to the problems under discussion is partially
unobtainable.

    Since HR does not register the probable *Vorlage* of the
Greek of Bar, we have used our own Greek-Hebrew and Hebrew-
Greek concordance of Bar 1:1-3:8 based on the Hebrew recon-
struction of Bar appended to ch. V.[45]

    Concordances to O, L, Sym and Th, all non-existent, would
undoubtedly have contributed to the issues under investigation.
Despite its defects,[46] Reider-Turner's *Index to Aquila*[47] is a
useful tool for the student of LXX revisions.

    c. Many of the examples listed in chapters II-VI were
previously mentioned by scholars (especially Thackeray), as indicated in footnotes in the beginning of each chapter.[48] But
upon comparison one notes that the majority of the common examples are presented below in a manner different from that of
previous discussions. Such differences result not only from
the fact that previously scholars have been trying to prove
multiple authorship for Jer-LXX, while we hope to establish a
different theory; variation in detail may also derive from differing opinions on the extent or form of the difference between
Jer a' and b' (one word/two words; word/root; word/meaning,
etc.). In order not to burden the discussion, no attempt is
made here to analyze all previous presentations or to refute
alleged oppositions (between Jer a' and b') which, in our opinion, do not exist.

    d. When referring to sub-divisions of books of the LXX
other than Jer-LXX, we use the divisions suggested by some

scholars, without intending to imply that their assumptions are considered proved or even likely.

The subdivision of 1-4 Reigns follows Thackeray, "Kings", that of Is follows Baumgärtel in Herrmann-Baumgärtel, *Beiträge* and that of Ez corresponds with Thackeray, "Ezekiel".

e. Greek words are accented, unless quoted as variants from MSS.

f. A notation such as "not found elsewhere in the LXX" relates only to the canonical and apocryphal books which were translated from Hebrew and Aramaic into Greek and whose *Vorlagen* are listed in HR.

g. Within each section, examples are arranged according to their assumed persuasion.

4. *Explanation of Symbols Employed in the Discussion.*

Jer-LXX	- The LXX of Jer in its present form.
Jer a'	- Chapters 1-28 of Jer-LXX.
Jer b'	- Chapters 29-52 of Jer-LXX together with Bar 1:1-3:8.
Jer-OG	- The Old Greek translation of Jer; often used to denote the translator of Jer a'.[49]
Jer-R	- The reviser of the OG translation of Jer b', now lost.
Bar	- The Greek translation of the Hebrew text of Baruch, now lost.
Dan-LXX	- The LXX translation of Daniel.
Dan-Th	- Theodotion's (Th) revision of Daniel.
MP	- The Minor Prophets.
The "Three"	- Aquila (Aq), Symmachus (Sym) and Theodotion (Th).
(the) Heb	- The Hebrew word/root/phrase reflected in Greek by...
Gk 1, Gk 2	- The (two) main rendition(s) of the Heb.
*	- The Greek *word* occurs only in the following verses, e.g. only in Jer-LXX or Jer a'.
!	- The mentioned *rendition* occurs only in the following verses, e.g. only in Jer-LXX or Jer a'.

14

---→   - The Hebrew word is further rendered with the fol-
          lowing renditions (occurring in Jer-LXX or in the
          whole LXX, as indicated).

parall   - The two renditions occur in two parallel verses
          (see p. 23).

NOTES

CHAPTER I

1. J. G. Janzen, *Studies in the Text of Jeremiah*, *Harvard Semitic Monographs 6* (Cambridge, Mass. 1973); E. Tov, "L'incidence de la critique textuelle sur la critique littéraire dans le livre de Jérémie," *RB* 79 (1972) 189-199; *id.*, "The Contribution of Textual Criticism to the Literary Criticism and Exegesis of Jeremiah: Some Remarks on the Hebrew *Vorlage* of the LXX of Chapter 27," *Shnaton* 1 (1975) 139-156.

2. E. Kühl, *Das Verhältniss der Massora zur Septuaginta in Jeremia* (Halle 1882) 8 stated explicitly that one person was responsible for the Greek translation of Jeremiah.

3. M.G.L. Spohn, *Ieremias Vates e Versione Iudaeorum Alexandrinorum* (Lipsiae 1794-1824) 9-10, 17, 20.

4. *Ib.*, 17, 20.

5. P. F. Frankl, "Studien über die Septuaginta und Peschito zu Jeremia," *MGWJ* 21 (1872) 448-449.

6. C. Workman, *The Text of Jeremiah* (Edinburgh 1889) XXVII.

7. A. W. Streane, *The Double Text of Jeremiah* (Cambridge 1896) 1, n. 1. In fact, the examples mentioned by Streane do not justify his assumption.

8. J. J. Kneucker, *Das Buch Baruch* (Leipzig 1897) 83, n. 8.

9. H.St.J. Thackeray, "The Greek Translators of Jeremiah," *JThSt* 4 (1903) 245-266; henceforth: Thackeray, "Gr.Tr. Jer."

10. For further details concerning Thackeray's views, see "Gr.Tr.Jer."

11. *A Grammar of the OT in Greek* (Cambridge 1909) 11ff.; *The Septuagint and Jewish Worship, Schweich Lectures 1920* (London 1921) 29-37, 116-117. See also his commentary on Bar *apud* C. Gore (ed.), *A New Commentary on Holy Scripture* (London 1928) II, 105.

12. "The Greek Translators of Ezekiel," *JThSt* 4 (1902-1903) 398-411; see also "The Greek Translators of the Prophetical Books," *ib.*, 578-585; "The Greek Translators of the Four Books of Kings," *JThSt* 8 (1906-1907) 262-278.

13. Epiphanius, *De Mensuris et Ponderibus*, 3ff.

14. For bibliographical references to the theories on 1-4 Reigns, Is and Ez, see ch. VII, notes 25-40.

15

15. Thus I. L. Seeligmann, *JEOL* 7 (1940) 373; Bickerman, "Transmission," 161, n. 43; E. Würthwein, *Der Text des AT*[4] (Stuttgart 1973) 54, n. 1.

16. H. A. Redpath, *JThSt* 7 (1906) 608-9 mentions the rendering listed below as III 37.

17. L. Köhler, "Beobachtungen am hebräischen und griechischen Text von Jeremia Kap 1-9," *ZAW* 29 (1909) 1-39, esp. 5, n. 4; 9, n. 3; 12-13, 25.

18. W. W. Graf von Baudissin, *Kyrios als Gottesname im Judentum und seine Stelle in der Religionsgeschichte* (Giessen 1929) I, 191, n. 1.

19. The importance of Ziegler's contribution to the study of Jer-LXX cannot be overstated. As for the two-translator theory, see his *Beiträge zur Ieremias-Septuaginta*, *NAWG*, *Phil.-Hist. Kl. 1958, 2* (Göttingen 1958) *passim*, and the remark quoted below (p. 113, n. 1). In his *Beiträge*, Ziegler frequently referred to previously recognized differences between "Ier.I" and "Ier.II" and he also mentioned some new criteria for the distinction between the two.

20. R. A. Martin, *The Syntax of the Greek of Jeremiah, Part I: The Noun, Pronouns and Prepositions in their Case Constructions*, unpubl. diss. Princeton Theol. Sem. (Princeton, N.J. 1957); subsequent volumes have not been written. Martin's study frequently touches upon differences between the two parts of the Jer-LXX and, in fact, "the theory of Thackeray...is one of the reasons Jeremiah was selected for this syntactical study" (*ib.*, 7). Prof. Martin kindly permitted us to quote from his unpublished dissertation.

21. I. Soisalon-Soininen, *Die Infinitive in der Septuaginta*, *AASF B 132* (Helsinki 1965) 169-176. Cf. further n. 25 below.

22. P. Walters, *The Text of the Septuagint, etc.* (Cambridge 1973) 314, n. 14.

23. E. Duval, "Le texte grec de Jérémie d'après une étude récente," *RB* 12 (1903) 394-403; R. R. Harwell, *The Principal Versions of Baruch*, diss. Yale Univ. (New Haven, Conn. 1915) 53, 65-66; E. J. Bickerman, "Transmission" 161, n. 43; W. Rudolph, *Jeremia*[2], *HAT* (Tübingen 1958) XXI.

24. Baudissin, *Kyrios*, I, 198.

25. Recognizing a distinct difference between the two parts of Jer (see IV 7), Soisalon-Soininen concluded: "obwohl also das Material hier schon ziemlich deutlich auf zwei verschiedene Übersetzer hinweist, muss man die Frage trotzdem unbeantwortet lassen" (*Infinitive*, 174).

26. Unless otherwise indicated, "Jer" denotes both Jer 1-52 and Bar 1:1-3:8.

27. Since several LXX revisions have been labeled "R", we avoid using this siglum alone.

28. Our hypothesis, as well as Thackeray's, refers to the different renderings of the two sections of Jer-LXX in the LXX's sequence of chapters--the most salient feature of which is its location of the prophecies against the foreign nations (chapters 46-51 of MT) after Jer 25:13 of MT. It should be stressed that a rearrangement of the Greek text according to the sequence of MT would not basically change the distribution pattern in such clear-cut examples as III 18 and 43. Moreover, when rearranged, the lexical differences between Jer a' and b' cannot be explained at all, while our hypothesis offers at least one possible solution.

29. For example, the assumption (1) that the dividing line between the two parts of Jer lies between chapters 28 and 29 of the Greek (see the appendix to ch. IV), and (2) that Bar 1:1-3:8 was revised by Jer-R (ch. V).

30. An interesting corollary of the comparison of the LXX of Jer, Ez and the MP is that the similarity of Jer a' and the MP to Ez is almost exclusively limited to the first part of Ez (chapters 1-27 = Ez a'). It is therefore possible that Ez a' (and c'?) reflects the OG of Ez, while Ez b' was retouched by an unknown hand. This supposition is corroborated by the fact that in approaching the question along a different line of reasoning, Barthélemy ascribed Ez b' to a *kaige*-like revision (cf. p. 164).

31. In any event, differences between the characteristic renditions of the OG of Jer, Ez and the MP have not been evidenced.

32. J. Ziegler, *Die Einheit der Septuaginta zum Zwölfprophetenbuch, Beilage zum Vorlesungsverzeichnis der Staatl. Akademie zu Braunsberg* (1934/1935) 1-16 = *Sylloge* (Göttingen 1971) 29-42.

33. Barthélemy, *Devanciers*.

34. For a summary, see E. Tov in R. A. Kraft (ed.), *SCS* 2 (1972) 1-15.

35. For bibliographical references, see ch. VII, notes 32-36 as well as in Tov, *Baruch* (see bibliography).

36. For bibliographical references, see ch. VII, notes 37-40.

37. For some similarities between the different sections of Ez, see Thackeray, "Ezekiel," 406; for Is, cf. the studies mentioned in ch. VII, n. 38.

38. J. Ziegler, *Ieremias, Baruch, Threni, Epistula Ieremiae. VT Graecum, Auctoritate Societatis Litterarum Gottingensis Editum,* vol. XV (Göttingen 1957); henceforth: Ziegler, *Ier*.

39. Ziegler did not commit himself as to whether his re-
construction refers to the archetype of all the known MSS of
Jer or whether this text is meant to represent the copy of Jer-
LXX prepared by the original translator(s).

40. Ziegler, "Einleitung," 56-60.

41. As a rule, variants found *only* in O and L are not included because by implication they are secondary in the textual
development of Jer.

42. S. Mandelkern, *Veteris Testamenti Concordantiae
Hebraicae atque Chaldaicae*[5] (Tel Aviv 1962).

43. E. Hatch and H. A. Redpath, *A Concordance to the
Septuagint* (Oxford 1897); henceforth: HR. The following tools
were used in addition to HR: X. Jacques, *List of Septuagint
Words Sharing Common Elements* (Rome 1972); E. Camilo dos San-
tos, *An Expanded Hebrew Index for the Hatch-Redpath Concordance
to the Septuagint* (Jerusalem [1973]).

44. Many of these emendations are discussed in the first
chapter of Ziegler, *Beiträge*.

45. The concordances are found in Tov, *Baruch* (see bibliography).

46. Cf. P. Katz and J. Ziegler, "Ein Aquila-Index in Vorbereitung," *VT* 8 (1958) 264-285; J. Barr, *JSS* 12 (1967) 296-
304; R. Hanhart, *ThR* 64 (1968) 391-4; E. Tov, *Textus* 8 (1973)
164-174.

47. J. Reider, *An Index to Aquila, completed and revised
by N. Turner, Suppl. to VT* 12 (Leiden 1966).

48. It should be pointed out, however, that the great majority of our examples were discovered by independent study.
References were added only later.

49. In chapters III-IV, the renditions in Jer a' are contrasted to those in Jer b'. In order that the discrepancy between the two sections be defined more precisely, they are also
designated Jer-OG and Jer-R, even though the substratum of Jer
b' belongs to the OG as well.

CHAPTER II

IMPORTANT SIMILARITIES BETWEEN JER A' AND JER B'

While the proof for a theory of multiple authorship necessarily begins with the demonstration of lexical differences between two or more sections of a book, any discussion of a revision should start with the agreements between the original
translation and the assumed revision. For if one wishes to establish that a certain translation contains a revision of
another one, one must prove first that the two translations
have a *common basis*. The ideal way of proving such a relationship would be by comparing two translations of one text, because translation equivalents for one and the same word in the
source language can be compared. In this way it is possible to
prove that *kaige*-Th and Lucian[1] revised the OG, that Aquila and
Symmachus revised the *kaige*-Th revision[2] and that "Theodotion"
revised the LXX of Daniel, etc.[3]

However, the problem under discussion is more complicated
than the ones mentioned above because it is difficult to demonstrate the common basis of two translations of *different* texts
(Jer a' and Jer b'). This common basis can be demonstrated
theoretically only if we succeed in pointing to important
agreements in translation vocabulary which distinguish the two
sections from the remainder of the LXX.

There are obviously many agreements in translation options
between Jer a' and Jer b', but we shall have to dismiss the
more obvious ones (such as אשה - γύνη) in order to concentrate
on the *distinctive* agreements. With the aid of concordances it
can be determined whether or not a certain agreement is distinctive, i.e., whether or not it recurs in other books.

In our discussion we shall list separately (1) unique and
rare renditions common to Jer a' and b', and (2) rare Greek
words, common to Jer a' and b', which sometimes render different Hebrew words. We shall refrain from giving here examples
of what we consider "distinctive" agreements, referring the
reader to the first examples of each section.

Before presenting the evidence, we shall discuss two alternative explanations of the agreements between Jer a' and b':

1. A few of the agreements between Jer a' and b' have been
    recognized by Thackeray. Probably because Thackeray rec-
    ognized only a few instances, he attributed them to a sec-
    ondary factor, supposedly during or after the process of
    the translation of Jer by two different translators (see
    below, p. 21).

2. If one does not adhere to a two-translator theory, the
    most obvious explanation of important agreements between
    two different parts of the same book is that they point to
    its original translator: Idiosyncracies of any translator
    naturally are visible in all parts of one book.

Of the two possibilities, the second one needs no special
proof. No attention need be paid to important agreements between two parts of homogeneous composition because they are expected. Only when doubts arise about the unity of a composition are such agreements studied. In our view, if the first
explanation is dismissed, it follows by implication that the
second one is correct.

The first possibility was formulated by Thackeray in different ways:

(a) Jer. β' imitated Jer. α' ("Gr.Tr.Jer.", 253-4);
(b) Later redactors or scribes were responsible for "a
     certain amount of mixture of the two styles" (*ib.*,
     254);
(c) The similarities resulted from "imperfect collabora-
     tion of two workers, the second of whom only partial-
     ly followed the lead of the first" (*Septuagint*, 35).

Concerning Thackeray's views as a whole, the following may
be maintained:

1. An adaptation of the vocabulary of Jer b' to that of
Jer a', or *vice versa*, which could account for the above-mentioned agreements, would have required an extraordinary recall
of the translation of the other part. Since many words occur
in completely different contexts, it is nearly impossible that

a translator, redactor, or scribe could know of their occurrence in the other part of the book unless he had access to
some kind of a Hebrew-Greek and Greek-Hebrew concordance.

2. Some of the examples mentioned below cannot be accounted for by any of the explanations mentioned by Thackeray:
Group (2) contains several instances of rare Greek words common
to the two sections and in ten of these examples (35-45) the
rare Greek word reflects more than one Hebrew word. There
seems to be no reason why anyone would copy a certain rare
Greek word (reflecting a given Heb 1) from one section to the
other as a representation of a different Heb word (Heb 2).

3. Differences between Jer a' and b' are more numerous
and salient than the similarities between the two. It is thus
a priori very unlikely that the similarities were inserted or
developed secondarily while so many striking differences were
left untouched. In Jer a', for example, τάδε λέγει κύριος renders כה אמר ה׳ 58 times, whereas the same phrase is translated
69 times in Jer b' by οὕτως εἶπε κύριος (III 18).

More detailed observations regarding Thackeray's theory
follow:

1. The attribution of the important agreements between
Jer a' and b' to a "mixture of the two styles" is a misnomer
and a misrepresentation of the evidence. The situation could
have been called a "mixture of the two styles" only if renditions which manifestly characterize either Jer a' or Jer b' had
occurred several times in the other part as well. The below-
mentioned correspondences, on the other hand, cannot be considered to constitute such a mixture since they do not represent characteristic features of the *style* of either Jer a' or
b', but rather are rare renditions and words found in two parts
of one book.

2. The suggestion that a given translator *imitated* the
vocabulary of a colleague has no parallel in the LXX. The only
book whose translation options were repeated elsewhere was the
Pentateuch, but the "Sitz im Leben" of borrowings from the Pentateuch was completely different: Those who embarked upon the
translation of the Prophets and Hagiographa leaned on the Greek
translation of the Pentateuch because they employed its

vocabulary and in some instances it provided them with needed lexical assistance.

Moreover, can it be claimed that Jer. β' imitated the *vocabulary* of his colleague? After all, he did not reproduce characteristic elements of Jer. α', but he supposedly copied some renditions which characterize only Jer a' and b'. This cannot be called the "imitation of a colleague's vocabulary."

3. The assumption that redactors were needed to weld together Jer a' and Jer b' seems farfetched. Furthermore, there is no proof for the existence of such redactors. If there had been redactors, they probably would have attempted to erase the differences between Jer a' and b'; and if they had introduced similarities between the two sections, they would have chosen more easily recognizable similarities.

4. In our previous remarks we alluded to the "imperfect collaboration of two workers" mentioned by Thackeray. It seems to us that given the present data, such a possibility exists only if the two translators cooperated (or if one translator used a written copy of the other's translation) in the representation of Hebrew words which might have caused lexical difficulties. This possibility can only be taken into consideration in a few of the examples given.

We conclude that there is no reason to accept any of Thackeray's explanations for the similarities between Jer a' and b'. As a result, we consider them to be indications of the OG translation of Jer. Special importance must be attached to the renderings which are indicated as (e) (see below, p. 23); doubts with regard to the relevance of "parallel" renderings (see p. 23) may be disregarded.

The next chapter (III) is intended to prove that the OG of Jer has been preserved only in Jer a' and was lost for Jer b', which, in its present form, represents a revised text. By this reasoning we hope to establish that it is the OG substratum of Jer b' which shares peculiar features with the OG of Jer a'. Of course, this OG substratum in Jer b' is more extensive than the 45 examples of this chapter suggest (see also pp. 167-68 for some criteria for the reconstruction of the OG of Jer b'), but additional elements of this stratum cannot be identified

with the same degree of certainty. Hence the number of similarities (ch. II) is smaller than the number of differences
(chapters III and IV).

The items listed below are represented in two columns.[4]
The left column refers to Jer a' (chapters 1-28) and the right
one to Jer b' (Jer 29-52 and Bar 1:1-3:8). For our purposes it
is very important to note that a given rendition occurs only in
a certain unit; hence the sign ! after a certain rendition
means that the *rendition* occurs only in the below-mentioned
verses (in this chapter only in Jer a' and b'). Similarly, the
asterish (*) means that a certain Greek *word* occurs only in the
below-mentioned verses (in this chapter only in Jer a' and b').

The examples cluster around a certain rendering of the Hebrew word common to Jer a' and b' which is listed at the beginning of each item. Additional renditions of the Heb are mentioned only when they emphasize the uniqueness of the rendition
discussed. When mentioned, such renditions are written after a
---→ sign. In this chapter the renditions which are mentioned
after the ---→ sign refer to the *whole* of the LXX.

Two additional notations are used:

(e): a few renditions (1, 14, 15, 27, 28, 30) reflect an
unusual common understanding of a certain Hebrew word and are
therefore of special importance for establishing the common basis of Jer a' and b'. Such readings are marked as (e), that is
"erroneous," because they reflect an incorrect understanding of
the Hebrew word. We shall not enter here into an analysis of
what is a 'correct' and what is an 'incorrect' rendering of the
Hebrew because such a discussion would lead us beyond the scope
of the present study. Suffice it to say that we are interested
in the peculiarity of the renderings marked as (e).[5]

(parall): some of the similarities are found in parallel
verses occurring in an identical or nearly identical fashion in
Jer a' and b' (items 27-31). Although it is possible that
these similarities derived from harmonization, internal evidence, as analyzed in item 31, seems to refute such a suspi-
cion. Moreover, it is very unlikely that parallel verses were
harmonized, since their vocabulary tends to be different.[6]
Nevertheless, for the sake of accuracy, these examples are de-
noted "parall".

1. *Unique and Rare Renditions Common to Jer a' and b'*

(1)   (אדני ה')‎ אהה - ὁ ὤν ! (e)

1:6(o ω 106^C)   4:10(MS 26; | 39(32):17
ω rel)   14:13(ω 106^C)

---→ אהה in (ה')‎ אדני אהה : δέομαι (Jos 7:7); ἆ ἆ (Jud 6:22); μηδαμῶς (Ez 4:14   20:49(21:5)); οἴμμοι (Ez 9:8   11:13); ὤ (2 Ki 3:10   6:5,15).

Since this is the first example of ch. II, we shall describe our notation in detail:

The word אהה in the phrase אהה אדני ה'‎ was rendered in
both parts of Jer with ὁ ὤν. This translation is not found
outside Jer (see the sign !); additional renditions in other
books of the LXX are listed in the second part of the notation.
ὁ ὤν occurs three times in Jer a' and once in Jer b'. The
translation option may be considered erroneous (e).

Ziegler is probably correct in assuming that the original
reading was ὁ ὤν not only in 1:6, 14:13 and 39(32):17, but also
in 4:10 where the manuscript support is very weak.[7]

The translator probably derived אהה ('alas') from the root
היה and, interestingly enough, translated it in accordance with
the LXX of Ex 3:14   אהיה אשר אהיה - ἐγώ εἰμι ὁ ὤν.[8]

(2) דמה , דמם - ἀπορρίπτω

8:14,14   28(51):6 | 29(47):5

cf. 27(50):30   ῥίπτω VI 32 and Jud 15:17   רמת לחי - ἀναίρεσις
σιαγόνος.

The two parts of Jer share a peculiar rendering which recurs a few times in the MP (see VI 32). It looks as if the
translation of דמה and דמם with ἀπορρίπτω reflects variants
from the root רמה (also reflected by the simplex ῥίπτω in
27(50):30), but probably the translator's *Vorlage* did not contain such variants. Rather, the renderings under investigation
reflect the text of the MT which the translator avoided, so to
speak, by representing the ambiguous grapheme *daleth/resh* as a

resh rather than a *daleth*. Even though such an assumption does not suggest itself easily,[9] further evidence in Jer-LXX also makes it likely that the original translator avoided the roots דמה and דמם: In 29(47):6 דמי is read as רמי (ἐπάρθητι). In 6:2 דמיתי is read as רמיתי/רמיכי (τὸ ὕψος σου). The translation of the Heb with διαλείπω in 14:17[10] and with πίπτω in 30:15(49: 26)[11] probably reflects the same uncertainty about the meaning of the Heb.[12]

(3) חמדה - ἐκλεκτός

3:19 ארץ חמדה - γῆν ἐκλεκτήν │ 32:20(25:34) חמדה ככלי -
│ ὥσπερ οἱ κριοὶ οἱ ἐκλεκτοί

and further Hagg 2:7 Zach 7:14 (cf. VI 34).

---→ Especially ἐπιθυμητός. Further ἔπαινος, ἐπιθύμημα, ἐπιθυμία, κάλλος, ὡραῖος.

(4) חזק - στερέω

5:3 10:4   │ 52:6
and Sir 34:11 50:1.

Cf. חזק - στερεός in 38(31):11 and Ps 34(35):10.
---→ Especially κρατέω.

(5) נפל , נֵפֶל - πτῶσις !

6:15   │ 29:22(49:21)
cf. מפלה (מפלת) - πτῶσις in Is. 17:1 and Ez 26-32 (6 x).

(6) היליל - ἀλαλάζω !

4:8   │ 29(47):2 30(49):3
│ 31(48):39[12] 32:20(25:34)

---→ θρηνέω (also Jer 28(51):8), ὀλολύζω (also Jer (31(48):20, 31). Cf. יללה - ἀλαλαγμός in Jer 32:22(25:36); this translation does not occur elsewhere.

(7) השכם - ὄρθρου !

7:25   25:4 | 33(26):5   39(32):33   42(35):14
                         | 51(44):4

---→ ὀρθρίζων 1 Sam 17:16   2 Chr 36:15   Jer 25:3 (cf. השכים - ὀρθρίζω passim).

(8) שאון - ὄλεθρος !

28(51):55 | 32:16(25:30)

---→ שאון - 'destruction' mainly: ἀπώλεια, ταλαιπωρία.   שאון - 'noise' mainly: κραυγή, ἦχος.

(9) קצוצי פאה !

9:26(25) περικειρόμενος τὰ | 30:10(49:32) κεκαρμένοι πρὸ
κατὰ πρόσωπον | προσώπου αὐτῶν   32:9(25:23)
                                | περικεκαρμένος κατὰ πρόσωπον
                                | αὐτοῦ (+ variants)

Cf. פאה - πρόσωπον in Lev 13:41.
---→ קצץ - compounds of κόπτω.
---→ פאה - variously (mainly rendering פאה - 'side', 'corner').

The aforementioned renditions of קצץ and פאה occur only here. Furthermore, περικείρω is a hapax in the LXX.

(10) מאס - ἀποδοκιμάζω

6:30,30   7:29   8:9   14:19 | 38:35(31:36)
and Ps 117(118):22; further passim in Sym.

---→ Especially ἀπωθέω (also Jer 2:37   4:30   6:19), ἐξουδενέω and -όω.

(11) שר - μεγιστάν

24:8   25:18(49:38)   27(50):35 | 32:5(25:19)   41(34):10
and 2 Chr 36:18   Prov 8:16   Is 34:12   Sir 8:8.

---→ Especially ἄρχων (cf. also III 47).

(12) חפץ - χρεία in כלי אין חפץ בו !

22:28 σκεῦος οὗ οὐκ ἔστι
χρεία αὐτοῦ
cf. Hos. 8:8 σκεῦος ἄχρηστον; Sir 11:23 χρεία = חפץ ?

31(48):38 ἀγγεῖον οὗ οὐκ ἔστι
χρεία αὐτοῦ

---→ Only here and in 1 Sam 15:22 18:25 is חפץ used as
'desire' (in a concrete matter).

(13) תן - στρουθός !

10:22

30:11(49:33)

---→ δράκων, ἐχῖνος, σειρήν.

(14) חוץ , חצות ('street(s)', 'open
spaces') - ἔξωθεν ! (e)

9:21(20) 11:6 28(51):4

40(33):10 44(37):21
51(44):6,9,17,21 Bar 2:23
(cf. V 29)

Except for 9:21(20) (חוץ), 28(51):4 (בחוצותיה) and 44(37):21,
ἔξωθεν occurs in the phrase ἐν πόλεσιν (γῇ) Ιουδα καὶ ἔξωθεν
Ιερουσαλημ.

---→ Mainly ὁδός or one of its compounds (cf. ὁδός in Jer 5:1
7:17, δίοδος in Jer 7:34 14:16, and ἔξοδος in Jer 11:13 - all
in the phrase בערי יהודה ובחצות ירושלם).

The translation of חוץ, חצות ('street(s)') with ἔξωθεν
probably resulted from the translator deriving the word incorrectly from חוץ ('outside').[14] It is not impossible that this
mistranslation was brought about by a faulty exegesis of the
phrase בערי יהודה ובחצות ירושלם, resulting from the attribution
of a similar meaning to the first and second parts of the
phrase.[15]
The simultaneous occurrence of "correct" and "incorrect"
renderings of the same word within Jer a'--or, for that matter,
within Jer--is hardly understandable, but the phenomenon is not
without parallel in the LXX and deserves a special investigation.[16]

(15) תְּעָלָה - ὠφέλεια (e)

26(46):11 | 37(30):13

cf. Sir 30:23 תעלה - ὠφέλεια; 41:14 תועלה - ὠφέλεια.

In the mentioned instances is the translation of תעלה derived from the root יעל, similar to תֹעֶלָה (תועלה) in Sir, also translated with ὠφέλεια.[17] In 31(48):2, on the other hand, MT תהלה was misread by the translator as תעלה and correctly rendered with ἰατρεία.[18] This rendition may be traced to Jer-R. In that case Jer-R left ὠφέλεια in 37(30):13 unrevised. See further n. 16.

(16) דְּבֶּר מִשְׁפָּטִים - λαλέω μετὰ κρίσεως !

1:16 | 52:9

---→ Literally: 2 Ki 25:6 Ps 36(37):30 Jer 4:12 12:1.

(17) ἐκλείπω - various *Vorlagen*

4:31 - עיף 6:4 - נטה 6:15 -	34:6(27:8), 43(36):23 44(37):
6:29, 6:29 - נחר עשה תועבה	21 49(42):17,22 (MT: מות)
24:10 - תמם 7:28 - אבד(כרת)	51(44): תמם - 51(44):12,18,27
9:10(9) - יצח 14:4 - חתת	27 - כלה 31(48):11 - מור
14:6, 15:10, 26(46):28 - כלה	42(35):19 - נתש 38(31):40
18:14 - עזב 28(51):30 - חדל	שבת - Bar 2:23 כרת 43(36):29,
28(51):58 - יעף	Bar 2:18 - כליון (?)

ἐκλείπω occurs more frequently in Jer-LXX than in the other books of the LXX[17] (only in Ps the verb occurs regularly as a translation of כלה). The verb was thus well-liked by the translators of Jer (cf. Ziegler, *Beiträge*, 20, 52; "Einleitung," 58) and of the MP (see VI 35) as a "stopgap" reflecting sundry *Vorlagen*, in particular when lexical difficulties were met.

(18) צפון - ἀπὸ βορρᾶ/ἀπηλιώτου

1:15 ממלכות צפונה - βασιλείας | מלכי הצפון (25:26)32:12 -
ἀπὸ βορρᾶ   25:9 משפחות צפון - | βασιλεῖς ἀπὸ ἀπηλιώτου
πατριὰν ἀπὸ βορρᾶ   26(46):24 |
עם צפון - λαοῦ ἀπὸ βορρᾶ |

---→ Literally, also in Jer (*passim*).

In a few instances Jer-LXX rendered צפון not with its
standard rending as '(the people) *of* the North', but as '(the
people coming) *from* the North' in accordance with Jeremiah's
frequent prophecies referring to a threatening people arriving
from the North. Note, however, that in Jer a' βορρᾶς is used,
in accordance with the regular practice in the LXX, as against
ἀπηλιώτης in Jer b'.

(19) כל - ἅπας

Occurrences listed in HR: Jer a': 9; Jer b': 16; elsewhere: 35.
Occurrences in MS B only: Jer a': 3; Jer b': 11; elsewhere:
17.[19]

ἅπας occurs more often in Jer-LXX than in any other book
of the LXX. One notes that ἅπας is nearly always used in the
LXX instead of πᾶς in order to preclude the harsh juxtaposition
of consonants (see Thackeray, *Grammar*, 138). The original
translator of Jer (or the first scribe?) thus used ἅπας more
than his fellow translators.

(20) הכין - ἀνορθόω

10:12 | 40(33):2
and 1 Chr 22:10. |

---→ Especially ἑτοιμάζω (also Jer 26(46):14 28(51):12,15),
κατευθύνω, κατορθόω (also Jer 10:23). ἀνορθόω renders also
כון, *niph'al*, *polel*, *hithpa'el*, and διορθόω renders כון, *polel*
in Jer 7:3,5 (and not elsewhere).

(21) ילד - τεκνοποιέω

12:2 (יָלְדֻּ; MT יָלְכוּ)   36(29):6 הולידו   38(31):8(7)

                   (יָלָדְהָ; MT יָלֶדֶת)

and Is 65:23 ילד; Gen 11:30 אין לה ולד - οὐκ τεκνοποιεῖ.

---→ Especially γεννάω, τίκτω, γίγνομαι.

(22) רחוק - πόρρω

12:2   31(48):24   32:12(25:36)

and Is 66:19.

Cf. further רחוק - πόρρωθεν in 2 Ki 20:14 Is 39:3. πόρρω and πόρρωθεν further render מרחק, ממרחק, למרחוק, מרחוק.

---→ Especially words derived from μακρ-.

(23) מאד - λίαν

24:3,3   30:8(49:30)   31(48):29

                     (Α σφόδρα)

and five times elsewhere in the LXX.

---→ In the LXX מאד is much more frequently rendered by σφόδρα (i.a. 10 times in Jer a' and 3 times in Jer b') than by λίαν.

(24) ערב - σύμμ(ε)ικτος !

27(50):37   32:6,10(25:20,24)

cf. Prov. 11:15 ערב - συμμείγνυμι and Ez 27 *passim* מערב - σύμμικτος.

---→ ἐπίμικτος.

(25) הלך - οἴχομαι

9:10(9)   16:11   27(50):6   31(48):11   35(28):11   48(41):

                                   10,12,15,17   52:7 AC

                                   (πορεύομαι rel)   Bar 1:22

οἴχομαι renders הלך 10(11) times in both parts of Jer
(and in addition נסרח in 29(49):7). Elsewhere in the LXX the
verb occurs only 10 times (of which 6 times reflect הלך). The
conglomeration of occurrences of οἴχομαι in Jer (generally =
הלך) thus sets both parts of the book apart from the remainder
of the LXX.

(26) צבאות 'ה - κύριος παντοκράτωρ[20]

3:19 5:14 15:16 23:16	29:29(49:18) 32:13(25:27)
27(50):34 28(51):5,57	37(30):3 SAVC (rel om) 39(32):
	14,19 40(33):11 51(44):7
	Bar 3:1,4

further: 2 Sam 4 x, 1 Ki 2 x, 1 Chr 3 x, MP 100 x, Sir 1 x.

---→ κύριος σαβαωθ Is 58 x and elsewhere 8 x; κύριος τῶν
δυνάμεων[21] 24 x.

Only in Jer and the MP (cf. VI 33) is the Hebrew phrase
rendered exclusively by κύριος παντοκράτωρ.

(27) מסגר - δεσμώτης ! (parall) (e)

24:1	36(29):2 Bar 1:9 (cf. V 28)

Cf. Is 42:7 מַסְגֵּר - δεσμός.

The word מַסְגֵּר ('smith'?)[22] was apparently unknown to the
translators of the LXX: While Jer-LXX vocalized the Heb as מְסֻגָּר
or מְסֻגָּר, both the translator of 2 Ki 24:14,16 (συγκλείων), Sym
in Jer 36(29):2 (συγκλείων) and Lucian in 2 Ki 24:14
(συγκλείστης) read מַסְגֵּר.[23]
The similarity between the two parts of Jer is more striking in view of the fact that δεσμώτης itself occurs elsewhere
only once (Gen 39:20 אסיר-).

(28) חול - ἥκω ! (parall) (e)

23:19	37(30):23, both: ἐπὶ (τοὺς)
	ἀσεβεῖς ἥξει

Only here in the LXX was חול ('to whirl') rendered with
ἥκω.[24] This rendition may have been influenced by the meaning
'to occur' of חול in post-Biblical Hebrew (cf. Levi, s.v.).

(29) הריץ - ἐκδιώκω ! (parall)

27(50):44 | 29:20(49:19)

---→ ἐξάγω, προφθάνω, τρέχω.

(30) הועיד - ἀνθίστημι (parall) (e)

27(50):44 | 29:20(49:19)
and further Job 9:19.

---→ הועיד does not occur elsewhere in the OT.

Because עמד was frequently rendered in the LXX with
ἀνθίστημι, the translators of Jer and Job must have derived
יועדני somehow from עמד, or otherwise their *Vorlagen* differed
from MT.[25] The latter assumption may be supported by the rendition of Aq and Sym in 29:20 (49:19): ὑφίστημι.

2. *Rare Greek Words Common to Jer a' and b'*

Jer a' and b' share several Greek words which recur rarely,
if at all, in the LXX. Several of these words also reflect
rare or unique renditions. The unique words are indicated with
an asterisk (*).

(31) ἐγχειρέω[26]

18:22 כרו שׂיחה - ἐνεχείρησαν | 29:17(49:16) - השׂיא
λόγον (ενεχιρωσαν S*) = כרו
שׂיחה[27] 28(51):12 זמם
(S* ἐγχειρίζω)
and further: 2 Chr 23:18 וישם...ביד... - ἐνεχείρησεν (-ισεν B^C)
διὰ χειρός.

ἐγχείρημα* (parall)

23:20 (מְזִמָּה ;MT מזמרת) | 37(30):24 מזמה

---→ מזמה - variously, i.a. βδέλυγμα (also Jer 11:15), ὀργή (also Jer 28(51):11).
---→ זמה - especially nouns from ἀσεβ- and νομ-. Cf. further Jer 13:27 ἀπαλλοτρίωσις.

The fact that the verb ἐγχειρέω is unique to Jer-LXX indicates that the word must have been an organic part of its first stratum. None of its occurrences could have been secondarily harmonized with the others because it renders three different verbs in Jer a' and b'. It seems reasonable to postulate the same original status for ἐγχείρημα since it does not occur outside Jer-LXX. However, since ἐγχείρημα occurs in two parallel passages in Jer a' and b', one passage could have been harmonized with the other. Moreover, such an assumed harmonization is very unlikely because 23:20 and the parallel verse 37(30):24 are differently phrased in Greek. Moreover, the fact that the cognate verb ἐγχειρέω was part of the OG of Jer considerably strengthens the first assumption.

(32) ארמון - ἄμφοδον* (parall?)

17:27 | 30:16(49:27)

There exists a double agreement between Jer a' and b':
1. In both verses ἄμφοδον denotes a 'block of houses surrounded by streets' (see LSJ, s.v., and Thackeray, *Septuagint*, 34) and not 'street',[28] a meaning which occurs more frequently (see the lexica, esp. Preisigke; the "Three" use ἄμφοδον as an equivalent of חָצוֹת).
2. Apparently the majority of the LXX translators were ignorant of the meaning of ארמון (the various renditions are conveniently listed by Blake[29]). In Jer a' and b', on the other hand, ἄμφοδον approaches our understanding of ארמון.[30]

(33) מהפכת - καταρράκτης !

20:2,3 | 39(29):26[31]

Ancient and modern sources are at variance about the meaning of מהפכת, which occurs only rarely in the OT.

The equivalent in Jer-LXX of מהפכת, καταρράκτης, should
probably be understood as 'dungeon' (thus Schleusner[32]). Several sources took מהפכת also as 'dungeon',[33] while others understood it as 'basement',[34] 'room',[35] or as an instrument used
for torture such as 'stocks'.[36]

(34) כונים - χαυῶνες or sim.* (parall)

7:18 | 51(44):19

---→ Both the Hebrew word and its Hellenized transliteration
occur only here.

(35) צהל - χρεμετίζω*

5:8 | 38(31):7

---→ κερατίζω (Jer 27(50):11),[37] ἀγαλλιάω, ταράσσω, βοάω,
χαίρω.

See also: χρεμετισμός*

8:6 - מלחמה (?) 8:16 - מצהלה |
13:27 - מצהלה; |
and further Am 6:7 - מרזח (cf. VI 21).

(36) ἰταμός, ἰταμία*

ἰταμός: 6:23 27(50):42 - | ἰταμία: 29:17(49:16) - זדון[38]
אכזרי

(37) συμψάω*

22:19 - סחב | 29:21(49:20) (συμψηφίζω AQ,
            | σύνειμι S) - סחב 31(48):33 -
            | אסף

(38) προμαχών

5:10 - שׁוּר (MT שׁרותיה) | חרב[39] - 40(33):4
and Ez 4:2 - דיק (cf. VI 55). |

(39) ἀλγηρός*

10:19 - נחלה (מכתי) | נחלה (מכתך) - 37(30):12
                            | למזור - εἰς ἀλγηρόν 37(30):13
Cf. Jer 4:19 אחולה (Q: אחילה) - ἀλγῶ; this translation does not
occur elsewhere.

ἀλγηρός is very rare in Greek literature (*Thesaurus*).

(40) ἀπολογέομαι*

12:1 - ריב | נצרים - ἀπολογούμενοι 38(31):6

Cf. further: ἀπολόγημα*
20:12 - ריב

(41) τρυμαλία

13:4 16:16 - נקיק | חגו - 29:17(49:16)
and further Jud 6:2 - מנהרה; Jud 15:8,11 - סעיף.

(42) ἀποικισμός*

26(46):19 (S* ἀποικία) - גולה | גולה - 31(48):11   50(43):11,11
                           | שבי - Bar 2:30,32 (cf. V 31)

---→ שבי and גולה were usually rendered with ἀποικία and
αἰχμαλωσία (also in Jer).

(43) ἀμελέω*

4:17 - מרה | בעל[40] - 38(31):32

Cf. further: ἀμελῶς*
             | רמיה - 31(48):10

(44) σύλληψις

חפש - 41(34):3 | הרה - 20:17   לכד - 18:22
and Hos 9:11 - הריון; Job 18:10 - מלכדת. See also VI 36.

(45) πάντοθεν

כְּלֹה - 31(48):31 | (כַּלְכֵל) MT) 20:9
and 2 Sam 24:14 (not in MT); Sir 51:7 - סביב.

NOTES

CHAPTER II

1. See A. Rahlfs, *Lucians Rezension der Königsbücher*, *Septuaginta-Studien* 3 (Göttingen 1911) 192ff.

2. See Barthélemy, *Devanciers*, 246ff. who discussed isolated readings of the "Three" in order to establish that Aq and Sym depend upon *kaige*-Th. It may be added that better proof of such a relationship can be provided through comparison of running texts. This is possible for the book of Psalms with the aid of texts published by G. Mercati, *Psalterii Hexapli Reliquiae* (Vatican 1958), as well as for the Aquila text of 2 Ki published by F. C. Burkitt, *Fragments of the Book of Kings according to the Translation of Aquila* (Cambridge 1897). The present writer's own pilot studies performed on both texts support Barthélemy's assumptions.

3. By the same method the present writer has attempted to prove that the Giessen Papyri 13,19,22 and 26 of Deut and the Samaritan inscription from Saloniki contain a revision of the LXX rather than a translation of the Samaritan Pentateuch, see *RB* 78 (1971) 355-383 and 81 (1974) 43-48.

4. The following items adduced in this chapter were mentioned by Thackeray and Ziegler: Thackeray, "Gr.Tr.Jer.", 253-54: 15,32,36,37; *id.*, *Septuagint*, 33: 1,7,14,26,34; Ziegler, *Beiträge*, 30: 6.

5. These and other examples cited in ch. II could undermine our working hypothesis, according to which Jer-R would probably have revised these words in Jer b'. However, this and other inconsistencies of Jer-R are explained below (pp. 44-45) as one of the traits of all revisions of the LXX.

6. For examples see Tov, *Diss. Jeremiah*, chapter III, appendix 1. Lists of parallel verses are provided by Spohn, *Ieremias Vates*, 9; Workman, *Jeremiah*, ch. V; S. R. Driver, *An Introduction to the Literature of the OT*[7] (N.Y. 1898) 276-277; Giesebrecht, *Jeremia*, XXXVIII.

7. Spohn, Streane (both *ad loc.*) and Rahlfs read ὧ (better ὦ) in all four verses. Though supported by ὧ-אהה אדני κύριε in 2 Ki 6:5,15 and ὧ-אהה in 2 Ki 3:10, this conjecture has a strong foundation only in Jer 4:10. It is unlikely, however, that the same textual development (ὧ→ ὸ ὦν) took place in three different verses in Jer. Moreover, this substitution did not occur in the MSS of the above-mentioned verses 2 Ki 3:10, 6:5,15, nor in Jer 6:6, 22:13,18, 23:1, 41(34):5, in all of which ὧ reflects הוי (Jer 6:6 MT היא). On ὧ and ὦ see also Walters, *Text*, 229-236.

8. Cf. Ziegler, *Beiträge*, 40 (where earlier literature is mentioned) and further Thackeray, *Septuagint*, 34; C. H.

Dodd, *The Bible and the Greeks* (London 1935) 4; Fritsch, *Pentateuch*, 22-23; F. Büchsel, *ThWNT*, s.v. εἰμι, ὁ ὤν.

9. For the background of this and similar renderings, see the present author's "On 'Pseudovariants' Reflected in the Septuagint," *JSS* 20 (1975) 165-177.

10. The employment of διαλείπω in Jer-LXX suggests that the translator availed himself of this verb as a "stopgap," like ἐκλείπω (cf. II 17), indicating that he had experienced difficulty.

11. יפלו...ידמו-πεσοῦνται...πεσοῦνται. The repetition of πίπτω indicates that the translator either was ignorant of the Heb or had no recourse to Greek synonyms (see Ziegler, *Beiträge*, 29, n. 1, where this practice is further exemplified). The former possibility is more likely.

12. In 31(48):2 and 32:23(25:37) the Heb is correctly represented by παύω. These renditions may have been inserted by Jer-R. Cf. further n. 16.

13. חחה הילילו-Ατατ ἠλάλαξε(ν) Katz and Ziegler] ηττηθη ολολυξατε L'; κατηλλαξε(ν) (+ ✕ ολολυξατε O Arm = MT) rel. Cf. Ziegler, *Beiträge*, 30. The fact that ἀλαλάζω is characteristic of Jer-LXX, in its turn supports the proposed emendation of the corrupted reading found in nearly all MSS.

14. Thackeray, *Septuagint*, 34, surmised that the translator misrepresented חצרות(חצרות) as ἔξωθεν because חוצות was abbreviated in his *Vorlage* as ׳חצ. However, while a scribe might conceivably have abbreviated חוצות in the recurring phrase בערי יהודה ובחצות ירושלם, the abbreviation of בחוצותיה in 28(51):4 cannot be accounted for, despite G. R. Driver's few examples of abbreviated pronominal suffixes described in *Textus* 1 (1960) 117. Moreover, while חוץ-'outside' is almost exclusively written *plene* in MT, the occurrences in Jer of חצות-ἔξωθεν are written defectively. This fact makes Thackeray's assumption even more difficult.

On the other hand, Thackeray's explanation accounts well for the simultaneous occurrence of "correct" and "incorrect" renditions in the same book. According to his explanation, in some instances the translator might have identified חוץ' correctly as חוצות, while in others he failed to do so.

15. See especially the construction of 40(33):10 ἐν πόλεσιν Ιουδα καὶ ἔξωθεν Ιερουσαλημ ταῖς ἠρημωμέναις (בערי יהודה ובחצות ירושלם הנשמות) which may indicate that the two parts were considered coordinate.

16. See, e.g., the different renditions of תעלה and ארמון in Jer (II 15,32) and the differences between the LXX translations of Is 18:2 and 18:7.

17. According to J. Ziegler, *ZAW* 77 (1958) 281, the grandson of Sirach depended in this instance on Jer-LXX.

18. אין עוד תהלת מואב - οὐκ ἔστιν ἔτι ἰατρεία Μωαβ Ziegler] αγαυριαμα Μωαβ QVO...; ιατρεια Μωαβ αγαυριαμα B-S A C'...;

γαυριαμα....τη Μωαβ L'. The greater part of the MSS thus contain a doublet composed of ἰατρεία (= מְעָלָה) and ἀγαυρίαμα (= MT חֵלְאָה). ἰατρεία unquestionably was the original rendition in this verse, subsequently approximated to MT (thus also Ziegler, *Beiträge*, 102).

19. As expected, for nearly all occurrences of ἄπας, variants of πᾶς are recorded.

20. Dodd, *op. cit.* (n. 8), 19, surmised that παντοκράτωρ, as a rendition of צבאות('ה), was coined on the model of κοσμοκράτωρ, meaning "the one God who rules and controls all other cosmic powers. As these powers are δυνάμεις, κύριος παντοκράτωρ may be regarded as a paraphrase (rather than a translation) of צבאות 'ה in the sense represented by κύριος τῶν δυνάμεων." See further AR, s.v.; W. Michaelis in *ThWNT* 3, 913-14; W. H. Roscher, *Ausführliches Lexicon der griechischen und römischen Mythologie* (Leipzig 1897-1909), s.v. and recently B. Lifshitz, *Donateurs et Fondateurs dans les Synagogues Juives* (Paris 1967) 28-29.

21. This is also Th's main rendition (see Schmitt, *Theodotion*, 27) adopted by O (see Sois.-Soin., *Zusätze*, 154). That of Aq was στρατιῶν (see Ziegler in Katz-Ziegler, "Aquila Index", 275; Katz, *Philo's Bible, etc.* (Cambridge 1950) 149 and that of Sym was ...στρατιῶν and ...δυνάμεων (Katz, *ib.*).

22. For the various opinions on the meaning of this מַסְגֵּר and its relationship to מַסְגֵּר - 'dungeon', see Rudolph, *Jeremia*, 144.

23. Cf. הסגיר - συγκλείω in Aq's translation of Lam 2:7.

24. Cf. the translation of חול with ἔρχομαι by Sym in 2 Sam 3:29 and also that of מחול with συναγωγή in Jer 38(31):4, 13. The latter equivalent, however, is problematic.

25. A third possibility must be excluded because it holds true for Jer only: In Jer the translation may have resulted from a parallelism of יעמד...יעדני - ἀντιστήσεται...στήσεται.

26. For the interchangeability of ἐγχειρέω, -όω and -ίζω, see Ziegler, "Einleitung," 110.

27. Having erroneously read שׂיחה as שׂיחה, the translator adapted the verb to its object. A similar development occurred in Jer 18:20 כרו שׂוחה - συνελάλησαν ῥήματα and Ps 118(119):85 שׂיחות...כרו - διηγήσαντο...ἀδολεσχίας. See M. L. Margolis, *ZAW* 27 (1907) 249.

28. However, ἄμφοδον in Jer 17:27 was incorrectly understood as 'street' by the Old Latin *apud* Tyconius (itinera; see F. C. Burkitt, *The Book of the Rules of Tyconius, Texts and Studies* III, 1 [Cambridge 1895] 62) and by E. A. Sophocles, *Greek Lexicon of the Roman and Byzantine Periods* (Boston 1870) s.v. ἄμφοδον, quoting Jer 17:27 as 'street'.

29. R. P. Blake, *HThR* 25 (1932) 254ff. See also Seelig-mann, *Isaiah*, 52; P. J. Heawood, "ארמון and ארם", *JThSt* 13 (1911-2) 66-73; G. B. Caird, *JThSt* 19 (1968) 460-61.

30. ארמון is further rendered in Jer with θεμέλιον (6:5), γῆ (9:21(20)) and ναός (37(30):18).

31. אל המחפכת ואל הציגק - εἰς τὸ ἀπόκλεισμα καὶ εἰς τὸν καταρράκτην. The word order of the LXX's *Vorlage* was probably inverted (thus Streane, *Jeremiah*, 206 and BDB, s.v. מחפכת).

32. "Locus subterraneus quo pro carcere utebantur." Schleusner's explanation was not documented by him but the as-sumed meaning 'dungeon' may have been extended from another meaning of καταρράκτης, viz. 'portcullis' (see LSJ, s.v.; in the LXX καταρράκτης also renders ארבה - 'sluice'; cf. Sym ארבות - καταρράγματα in Is 25:11).

33. 1. LXX 2 Chr 16:10 and Sym in Jer 36(29):26 : φυλακή.
     2. Aq in Jer 36(29):26 : καταπατάκτην (leg. καταπηκτην ? Ziegler, *Ier.*; See LSJ, s.v.), cf. Sym in Job 36:6 אדן - κατάπηξ ('trap door').
     3. The Peshitta in Jer 29:26 : בית אסירא.
     4. The Vulgate in Jer 20:2,3 29:26 : nervus.
     5. "Iosippos" in Jer 20:2 : δεσμωτήριον·
     6. Cf. also Rashi *ad* Jer 20:2.

34. Targum to Jer : כיפחא.

35. The Peshitta in Jer 20:2,3 : חדרא.

36. 1. Sym in Jer 20:2 βασανιστήριον (86, Syh).
     2. Sym in Jer 20:3 στρεβλωτήριον (86) and in 20:2 (Jerome: "βασ. sive στρεβλ.").
     3. R. David Qimḥi on 20:2.
     4. BDB, s.v.
     5. Rudolph, *Jeremia*, 118.
     6. LSJ, *Suppl.*, s.v.: "dub.sens.,perh. *stocks* or *pillory*, LXX Je. 36(29).26".

37. F. Wutz's emendation (χρεμετίζω) in *Die Transkrip-tionen von der Septuaginta bis zu Hieronymus* (Stuttgart 1924) 34 was rightly rejected by Ziegler, *Beiträge*, 25.

38. See further 30(49):4 הבת השובבה - θύγατερ ἀτιμίας 239] τῆς ἀτιμίας L⁻⁵¹ ³¹¹ Bo Tht; τῆς ἰταμιας rel. Although ἰταμία has good manuscript support in this verse, its correct-ness may be doubted in view of the translation of the same He-brew word with the similar θυγάτηρ ἠτιμωμένη in 38(31):22. The majority reading in 30(49):4 must have developed from ἀτιμία under the influence of the adjacent 29:17(49:16). Cf. further Ziegler, *Beiträge*, 48-49 and Walters, *Text*, 294, n. 88.

39. This rendition was probably influenced by that of סללה with χάραξ in the same verse.

40. This rendition should be considered a free, context-ual translation.

CHAPTER III

DIFFERENCES BETWEEN JER A' AND B' PROBABLY RESULTING
FROM JER-R'S REVISIONS IN JER B'

The first translators who embarked upon translating the
Hebrew Bible chose their Greek equivalents mainly on the basis
of linguistic identifications, but they were also guided by
literary and contextual considerations and several of their
choices were tendentious. The results of the translators'
search for equivalents are not the same in the various books of
the Canon, nor in the different semantic fields. One of the
reasons leading to these differences is the fact that within
the books of the LXX there are opposing tendencies with regard
to the representation of individual Hebrew words. "Literal"
translators not only attempted to choose those equivalents
which would express the meaning of the Hebrew word in the best
way, but they also tended to use the same rendition as much as
possible. In this way a translator's jargon developed in which
certain Hebrew roots and words were represented with one standard ("stereotyped") translation. This system facilitated the
translation process and, in a way, was also of help to the
reader. Less literal and "free" translators used only that
part of the system which was needed to make their translation
understandable within the framework of the LXX--mainly some
basic concepts and frequently occurring words--but they often
deviated from it in accordance with the special requirements of
the context and their feeling for style.

Differences in the translation vocabulary should be expected not only between different books, but also within any
given unit that may be considered homogeneous. For a translator may vary the use of translation equivalents, often without
any apparent reason and often in accordance with literary or
contextual considerations and/or exegetical traditions.[1]

As a result of this situation, consistency in the representation of a given Heb 1 with Gk 1 is not to be expected in
any single book of the LXX. Only very literal translations,
such as Aquila's revision of the LXX, may be regarded as

41

consistent with regard to the employment of translation equivalents. By way of example, we may mention the verb הלך which is represented in the various books of the LXX with more than 80 equivalents, while in Aquila's revision mainly with πορεύομαι.

It needs, therefore, hardly to be stressed that one should be very cautious in drawing conclusions with regard to a peculiar distribution of translation options within any book of the LXX. Only when the distribution does not reflect types of variation or exegesis may it be regarded as reflecting a special situation. Conversely, if the variation follows a clear pattern, it cannot be considered mere "variation" and an alternative explanation is needed. Such, apparently, is the case in Jer-LXX:

It seems to us that the differences in translation equivalents of one Hebrew word within the book of Jer cannot be ascribed to mere variation,[2] nor do they result from the occasional insertion in Jer-LXX of readings from other translations. The differences are too numerous and they follow a relatively clear pattern: Many Hebrew words, roots, and phrases are rendered in Jer 1-28 differently from their translation in chapters 29-52 and Bar.

It is improbable that after ch. 28 a single translator would have changed his vocabulary as drastically as the observed evidence would necessitate; it was therefore suggested by Thackeray, "Gr.Tr.Jer.", that two different translators were responsible for Jer a' and b'. However, we have attempted to demonstrate in the preceding chapter that Jer a' and b' exhibit many important agreements which make such a two-translator theory untenable. We therefore turn to an alternative explanation of the facts which takes account both of the differences and of the agreements: The two sets of data are best explained by a theory which supposes a partial revision of the book of Jer, or, more precisely, a revision of Jer-LXX, now preserved only in part. We hope to demonstrate in this chapter that it was Jer b' which was revised. The *per contra* assumption that Jer a' embodies a revision (of a different kind) is discussed in appendix 1 to this chapter.

Data provided in this chapter are intended to show how a
Hebrew word was rendered in Jer a' mainly by Gk 1, while in Jer
b' mainly by Gk 2. We hope to demonstrate that the relationship between Gk 1 and Gk 2 is that of an original to its revision. It is further assumed that, as a rule,[3] the Gk 1 rendition originally formed part of the OG of Jer b'.[4]

Differences[5] between Jer a' and b' are classified according to the presumed tendencies of Jer-R's revision, viz.,

1. more precise renditions;
2. corrections of erroneous renditions;
3. stereotyped (literal) replacing non-stereotyped (free)
   renditions;
4. renditions reflecting the Heb more consistently;
5. other changes.

Although we described above in a general way what we mean
by 'stereotyped', the characterizations 'literal' and 'stereotyped' need to be discussed more thoroughly, though not in the
present context.[6]

Our suggestion is not without difficulties. They may be
summarized as the following:

1. A major problem in the recognition of Jer-R as a revised text is the question of what may be expected from a revision of the LXX. Unfortunately, the rich literature on the LXX
revisions contains only few descriptions of the revision techniques employed, so that the reader may get an imprecise picture from knowing only one or two revisions.

We shall first attempt to define the essence of the LXX
revisions:
A given textual tradition can be considered a revision of the
LXX if the following two conditions are met:

(a) The LXX and the revision share a common textual basis, established by the recognition of distinctive agreements.

(b) The reviser retouched the LXX in a certain direction,
generally towards a more precise reflection of his Hebrew
source. Other revisions aim at greater clarity as well as at
improvement of the Greek language.

The first of these conditions is met with regard to Jer-R as has been shown in ch. II. The second condition is met once we can show that there exists a common denominator to the various changes which presumably were introduced by Jer-R. It seems to us that this common denominator is a trend towards a more precise and consistent representation of the Hebrew *Vorlage*. Similar tendencies are found in the "Three" (Aq, Sym and Th), the revisions of Origen and Lucian and, to a lesser extent, in several pre-Hexaplaric revisions such as Pap. Ryl. Gk. 458 of Deut, Pap. Chester-Beatty-Scheide 967 of Ez, Pap. Antinoopolis 8 of Prov, 4QLXX Num, 7QLXX Ex. It is noteworthy that a much smaller number of Greek words was changed in the revisions of the latter kind than in the revisions of the "Three", Origen and Lucian. By way of example, we may quote Ziegler's description of Pap. Chester-Beatty-Scheide 967 of Ez: "Diese Bearbeitung nach dem hebr. Text war keine durchgehende, sondern nur gelegentliche Verbesserung."[7] It is hard to determine why certain revisions were thorough while others were merely superficial. As a rule the earlier revisions were less thorough than the later ones; beyond this we can say only that the character of the reviser determined the scope of the revision.

Within the framework of the known revisions of the LXX the revision of Jer-R will thus be no exception, if we describe it in the following as a revisionwhich, as far as we know, retouched only a limited number of words.

2. Closely related with the aforementioned problem is the question of the *inconsistency* of the assumed revision of Jer-R. Different renditions of one Hebrew word found in Jer a' and Jer b' are described here as the original rendition and its revision. However, if this assumption is correct, one must acknowledge that the reviser was rather inconsistent, because he left many renditions unrevised which he retouched in other instances. Furthermore, he did not revise certain words which he would have retouched according to what we know about his revision technique (e.g., some of the examples of ch. II, in particular some "incorrect" renditions). Moreover, his revision is characterized by several revisional tendencies which are at

times opposed; contrast, e.g., literal non-stereotyped renditions with stereotyped non-literal renditions (see below).

While recognizing these difficulties, it seems to us that
they are not insurmountable because similar phenomena are found
in other revisions of the LXX.

A good example of this point is the revision of Lucian.
For (the historical) Lucian left many readings unrevised which
he retouched in other instances. Moreover, since the days of
Rahlfs,[8] Lucian's revision has been characterized as containing
both elements which bring the LXX into closer conformity with
MT and elements which are meant to improve the Greek style of
the translation. This situation was partly caused by the
discrepancy between Lucian's source and his own preferences,[9]
but in practice the two tendencies are incompatible. Another
example is the revision of Symmachus, containing both literal
elements apparently derived from *kaige*-Th's revision,[10] as well
as paraphrastic renditions issuing from Symmachus himself.[11]
Opposing tendencies of another type are also present within
kaige-Th: on the one hand one notices stereotyped renditions,
such as the translation of איש with ἀνήρ also when the Heb is
used as 'everyone',[12] and on the other hand one finds etymological, non-stereotyped translations such as נצב/יצב - στηλόω
(based upon מצבה - στήλη),[13] as well as the unusual, non-
stereotyped translation of אנכי with ἐγώ εἰμι.[14] The co-
existence of literal non-stereotyped renditions and stereotyped non-literal translations in Jer b' should therefore certainly not surprise us.

The list of inconsistencies of the LXX revisions can be
extended. However, for us it is of importance to stress that
the mere fact of the inconsistencies should not prevent the
very assumption that Jer b' contains a revision. The fact that
a given revision is inconsistent did not undermine previous
analyses of revisions.[15] See further below, pp. 157ff.

As indicated above, we suggest our working hypothesis in
spite of the mentioned difficulties because the agreements discussed in ch. II do not seem to leave any other possible explanation of the differences between Jer a' and b'.

The evidence is classified according to the presumed tendencies of Jer-R's revision, and those items which are the most

46

convincing for the assumption of a revision are found at the
beginning of each section. The reader who wants to get an impression of the more important examples before reading them in
our sequence is advised to read first the data collected in
items 1,18,19 and 43.

The data listed below are presented as in the preceding
chapter: In this chapter the left column contains renditions
of Jer a' which are contrasted to renditions of Jer b' found in
the right column. Renditions found only in Jer a' or b' are
marked ¹; Greek words found only in Jer a' or b' are marked *.
In this chapter the additional renditions of the Heb mentioned
after the sign ---→ refer respectively to Jer a' or Jer b'
only.

1. *More Precise Renditions*

Jer-R replaced some renditions of Jer-OG with renditions
which in his opinion better expressed the meaning of the Heb.

(1) שממה , שמה

ἀφανισμός (18 x)	ἄβατος , noun ¹ (12 x) [16]
9:11(10) 10:22 12:11,11	29:14,18(49:13,17) 30:11(49:
18:16 19:8 25:9,11,12	33) 31(48):9 32:4,24(25:18,
26(46):19 27(50):3,13,23	38) 39(32):43 49(42):18
28(51):26,29,37,41,62;	51(44):6,22 Bar 2:4,23
this is also the chief rendi-	
tion of Ez and the only one	
of the MP (VI 61); elsewhere	
2 x.	
---→ ἄβατος, adj. 6:8	---→ ἔρημος 41(34):22 BSC'
12:10 28(51):43; ἀπορία 8:21;	(ἄβατος AQVO = Bar 2:23);
ἔρημος 4:27; ἐρήμωσις 4:7;	ἀπώλεια 30(49):2 51(44):12.
ἔκστασις 5:30.	

Since this is the first example of ch. III, we shall describe our notation in detail. A comparison of the two columns
shows that שממה (שמה) is differently represented in Jer a' and
Jer b'. ἀφανισμός is the main rendition of the Heb in Jer a'

(18 x), where it is in addition rendered seven times in other
ways. In Jer b' the Heb is mainly rendered with ἄβατος (12 x);
other renditions are used on three occasions.

As indicated by the sign !, the rendition ἄβατος does not
occur outside Jer b' (in the three mentioned verses in Jer a',
the word is used as an adj.). Jer a''s main rendition,
ἀφανισμός, is also the main rendition of Ez.

שמם ('to destroy', 'to be desolate')[17]

ἀφανίζω (3 x)	ἀβατόω* (1 x)
12:11 27(50):21,45 (both *hiph'il*); and frequently in the MP, Ez and Lam (VI 61).	29:21(49:20)
---→ ἐρημόω 10:25	---→ ἐρημόω 40(33):10.

Jer-OG's ἀφανισμός ('the act of destroying') has been replaced by Jer-R with ἄβατος (literally 'untrodden'[18]) because
the former does not precisely represent the Heb.[19] Jer-R even
went so far as to innovate a corresponding verb ἀβατόω, which
occurs only here in Greek literature (cf. *Thesaurus*), and which
relates to ἄβατος as ἐρημόω to ἔρημος, both of which occur frequently in the LXX.

(2) שדד

ταλαιπωρέω (6 x)	ὄλλυμι (7 x)
4:13,20,20 9:19(18) 10:20 12:12; and further 7x in the MP (VI 1) Is 33:1 Ps 16(17):9.	29:11(49:10) 30(49):3 31(48):1,15,18,20 38(31):2(MT שרידי)
---→ (ἐξ)ολεθρεύω 5:6 28(51):53,55	ἀπόλλυμι
	29(47):4; and further Is 23:1,14 Ez 32:12.
	---→ ἐξολεθρεύω 29(47):4; πλήσσω 30:6(49:28).[20]

שֹׁד

ταλαιπωρία (2 x)[21]	ὅλεθρος (1 x)
6:7 20:8;	31(48):3;
and 11x in the LXX.	and further Prov 21:7.

שַׁדֵד

ταλαιπωρία (2 x)	ὅλεθρος ! (2 x)
6:26 15:8 28(51):56;	31(48):8,32
cf. further Mich 2:4 (VI 1).	

Since the root ταλαιπωρ- ('to endure hardship')[22] does not precisely represent שדד ('to devastate', 'to plunder'; generally in passive: 'to be destroyed'), it was revised by Jer-R to the stronger (ἀπ)όλλυμι.

The renditions of שֹׁדֵד are instructive for understanding Jer-R's revision technique: The *nomen agentis* שֹׁדֵד[23] is reflected in Jer a' (ταλαιπωρία), Jer b' (ὅλεθρος), and elsewhere[24] as a *nomen actionis*.[25] In 31(48):8,32 Jer-R presumably altered an earlier ταλαιπωρία to ὅλεθρος, replacing the translation option, but not altering the basic understanding of the Heb. The latter action was completed only by Aq and Sym.[26]

(3) אָמֵן

γένοιτο (3 x)[27]	ἀληθῶς ! (1 x)
3:19 (not in MT) 11:5 15:11	35(28):6
(MT אמר);	Elsewhere ἀληθῶς renders sev-
and thus generally in the LXX.[28]	eral times אמנה, אָמְנָה and אָמְנָם.

While אָמֵן is rendered in Jer a' with a verb ('let it be'), it is rendered in Jer b' with an appropriate adverb.

(4) זְרֹעַ

βραχίων (2 x)	ἐπίχειρον* (3 x)
17:5 21:5;	29:11(49:10) MT זְרֹעַ - ἐπίχειρα
and *passim* in the LXX.	Rudolph] MSS δια χειρα[29]

31(48):25 (ἐπίχειρον V)
34:4(27:5) BSA (βραχίων rel)

---→ βραχίων 39(32):17,21
Bar 2:11.

Jer-R apparently considered ἐπίχειρον ('that which is
above the hand') a more precise rendition of זְרֹעַ than βραχίων
although he left this rendition twice unrevised.

ἐπίχειρον is not attested elsewhere in Greek literature
(cf. *Thesaurus*)[30] and may have been coined by Jer-R.

(5) אחר(י)

μετά (3 x)	ὕστερον + gen. ¦ (4 x)
3:7 12:15 24:1;	36(29):2 38(31):19,19
and *passim* in the LXX.	47(40):1(?)[31]
	---→ μετά 35(28):12 38:33(31:
	32) 39(32):16 41(34):8
	43(36):27 Bar 1:9.

In place of the stereotyped LXX rendition אחר(י) - μετά
Jer-R used a rendition which may have been chosen because it
shows the etymological connection between אחר(י) and אחרון -
ὕστερος.

Jer-R used ὕστερον + gen. in a sense which, according to
our lexica,[32] is not documented before the LXX.[33] Cf. also VII
4.

(6) לבלתי

τοῦ μή (10 x)	πρὸς τὸ μή ¦ (12 x)
16:12 17:23,23,24,24,27	39(32):40 41(34):9 42(35):8,
18:10 19:15 23:14	9,14 43(36):25 45(38):26
28(51):62; and *passim* in the	49(42):13 51(44):5,7
LXX.	Bar 1:19 2:5
---→ 7:8 לבלתי הועיל - ὅθεν	---→ τοῦ μή 33(26):24.
οὐκ ὠφεληθήσεσθε.	

The most frequent rendition in the LXX of לבלתי is that of
Jer-OG (τοῦ μή). Since many of the LXX translators felt that
this rendition did not adequately express both components of
לבלתי, several new renditions were introduced, especially (1)
ὅπως μή, ἵνα μή, ὥστε μή, all starting a final clause, and (2)
παρά τὸ μή, τὸ παράπαν μή, τοῦ μή εἰς τέλος, τὸ καθόλου μή and
πρὸς τὸ μή.[34] Yet, none of these more precise renditions outnumber τοῦ μή in any one book of the LXX. Jer-R, on the other
hand, was the only translator who almost consistently employed
a more precise rendition than τοῦ μή, i.e., πρὸς τὸ μή (τοῦ μή
in 33(26):24 was probably left unrevised).[35] See further pp.
165-66.

<h2 style="text-align:center">(7) למען + inf.</h2>

finite clause (3 x)	πρὸς τό + inf. ! (4 x)
ἵνα 7:18 ὅπως 11:5 27(50):34; and *passim* in the LXX.	34:8,12(27:10,15) 39(32):29, 35
---→ 7:10 נצלנו‸למען‸עשות - ἀπεσχήμεθα τοῦ μὴ ποιεῖν.[36]	---→ ἵνα 50(43):3 51(44):8.

Jer-OG's rendition is the usual one in the LXX,[37] revised
by Jer-R to the more literal πρὸς τό + inf.

The evidence gathered in this and the preceding items indicates that in the LXX the use of πρός + art. inf. is limited
to Jer-R, with the exception of Ex 1:16 where, however, πρός
governs the dative.

<h2 style="text-align:center">(8) עבד ('to serve someone')</h2>

δουλεύω (10 x)	ἐργάζομαι ! (15 x)
2:20 5:19,19 8:2 11:10 13:10 16:11,13 22:9 25:6; and *passim* in the LXX.	34:5,7,9,9,10(27:6,9,11,11,12) 35(28):14 37(30):8,9 41(34): 14,18 47(40):9 Bar 1:22 2:21,22,24
---→ עבד ב - ἐργάζομαι παρά 22:13.	---→ δουλεύω 34:5(27:6) 41(34):9 42(35):15 Bar 1:12.

Instead of Jer-OG's equivalent עבד - δουλεύω, Jer-R preferred to render עבד with ἐργάζομαι. This lexical choice is significant because ἐργάζομαι is not used in classical Greek as 'to serve someone'.

Jer-R's choice of this verb may have been motivated by his wish to represent both meanings of עבד ('to carry out work', 'to serve someone')[38] with one verb.[39] He also may have opted for a verb which was connected with עבודה - ἔργον.[40]

(9) נֶחַם

μετανοέω (4 x)	παύομαι (4 x)
4:28 8:6 18:8,10; and 6 x in the MP (see VI 3) and elsewhere 3 x (once in Jer b').	33(26):3,13,19 38(31):15 (παρακαλέω B^mg AVC=Matth 2:18); and Is 1:24.
μεταμέλομαι (1 x)	ἀναπαύομαι ! (1 x)
20:16; and *passim* in the LXX.	49(42):10; cf. Gen 5:29 διαναπαύω.
---→ 15:6 הַנָּחֵם - ἀνήσω αὐτούς = הַנַּחֵם.	---→ μετανοέω 38(31):19.

Jer-OG's μετανοέω and μεταμέλομαι, together with παρακαλέω[41] the stereotyped renditions of נחם in the LXX, were revised by Jer-R to (ἀνα)παύομαι.[42] It is possible that μετανοέω in 38(31):19 was left unrevised.

Jer-R probably rendered forms of נחם as if they were derived from נוח (generally represented with (ἀνα)παύομαι).[43] If so, he made an erroneous revision.[44]

(10) עת

καιρός (25 x)	χρόνος ! (3 x)
2:27,28 3:17 4:11 5:24 6:15 8:1,7,15 10:15 11:12,14,14 (MT עד) 14:8,19 15:11 18:23 26(46):21 27(50):4,16,20,27,31 28(51):6,18; and further *passim* in the LXX.	29:9(49:8) 37(30):7 38(31):1 BSA (καιρός rel)

καιρός (Jer-OG), denoting both 'the right moment' and 'time' (the latter from the Hellenistic period onwards), is a somewhat ambiguous rendition of עת. It was possibly for this reason that Jer-R replaced it with the unambiguous χρόνος.[45]

(11) שׂים(פנים)

στηρίζω (1 x)	ἐφίστημι ! (1 x)
21:10;	51(44):11
and further Am 9:4 and Ez (9 x;	
cf. VI 68).	δίδωμι ! (1 x)
Cf. שׂים - στηρίζω in 17:5	49(42):15
24:6; הפיל פנים - στηρίζω	
3:12.	τίθημι (1 x)
	49(42):17;
	and elsewhere in the LXX (3 x).

Jer-OG's free rendition ('to fix') may have been revised by Jer-R to three more precise ones.

2. *Corrections of Erroneous Renditions*

Jer-R revised some renditions of Jer-OG, which he presumably considered incorrect.[46]

(12) נפץ

διασκορπίζω ! (9 x)	συγκόπτω ! (1 x)
13:14 28(51):20,21,22(3 x),	31(48):12 BSAC' (συντρίβω rel)
23(3 x); cf. Th in Dan 9:7	
נפץ - διασκορπισμός.	

Jer-OG διασκορπίζω ('to scatter') is an incorrect rendering of נפץ ('to shatter'), based upon the meaning of the root in Rabb. Hebrew ('to scatter' = Targum *ad loc.*), of which διασκορπίζω is an equivalent (9:16(15) 10:21 23:1,2).[47] Jer-R corrected this rendition.

דמן (על פני האדמה) (13)

παράδειγμα ! (3 x)	κόπριον (1 x)
8:2 9:22(21) 16:4;	32:19(25:33);
cf. Dan 2:5 הדמין תתעבדון –	and further 2 Ki 9:37 (κοπρία)
παραδειγματισθήσεσθε.	Ps 82(83):11 (κόπρος).

Jer-OG, ignorant of the precise meaning of דמן,[48] probably
derived it from דמה[49] and rendered it in accordance with the
context.[50] Jer-R corrected παράδειγμα to κόπριον.

התהלל (14)

various (3 x)	μαίνομαι ! (1 x)
התהללו הרכב – 26(46):9	32:2(25:16) BSA (εκμαιν. rel)
παρασκευάσατε (κατασκ.Α)	
τὰ ἅρματα 27(50):38 יתהללו –	
κατεκαυχῶντο(= יתהללו)	
28(51):7 – σαλεύω	

Presumably unacquainted with the precise meaning of התהלל,
Jer-OG rendered it in three different ways:

1. In 26(46):9 the Heb is reflected by a "passe partout"
    translation (cf. III 25), conforming with its context.[51]
2. In 27(50):38 he vocalized the Heb differently from MT.[52]
3. The rendition in 28(51):7 may have resulted from ignorance
    or from a different exegetical tradition (cf. Targ
    ישתגשון).
    Jer-R rendered the Heb correctly.

נגב (15)

νότος (2 x)	Ναγεβ (2 x)
13:19 ערי הנגב – πόλεις αἱ	39(32):44 and 40(33):13 בערי
πρὸς νότον 17:26 מן הנגב –	הנגב – ἐν πόλεσι τῆς Ναγεβ;
ἐκ τῆς πρὸς νότον;	and passim in the LXX.
and passim in the LXX.	

In the OT נגב denotes (1) 'a certain region in the South'
and (2) 'the South'. Since in the four above-mentioned verses

נגב is used in its first meaning, Jer-OG's rendition (νότος)
was probably considered inappropriate; Jer-R preferred a transliteration.

(16) מגור ('fear', 'terror')

various (5 x)	ἀπώλεια (1 x)
6:25 לאיב מגור - τῶν ἐχθρῶν	30:7(49:29);
παροικεῖ (= לאיבים גר)	cf. Prov 10:24 מגורה - ἀπώλεια.
20:3 μέτοικος 20:4 μετοικία	
20:10 רבים מגור מסביב - πολλῶν	
συναθροιζομένων κυκλόθεν	
(= רבים גרים (מ)סביב)	
26(46):5 מגור מסביב -	
περιεχόμενοι κυκλόθεν;	
cf. Ps 30(31):14 רבים מגור מסביב -	
πολλῶν παροικούντων κυκλόθεν	
(= רבים גרים (מ)סביב) Ps 33(34):5	
מגור - παροικία Lam 2:22 מגורה	
מגורי Ez 21:12(17) παροικία	
παροικήσουσι	

Probably unfamiliar with the meaning 'fear', 'terror', of
מגור, Jer-OG rendered it with various equivalents, some of
which were based on a consonantal reading different from that
of MT. The deviations from MT and the variation in representing the Heb show Jer-OG's hesitations:
1.   The translation in 6:25 was based upon גור - 'to dwell'.
2.   The renditions in 20:3,4 were founded on גור - 'to sojourn',
     possibly also influenced by הגלה - μετοικίζω in the same
     verse.
3.   The rendition in 20:10 may have been derived from גור - 'to
     dwell', גרר - 'to assemble',[53] or אגר.
4.   The rendering of מגור with περιεχόμενοι in 26(46):5 should
     probably be considered a guess equating מגור with מצור
     (cf. מצור - περιοχή *passim* and see the article quoted in
     II, n. 9.).
The LXX translators of Ps, Lam and Ez were likewise unacquainted with the meaning מגור - 'fear'.

Jer-R's ἀπώλεια, although not a literal equivalent of
מגור, was probably meant to render the Heb as 'terror'.[54] It
is not impossible, however, that Jer-R and the translator of
Prov derived מגור from מגר - 'to destroy'.[55]

(17) אולי

εἰ (2 x)	ἴσως (3 x)
20:10 21:2;	33(26):3 43(36):3,7;
and further 4 x in the LXX.	and elsewhere Gen 32:21.
εἰ πῶς (1 x)	
28(51):8;	
and further 3 x in the LXX.	

Although אולי originally served as an adverb, at times,
when "followed by another clause ἀσυνδέτως, it expresses vir-
tually the protasis = if peradventure" (BDB, s.v.). But the
majority of LXX translators, including Jer-OG, rendered אולי as
'if peradventure...'[56] (starting a dependent clause), making an
infrequent use of אולי the basis of their main rendition.
    Jer-R revised the OG to ἴσως, starting off an independent
sentence.[57]

3. *Stereotyped (literal) Replacing Non-stereotyped (free) Renditions*

Several examples show a certain tendency of Jer-R to prefer stereotyped to non-stereotyped renditions (cf. p. 43 above).
Two similar phenomena are distinguished according to Jer-OG's
techniques:

a. *Gk 1 (non-stereotyped) in Jer a' versus Gk 2 (stereotyped) in Jer b'*

In the following instances, Jer-OG justifiably represented
the Heb with non-stereotyped renditions when it occurred in
certain phrases, combinations or situations which are best rendered as such. Jer-R tended to replace these renditions with
stereotyped ones.
    The examples listed below may be schematically represented
in the following way (example 18):

כה Heb

Jer-OG: Gk 1 τάδε (representing the Heb in כה אמר ה');
Gk 2 οὕτως generally representing the Heb in other circumstances

Jer-R: Gk 2 οὕτως only.

כה אמר ה' (18)

τάδε λέγει κύριος (58 x)	οὕτως εἶπε κύριος (69 x)
2:31 4:3(ουτωςS*) 4:27 5:14	30(49):1 30:6(49:28) 31(48):
6:6,9,16,21,22 7:3,20,21 8:4	1,40 32:1,13,14,18(25:15,27,
9:7,15,23(6,14,22) 10:2,18	28,32) 33(26):2,4,18 34:1,3,
11:3,11,21 12:14 13:1,9,13	16(27:1,4,19) 35(28):2,11,13,
14:15 15:2,19 16:3,5,9	14,16 36(29):4,8,10,21,31,32
17:19,21 18:13 19:3,11,15	37(30):2,5,12(λεγει A),18
20:4 21:4,8,12 22:1,3,6,11,18	38(31):2,7,15,16,23,36(35)
23:2,15,38 24:5,8 25:8,15(49:	39(32):3,14,15,28,36,42
35) 27(50):18,33 28(51):1,33,	40(33):2,4,10 41(34):2,13,17
58	42(35):17,18 43(36):29,30
	44(37):7,9 45(38):2,3,17
	46(39):16 49(42):9,15,18
	50(43):10 51(44):2,7,11,25,
	30,32(45:2),34(45:4) Bar
	2:21
---→ οὕτως λέγει κύριος 14:10	---→ τάδε λέγει κύριος[58]
(ειπεν S) 21:7 23:16.	29:2,8(47:2,7) 29:13(49:12;
	BS ειπεν); οὕτως λέγει κύριος
	41(34):4 42(35):13.

Since an investigation of the renderings of כה אמר ה' should not be separated from an examination of all *verba dicendi* with כה, the following chart lists the renditions of (1) כה[59] + *v.d.* (= *verba dicendi*) (נבא, צוה, דבר, אמר), excluding renditions of the formula כה אמר פלוני, listed in (2).

| | (1) כה+v.d. | | (2) כה אמר פלוני | | | |
| | a | b | a | b | c | d |
	v.d. + οὕτως	v.d. + τάδε	οὕτως λέγει	τάδε λέγει	οὕτως εἶπε	τάδε εἶπε
Gen	4		1	1		
Ex	2	2		11		
Num	1	1		2		
Jos				3		
Jud		1	1	2		
Reigns a'		5		1		3[61]
b'b'		1		2		
b'c'	1	1		3	1[60]	
c'c'	2	4		15		
c'd'		2		28	1	
1 Chr	1		1	1	1	
2 Chr	3		3	5	3	
MP				43		
Is a'	3		4	13	4	
Is b'			21	6		
Jer a'	2		3	58		
Jer b'	2		2	3	69	
Ez				122	2	

The stereotyped LXX rendition of כה, also when connected
with a v.d., is οὕτως (1a). In this situation, however, the
rendering with τάδε (1b) is just as frequent because the Hebrew
v.d. + כה is best represented with a Greek v.d. + τάδε. The
same applies to the formula כה אמר פלוני, whose predominant
rendition τάδε λέγει δεῖνα (2b) is used also in classical Greek
as 'he says/said the following' (LSJ, s.v. λέγω III,8).

In addition to the predominant LXX rendition of כה אמר
פלוני, τάδε λέγει δεῖνα (2b), the LXX translators used three
more literal renditions: in renditions 2a, c and d the present
tense was replaced by the aorist and/or כה is represented with
its stereotyped equivalent, with οὕτως.[62] Only in two translation units is the non-stereotyped rendition of the phrase out-
numbered by more stereotyped ones:
Is b'   οὕτως λέγει :   τάδε λέγει = 21:6.[63]
Jer b'   οὕτως εἶπε :   τάδε λέγει = 69:3.

While the relationship between the two parts of Is needs further study, it is reasonable to assume that Jer-R's renditions
bear the mark of a revision.[64]

It is noteworthy that the known revisers of Jer-LXX, while
generally leaving τάδε λέγει κύριος and οὕτως εἶπε κύριος unrevised, often altered οὕτως εἶπε κύριος to τάδε λέγει κύριος,[65]
probably because the latter is the main LXX rendition. Likewise, the "Three", O and L added τάδε λέγει κύριος to the LXX
in many asterized passages in Jer.[66] τάδε λέγει κύριος is also
in other parts of the LXX their most frequent rendition.[67] It
is remarkable that in the reproduction of כה אמר ה' Jer-R's
lexical choice was more literal than those of the other revisers of the LXX.

(19) אלהים אחרים

θεοὶ ἀλλότριοι (12 x)	θεοὶ ἕτεροι (7 x)
1:16 5:19(ετεροι A) 7:6,9,18	39(32):29 42(35):15(αλλοτριοι
11:10 13:10 16:11 19:4,13	SA) 51(44):3,5,8,15 (om BS)
22:9 25:6;	Bar 1:22;
and further Hos 3:1 (VI 2) and	and further *passim* in the LXX.
elsewhere 6 x.	
---→ θεοὶ ἕτεροι 16:13	
(αλλοτριοι QV).	

Jer-R substituted the stereotyped rendition of אחר for
Jer-OG's rendering.[68]

(20) הטה אזן

προσέχω τὸ οὖς (τὰ ὦτα) (3 x)	κλίνω τὸ οὖς(τὰ ὦτα) (4 x)
7:24,26 25:4;	41(34):14 42(35):15 51(44):5
and Is 55:3 Dan 9:18.	Bar 2:16;
	and *passim* in the LXX.
---→ κλίνω τὸ οὖς 17:22.	

The employment of προσέχω τὸ οὖς in classical Greek probably influenced Jer-OG in the choice of this non-stereotyped
rendition, subsequently altered by Jer-R.

59

(21) בעיני

ἐναντίον (2 x)	prep. + ὀφθαλμός (5 x)[69]
7:30 (ενωπιον AQ) 18:10	34:4(27:5) 39(32):30 41(34):
	15 47(40):5 Bar 1:22;
ἐνώπιον (1 x)	and *passim* in the LXX.
7:11	
	---> ἐναντίον 47(40):4
Both renditions are well-	Bar 1:12; dat. 33(26):14.[70]
represented in the whole LXX,	
cf. Johannessohn, *Präposi-*	
tionen 191, 196.	

While leaving three renditions untouched, Jer-R chose to express the two constituents of the preposition with their stereotyped renditions.[71]

(22) לפני

ἐναντίον (6 x)	κατὰ πρόσωπον (20 x)
1:17 2:22 15:9 18:23 19:7	29:20(49:19) 33(26):4 37(30):
25:17(49:37)	20 38:37(31:36) 41(34):15,18
	42(35):5,19 43(36):7,9,22
ἐνώπιον (1 x)	44(37):20 49(42):2 51(44):10
7:10	52:12,33 Bar 1:11 2:10,14,19
κατὰ πρόσωπον (5 x)	---> εἰς πρόσωπον 30(49):5;
	ἐναντίον 47(40):10 Bar 2:28;
18:17,20 24:1 27(50):8,44	πρότερος 35(28):8,8 41(34):5.
πρὸ προσώπου (4 x)	
9:13(12) 15:1,19 21:8	

Contrary to Jer-OG, Jer-R for the most part rendered לפני as κατὰ πρόσωπον, which faithfully represents the two components of the Heb.[72]

It should be noted that Jer-R substituted ἐναντίον not only as an equivalent of לפני, but also of בעיני (III 21) and of חטא(ל- (III 27).

All the renditions occur *passim* in the LXX.

60

לקח מוסר (23)

δέχομαι παιδείαν (4 x)	(ἐκ)λαμβάνω παιδείαν (2 x)
2:30 5:3 7:28 17:23; and Zeph 3:2,7. Cf. also Prov. 1:3 δέχομαι στροφὰς λόγων.	39(32):33 ἐκλαβεῖν (ετι λαβειν BSA) 42(35):13 λαμβάνω; and further Prov 8:10.

Jer-OG's δέχομαι correctly rendered לקח denoting 'to receive' in the above-mentioned expression.[73] Jer-R employed the stereotyped rendition of לקח ('to take') - (ἐκ)λαμβάνω.

(24) Various

ἔχω (6 x)

3:3 - מנע 9:8(7) - שים 15:18
17:5 - בטח - ἐλπίδα ἔχω 18:15 - Ø
27(50):42 - החזיק

Four of the six occurrences of ἔχω represent non-stereotyped renditions of the Heb. Since this use is not found in Jer b', it may be assumed that the reviser eliminated the use of ἔχω for this reason.

(25) Various

παρασκευάζω (5 x)

6:4 קדשו עליה מלחמה - παρασκευάσασθε ἐπ'αὐτὴν εἰς πόλεμον

12:5 תתחרה את הסוסים - παρασκευάσῃ ἐφ'ἵπποις[74]

26(46):9 התהללו הרכב - παρασκευάσατε (κατασκ. A) τὰ ἅρματα[75]

27(50):42 ערוך...למלחמה - παρασκευασμένοι...εἰς πόλεμον

28(51):11 הברו החצים - παρασκευάζετε τὰ τοξεύματα

Occurring in only six additional places in the LXX, this
verb was clearly cherished by Jer-OG. The mentioned examples
show that Jer-OG availed himself of this verb particularly when
he felt uncertain about the meaning of the Heb. The broad
meaning of παρασκευάζω made it an adequate "passe-partout" rendition.[76]

Since this general use of παρασκευάζω is not found in Jer
b', it was probably eliminated by Jer-R.

(26) ישב

κατοικέω : *passim*	κατοικέω : *passim*
κατοικέομαι (10 x)	
2:15 4:7 6:8(-ίζω B) 9:11	
(10) 17:6 22:6 27(50):13	
(-ίζω QV),39 28(51):29,37;	
and the MP, Is and Ez, cf.	
VI 69.	
---→ In Jer a': especially	---→ In Jer b': especially
καθίζω, κάθημαι.	ἐνοικέω, καθίζω, κάθημαι.

Jer-OG often represented active forms of ישב[77] with
κατοικέομαι because either the *Vorlage* has a passive meaning,[78]
or because the translator chose to render the phrases מאין ישב
and מבלי ישב with passive forms (see III 28). Jer-R possibly
eliminated this use of κατοικέομαι (Cf. 30(37):18 and the examples mentioned in item 28).

(27) חטא ל- - ἀμαρτάνω +...
(in all the obj.: God)

ἔναντι/ἐναντίον (4 x)	dat. (6 x)
3:25 8:14 14:20 16:10;	40(33):8,8 47(40):3 51(44):
and *passim* in the LXX.	23 Bar 1:13 2:5;
	and *passim* in the LXX.
---→ dat. 14:7[79] 27(50):7;	---→ ἔναντι/ἐναντίον Bar 1:17
and *passim* in the LXX.	2:33 3:2,4,7; cf. further

44(37):18 ἀδικέω (different object).

Since Jer-OG wanted to avoid the slightly harsh expression 'to sin to (God)', he rendered the Heb with ἁμαρτάνω ἔναντι/ ἐναντίον.[80] This translation was frequently revised by Jer-R to its literal rendition.[81] The number of renditions left unchanged by the reviser is rather large; but, since all of them are concentrated in Bar 1-3, an alternative explanation may be suggested.[82]

(28) מאין + noun

verb, esp. διά/παρά + art. inf. (5 x)	ἀπό + noun (5 x)
4:7 מאין יושב - παρὰ τὸ μὴ κατοικεῖσθαι αὐτάς 7:32 מאין מקום - διὰ τὸ μὴ ὑπάρχειν τόπον 26(46):19 מאין יושב - διὰ τὸ μὴ ὑπάρχειν κατοικοῦντας ἐν αὐτῇ 28(51):29 מאין יושב - καὶ μὴ κατοικεῖσθαι αὐτήν 28(51):37 מאין יושב - καὶ οὐ κατοικηθήσεται; and *passim* in the LXX. Cf. מבלי + noun - παρὰ τὸ μὴ + inf.: 2:15 9:10,11,12(11, 12,13).[84]	מאין יושב 33(26):9, 41(34):22- ἀπὸ κατοικούντων מאין אדם 39(32):43, 40(33):10- ἀπὸ ἀνθρώπων Bar 2:23 ἀπὸ ἐνοικούντων ---→ παρὰ τὸ μή + inf. מאין 40(33):10;[83] 31(48):9 יושב - πόθεν ἔνοικος αὐτῇ (= מֵאַיִן) BQ (αυτης SOQV)] απο ενοικουντων αυτας A.

Occurring also *passim* in the LXX, in the "Three" and in O,[85] the rendering found in Jer-OG represents the short Heb expression adequately, although not literally, since it adds an infinitive to the Heb.[86] Jer-R's ἀπό + noun,[87] on the other hand, was meant to reflect מאין + noun more precisely.[88] It is noteworthy that Jer-R's renderings are more successful from a reviser's point of view than those of the "Three" and O (cf. n. 85).

(29) ὑπάρχω

ὑπάρχω (4 x)

5:13 7:32 (מאין) 26(46):19
(מאין) 27(50):20;
and *passim* in the LXX.

In many sentences lacking a copula in the Heb, the LXX translators added ὑπάρχω, especially in negative sentences. This usage is not found in Jer b' (for מאין, see III 28).

(30) διότι

ὅτι : *passim* in Jer a'	ὅτι : *passim* in Jer b'

διότι (25 x)

1:12,15 2:10 3:8,14,25 4:8,
15,22,28 8:17 15:20 16:9
20:4 21:10(οτι S*) 22:4,11
(οτι S) 23:12 26(46):21,27
27(50):11 28(51):5,14,29,33;
cf. further VI 70.

As in the remainder of the LXX, Jer-OG generally used both ὅτι and διότι for כי, employing διότι particularly to avoid a hiatus (see Thackeray, *Grammar*, 139). Jer-R limited himself to ὅτι.

(31) δέ

δέ : καί = 1:42	δέ : καί = 1:148
(22:917 occurrences)	(6:889 occurrences) [89]

Turner observed that the relation between δέ and καί ranges from 1:1 in 4 Macc to 1:188 in Jer b' (*Syntax*, 331-2), the latter displaying an un-Greek style in this respect. The situation in Jer a' is somewhere in the middle (1:42). It is therefore significant that Jer-R, more than any other translator of the LXX, avoided using δέ where καί would represent the Heb *waw* in a stereotyped way.[90]

(32) <u>The Employment / Lack of the Gk</u>
<u>Article in Accordance with the Heb</u>

In the concluding remarks to his penetrating study of the
article in Jer-LXX (*Beiträge*, ch. IV), Ziegler remarked: "Der
Artikel ist oftmals in der Ier.-und Thr.-LXX im Anschluss an MT
(also besonders beim Status constructus) nicht gesetzt worden.
Er fehlt häufiger in Ier. II und Thr. als in Ier. I" (*ib.*,
167).[91] On the other hand, the *addition* of the article against
the Heb follows the rules of the Greek language. In the following syntactical conditions a more or less different trend in
Jer a' and b' is discernible:

a. *prep. + noun + suff.*,
e.g., במלכותו - ἐν (τῇ) βασιλείᾳ αὐτοῦ[92]

article : 125 x	article : 60 x
no article : 35 x	no article : 40 x

b. *prep. + double noun*

"gern der doppelte Artikel"	"...er fehlt dagegen in Ier.
(Ziegler, *ib.*, 127), e.g.,	II...gewöhnlich..." (*ib.*, 127)
13:22 διὰ τὸ πλῆθος τῆς	e.g., 29(47):3 ἀπὸ φωνῆς ὁρμῆς
ἀδικίας σου	αὐτοῦ

c. *prep. +* עיר *+ proper noun*
e.g., בערי יהודה

<u>article</u> (4 x)	<u>article</u> (1 x ?)
4:16 7:17,34 17:26	51(44):21[93]
<u>no article</u> (1 x)	<u>no article</u> (11 x)
11:6	38(31):24 39(32):44 40(33):
	10,13 41(34):7,7 51(44):2,6,
	17,21 Bar 2:23

(33) יום, followed immediately by a verb[94]

ἡμέρα + rel. pron. + rel. clause (2 x)	ἡμέρα + gen. abs. / part. conj. (4 x)
7:22, 11:4 ἐν ἡμέρᾳ ᾗ ἀνήγα-γον (η ημερα QV); and thus generally in the LXX (see Sois.-Soin., *Infinitive*, 24 - 27).	38:32(31:31) ἡμέρᾳ ἐπιλαβομέ-νου μου 43(36):2 ἀφ'ἧς ἡμέρας λαλήσαντός μου (om ης VQ^CL) 48(41):4 τῇ ἡμέρᾳ τῇ δευτέρᾳ πατάξαντος αὐτοῦ Bar 2:28 ἐν ἡμέρᾳ ἐντειλαμένου σου and elsewhere in the LXX (cf. Sois.-Soin., *Infinitive*, 26), Aq, Th and O.[95]
	---→ ἡμέρα + noun 38(31):6(5); ἡμέρα + rel. pron. + rel. clause 41(34):13 Bar 1:19,20

Jer-OG's translations render the Heb well, but since they include a relative pronoun not found in the Heb, they were replaced with a gen. abs. or part. conj., probably the closest a Greek translation can come to the Heb.

b. *Gk 1 (stereotyped) and Gk 2 in Jer a' versus*
   Gk 2 (stereotyped) only in Jer b'

Jer-OG rendered the Heb with two or more renditions, which the reviser tended to reduce to one, i.e., its stereotyped rendition in the LXX.

All renditions mentioned in this section occur *passim* in the LXX.

(34) הוציא

ἐκφέρω (5 x)	ἐξάγω (10 x)
8:1 17:22 27(50):25 28(51):10,44	33(26):23 38(31):32(31) 39(32):21 45(38):22,23 46(39):14 52:31 Bar 1:19,20 2:11
ἐξάγω (4 x)	
10:13 15:19 20:3 28(51):16	

ἀνάγω (2 x)   ---→ ἐξαιρέω 41(34):13;
7:22 11:4   ἐκφέρω Bar 1:8 2:24.

(35) שֶׁבֶר

συντριβή (4 x)   σύντριμμα (3 x)
4:6 6:1 27(50):22 28(51):54   31(48):3,5 37(30):12

σύντριμμα (4 x)
6:14 8:21 10:19 14:17

σύντριμμος (1 x)
4:20; cf. VI 29.

(36) יחדו

ἐπὶ τὸ αὐτό (4 x)   ἅμα (4 x)
3:18 6:12 26(46):12   30(49):3 31(48):7 38(31):24
27(50):4   48(41):1

ἐν τῷ αὐτῷ (1 x)
13:14

ἅμα (4 x)
6:11,21 27(50):33 28(51):38

ὁμοθυμαδόν (2 x)
5:5 26(46):21

(37) 'ה

κύριος : passim in Jer a'   κύριος : passim in Jer b'
θεός (7 x)[96]
1:1,2 3:21 4:4 9:20(19)
(κυριος AC) 14:10 27(50):15;
and elsewhere rather infrequently in the LXX.[97]

However, the *Vorlage* of 3:21
4:4 14:10 and 27(50):15 may
actually have read אלהים.

Reserving θεός for אלהים, Jer-R eliminated the non-stereotyped rendition of 'ה.[98]

(38) ידע *qal*

γιγνώσκω (25 x)

2:16(MT ירעוך),19,23 3:13
5:1,4 6:15,27 8:7,7 9:3,
16,24(2,15,23) 11:18,19
12:3 13:12,12 14:20
15:12(MT ירע),15 16:21
17:9 18:23 22:16,16
(27(50):24 QVOL')

οἶδα (11 x)

4:22 7:9 9:6(5) 10:23,25
14:18 15:14 16:13 19:4
22:28 24:7

ἐπίσταμαι (4 x)

1:5,6 2:8 17:16

ἐπιγιγνώσκω (2 x)

4:22(γιγν. AL'C) 5:5

γιγνώσκω (19 x)

31(48):30 33(26):15,15
38(31):34 39(32):8 40(33):3
43(36:19) 45(38):24 47(40):
14,15 48(41):4 49(42):19,19
51(44):3,15,28 Bar 2:15,30,31

---→ οἶδα 38(31):34(33).

Jer-R used mainly γιγνώσκω.

(39) כ־

ὡς : *passim* in Jer a'

ὡσεί (6 x)

3:2 14:8 26(46):8
27(50):37(AQ^txt-130-239-613

ὡς : *passim* in Jer b'

L^{-36} 311$_{ως}$) 28(51):14,30;
for further variants, see
Ziegler, *Ier*.

  Jer-R used only ὡς.

       (40) הלא

<u>οὐχί</u> (5 x)

2:16(17) 7:19 14:22 23:24
(μη ουχι) 23:29B*SQ*(ουκ B^{C};
ουχ rel)

<u>οὐ</u> (5 x)

3:1,4 5:3^{99} 13:21 22:15,16

<u>οὐχί</u> (3 x)

33(26):19 45(38):15
51(44):21

---→ οὐ μή 42(35):13.

  Limiting οὐ to לא,[100] Jer-R rendered הלא mainly with
οὐχί.[101]

    (41) <u>Emphatic Forms of the Greek Pers. Pronouns</u>

<u>ἐμοῦ</u> (1 x)

4:17

<u>ἐμοί</u> (5 x)

12:8,9 13:25 15:16 20:8

<u>ἐμέ</u> (10 x)

2:13,16(17),19 4:22 5:22
7:19 9:3(2) 16:11 22:16
24:7

<u>ἐμοί</u> (1 x)

38(31):20

  Nearly all the occurrences in Jer-LXX of the emphatic
forms of the pers. pronouns in the oblique cases (except when
preceded by a preposition) are limited to Jer a'.[102] Jer-R may
have discontinued the use of the emphatic forms, restricting
himself to the ordinary forms of the pronoun.[103] The ordinary
forms occur *passim* in Jer a' and b'.

4. *Renditions Reflecting the Heb in a More Consistent Way*

The phenomenon described as "translational consistency"
may come to light in different, even opposing, forms, whose
common characteristic is the tendency to represent the Heb according to preconceived principles.[104] While in section (3)
the revisional tendency is determined by the *character* of the
rendition (stereotyped versus non-stereotyped), the renditions
mentioned below (4a, 4b) are preferred by Jer-R by virtue of
their being the *only* rendition in Jer b', not necessarily more
stereotyped within the LXX.

a. *Gk 1 and Gk 2 in Jer a' versus Gk 1 only in Jer b'*

Instead of Jer-OG's two different renditions of the same
Heb, Jer-R tended to employ only one, thus representing the Heb
in a more consistent way.

(42) עבד

παῖς (3 x)	παῖς (18 x)
21:7 22:4 .26(46):28	32:5(25:19) 33(26):5(δουλος Q^{txt}) 41(34):9,10,11,16,16
δοῦλος (4 x)	42(35):15BS^c(δουλος rel)
2:14 7:25 25:4 26(46):27	43(36):24,31 44(37):18
	47(40):9 51(44):4(δουλος A)
	52:8 Bar 1:20 2:20,24,28

Jer-OG might have distinguished between παῖς and δοῦλος.[105]
Jer-R confined himself to παῖς.[106]

b. *Gk 1 (= Heb 1 + Heb 2) in Jer a' versus Gk 1 (= Heb 1) and Gk 2 (= Heb 2) in Jer b'*

Jer-OG used one Greek word to render two different Hebrew
words, while Jer-R tended to employ two different Greek words.

(43) נאם ה׳

λέγει κύριος (68 x)[107]	φησὶ κύριος (21 x)
1:8,15,17,19AQ (ειπεν κυριος BSVOC')[108] 2:2,9,12,17,19,	30(49):2(λεγει κ.QC'),15(49: 26) 31(48):12,35,38 36(29):23

22,29   3:1,12,13,14,16(φησι
κυριος Q),20   4:1,9,17   5:1
(MT סם וראה),9,15,18,22,29   6:12
7:11,19,30,32   8:1   9:9,24,25
(8,23,24)   13:14,25   15:3,6
16:1,11,16   17:24   19:6,12
(ειπεν κ. S)   21:7   22:5,16,24
23:4,5,23,24,30,33   26(46):
5,18,23,28   27(50):20,21,31
28(51):24,26,39,52,53;
and *passim* in the LXX (Pent,
2 Ki, MP, Is, Ez).

37(30):3,17,21(λεγει κ.Q)
38(31):20,27,28,31C'(λεγει κ.
rel = Hebr.8:8),32,33,35(37),
37(36; λεγει κ.Q), 38(37;
λεγει κ.C')   41(34):22   46(39):
18   49(42):11; and further
1 Sam 2:30   2 Ki 9:26   2 Chr
34:27.

---→ φησι κυριος 2:3(OL'
λεγει and sic Ziegler)   23:12
AQVOL'..(rel om)   25:12
AQVCOL'..(rel om)   27(50):20
AQVOL'...(rel om) - in the
last mentioned three verses
Ziegler correctly omits φησι
κυριος with BS...; ειπε
κυριος 27(50):30,40.

---→ λεγει κυριος 29:14(49:13)
32:17(25:31)   34:18(27:22)
51:35(45:5); ειπε κυριος
30:5,10(49:5,32)   34:6(27:8)
37(30):8   38(31):1   41(34):5.

While the rendition found in Jer-OG, λέγει κύριος,[109] is
by far the most frequent translation in the LXX of נאם ה', φησι
κύριος is almost exclusively confined to Jer b'.

It may be suggested tentatively that Jer-R, the "Three",
O and L endeavored to distinguish between אמר - λέγω, εἶπον (as
in כה אמר ה' - οὕτως εἶπε κύριος and אמר ה' - εἶπε κύριος) and
נאם - φημί. A few cases were left unrevised.[110]

While changing an earlier λέγει κύριος to φησι κύριος, the
revisers did not modify the basic understanding of נאם as a
verb rather than a noun.[111]

A fact which sheds further light on the background of Jer-
R's revision is that Jer-R shares the rendition of this formula
only with the "Three", O and L, and that this is their most
frequent rendition.[112]   See also VII 1.

c. *Exegetical consistency:*

Gk 1 (= Heb 1, meaning 1 and 2) in Jer a' versus Gk 1
(= Heb 1, meaning 1) and Gk 2 (= Heb 1, meaning 2) in Jer b'

Contrary to Jer-OG, Jer-R distinguished in some cases between two meanings or usages of a word. The few examples of this group do not conform with the implication of the preceding ones.

(44) דִּבֶּר

λαλέω : *passim*	1. *subject human:* λαλέω : *passim*
	2. *subject God or prophet:* χρηματίζω ! (7 x)

33(26):2,2(subject:Jer.) 36(29):23(false proph.) 37(30):2(Jer.) 43(36):2(BSQV λαλέω)(Jer.) 43(36):4(BS λαλέω)(Bar.) 47(40):2 VOQ^{mg}L (BSAQC' λαλέω)(God);[113] further 1 Ki 18:27(MT דרך) Job 40:3(8).[114]

---→ λαλέω 36 x in 33(26):7 - Bar 2:28; λέγω 35(28):7.

Cf. further שאג - χρηματίζω 32:16,16(25:30, 30).

The rendering of the divine and prophetic speech and the roaring of God (שאג) with χρηματίζω ('to give oraculum')[115] in Jer b' was exegetically motivated. Jer-R was highly inconsistent in the insertion of this verb. It is noteworthy that χρηματίζω is a distinct Jer b' word within the LXX.

(45) נביא ('false prophet')[116]

προφήτης : *passim*	ψευδοπροφήτης (8 x)
	33(26):7,8,11,16 34:7(27:9) 35(28):1 36(29):1,8; and elsewhere Zach 13:2.
---→ ψευδοπροφήτης 6:13.	---→ προφήτης 34:12,13(27:15, 16) 39(32):32.

72

Jer-R endeavored, however inconsistently, to make a distinction between the real and the false prophet (both נביא)[117]
by using ψευδοπροφήτης as the main rendition of נביא - 'false
prophet'.

Not attested to elsewhere in classical literature,
ψευδοπροφήτης was probably coined by the LXX translators[118] on
the basis of προφητεύω ψευδῆ which frequently occurs in Jer-
LXX.[119] See further p. 165.

(46) זֶרַע

σπέρμα (3 x)

7:15 22:30 26(46):27;
and *passim* in the LXX.

---→ 2:21 זרע אמת -
καρποφόρον...ἀληθινήν.

1. σπέρμα (4 x)

38(31):27 σπέρμα ἀνθρώπου καὶ
σπέρμα κτήνους
42(35):7 σπέρμα οὐ μὴ σπείρητε
42(35):9 σπέρμα οὐκ ἐγένετο
ἡμῖν (cf. v. 7)

2. γένος (5 x)[120]
36(29):32 (of Shemaiah)
38(31):35,37(36) τὸ γένος
Ισραηλ 43(36):31 (of Jehoia-
kim) 48(41):1 ἀπὸ γένους τοῦ
βασιλέως;
and further Lev 21:17 Esth
6:13 Dan 1:3.

Jer-R apparently wished to distinguish between 'seed',
'offspring' in general (= σπέρμα) and 'offspring of a certain
person or group' (= γένος). For the latter meaning, cf. זרעית
('family') in Rabbinic Hebrew.

(47) שַׂר

ἄρχων (8 x)

1:18 2:26 4:9 8:1 17:25,25
24:1 28(51):59;
and *passim* in the LXX.

---→ ἡγεμών 28(51):57 B-S-538
A O L' (ηγουμενος rel).

1. ἄρχων (26 x)

30(49):3 31(48):7 32:4(25:
18) 33(26):10,11,12,16,21
39(32):32 41(34):19,21
42(35):4 43(36):14,21
44(37):14,15 45(38):22,25,27

51(44):9,17,21 52:10 Bar 1:
9,16 2:1;
and *passim* in the LXX.

2. שר in שרי מלך בבל/
(12 x) ‘νṓή ἡγεμών שרי החילים

45(38):17 46(39):3 (ηγουμενοι
B),3(αρχοντες OL) 47(40):7,
13 48(41):11,13,16 49(42):1,
8 50(43):4,5

While Jer-OG used the stereotyped rendition of שר only--
the one occurrence of ἡγεμών is problematic[121]--Jer-R differentiated between 'leader' (ἄρχων) and 'military leader' (ἡγεμών);
the latter rendition does not occur elsewhere.[122]

(נוה)נוה[123] (48)

'habitation' - νομή (2 x)[124]	'habitation' - τόπος (2 x)
10:25 27(50):7	29:20(49:19) 32:16(25:30); and Ps 22(23):2(נָוֵה) 78(79): 7.
'abode of sheep' - νομή (3 x)[124]	'abode of sheep' - κατάλυσις ! (1 x)
23:3 27(50):19,45	29:21(49:20)
	'abode of shepherds' - κατά- λυμα (1 x) 40(33):12
נוה ('pasture') - νομή (1 x)[124]	נָוֶה ('pasture') - κατάλυμα (1 x)
23:10; cf. מרעית - νομή 10:21 23:1.	32:23(25:37) καταλύματα Spohn] καταλοιπα BSAC'Ω., καλα OL'V ...; and further Ex 15:13 (נָוֵה).
---→ בָּרָה ('pasture') - τρίβος 9:10(9).	

74

Jer-R not only chose translation options different from
those of the OG, but also distinguished between two different
meanings of נוה : נָוֶה ('habitation') - τόπος; נָוֶה ('abode'),
together with נָוָה ('pasture') - κατάλυσις and κατάλυμα.[125]

5. *Other Changes*

(49) שלל in רהיתה לו נפשו לשלל (or sim.)

σκῦλα (1 x)	εὕρεμα [!] (3 x)
21:9;	45(38):2 46(39):18 51:35(45:
and *passim* in the LXX.	5)
---→ שלל (in a different con-	
text) - προνομή 27(50):10.	

שלל ('booty') is here part of an idiom referring to the
returning soldier who discovers that his soul is the only
booty.[126] As a stereotyped rendition of שלל, Jer-OG's σκῦλα
did not convey this connotation in the target language. Jer-
R's lexical choice, on the other hand, achieved this goal.
This rendition does not occur elsewhere.

(50) נדח, mainly *hiph'il*

ἐξωθέω (10 x)	διασπείρω (6 x)
8:3 16:15 23:2(ἀπωθέω A),3,8	30(49):5 39(32):37 Bar 2:4,
24:9 25:16(49:36) 26(46):28	13,29 3:8;
(εἰσάγω V) 27(50):17 28(51):	and further Is 56:8; cf. also
35(הֲדִיחֲנִי MT);	Deut 30:4, Neh 1:9, Ps
and further 9 x in the LXX.	146(147):2 - διασπορά .
---→ διασπείρω 23:3 SC'(rel	σπείρω (1 x)
om): *ex* 39(32):37.	37(30):17

Jer-OG's ἐξωθέω is a perfect rendering of the Heb.
διασπείρω ('to scatter'), found in Jer b', seems inappropriate
at first glance, but since in the OT הדיח is interchangeable
with הפיץ ('to scatter'),[127] this rendition should not be

considered unapt. The fact that other translators and revisers rendered הדיח similarly[128] corroborates this point.

It is difficult to determine whether Jer-R was influenced by the technical meaning of διασπορά when he replaced ἐξωθέω with διασπείρω.[129]

גבור (51)

μαχητής (8 x)

20:11(μαθητης A) 26(46):9 (μαθητης A),12,12 27(50):9,36 28(51):30,56; and Jud 5:23 A (doublet) 1 Chr 28:1 and the MP (8 x; cf. VI 7).

ἰσχυρός (3 x)

9:23(22) 26(46):5,6

ἰσχυρός (3 x)

29:23(49:22) 31(48):14 39(32):18; and *passim* in the LXX.

δυνατός (5 x)

48(41):16 50(43):6 51(44):20 Bar 1:4,9, in the first three verses MT reads (גִּבְרִים) גֶּבֶר;[130] and *passim* in the LXX; cf. also 23:9 כְּגִבֶּר(1) - ὡς ἰσχυρός in Aq.

The main rendition of Jer-OG does not represent the usual equivalent of the Hebrew word in the LXX.[131] Jer-R preferred the two standard renditions of גבור.

APPENDIX 1

Is Jer a', and not Jer b', in the nature of a revision?

A two-translator theory would have been a natural explanation for the differences between Jer a' and b'. However, important agreements between the two parts have led us to look
for a translator-reviser theory. We have attempted to locate
this reviser in the second part of the book. However, from the
outset it would not be impossible that Jer a', and not Jer b',
includes a revision, although of a different nature. This possibility is considered here.

Several of the examples of chapter III may indicate that
Jer a' contains a revision towards a more flexible translation
technique, or, at times, towards better Greek.[132] Alternately,
some examples could be adduced to show that Jer a' was revised
towards greater literalness and a more stereotyped translation
(see items 44 and 48 above and items 4,12,17,19 of the next
chapter). The assumption of a revision of Jer a' could be supported by the following remarks of Thackeray and Ziegler: "The
words used in Jer. α generally have some Hexaplaric support,
whereas those in Jer. β do not" (Thackeray, "Gr.Tr.Jer.", 252);
"Da gewöhnlich der erste Ier.-Übers. wörtlich wiedergibt..."
(Ziegler, *Beiträge*, 103). However, neither Thackeray nor Ziegler documented their remarks.

An assumed revision of Jer a' is, however, unlikely:
1. If Jer a' were a revision, what kind of revision could
it be? It could hardly be a revision towards greater literalness, since the renditions indicating such a trend are too few.
It could be said that Jer a' embodies a revision towards a more
flexible translation technique, such as that of Sym. But one
immediately notes that, while in some examples the renditions
of Jer a' are more flexible than those of Jer b', as a rule
they are often identical to and certainly no more flexible than
the lexical choices used in the other books of the LXX. In
other words, if Jer a' were a revision, it would be a revision
towards the general LXX vocabulary. Such a supposed tendency

is not paralleled in any known LXX revision. Moreover, if the vocabulary of Jer a' is closer to that of the LXX in general than that of Jer b', it seems methodologically more sound to assume that Jer a' represents the OG itself rather than a revision towards its vocabulary.

2. Turning to external evidence, some of Jer-R's renditions are paralleled by identical ones of the later revisions (see p. 161). The renditions of Jer a', on the other hand, do not have any "Hexaplaric support" (against Thackeray as quoted above).

3. In ch. VI it is suggested that Jer a', Ez a' and the MP were probably produced by one translator. This translation presumably was the OG of these books. It is further hypothesized that renditions common to the OG of Jer a', Ez a' and the MP were subsequently altered by Jer-R in Jer b'. Such an assumption is more natural than supposing that Jer b' alone embodies the original text of Jer while a reviser retouched the whole of the MP, Ez a' or the whole of Ez and one half of Jer. Moreover, the renditions common to these three books bear no revisional traits.

APPENDIX 2

Chapter 52 = Jer. γ' ?

In "Gr.Tr.Jer.", 260, Thackeray adduced two arguments in favor of his tentative proposal that ch. 52 encorporates a third unit--in particular, a third translator--in addition to Jer. α' and Jer. β'.

1. Except for 52:24,31, φυλάττω is nowhere in the LXX[133] spelled with -ττ (see also Ziegler, "Einleitung", 120).

2. In 52:33 בגד is rendered with στολή, as frequently in the LXX, in contrast with ἱμάτιον in Jer 43(36):24 48(41):5 50(43):12. The latter rendition occurs frequently elsewhere in the LXX.

Probably more impressed by the secondary nature of ch. 52 in MT than by textual evidence relating to the LXX, Thackeray provided only these two arguments to support his assumption of a third translator. Thackeray's arguments are not convincing,[134] but on the other hand, there is little positive evidence that the substratum of ch. 52 was part of the OG,[135] and was subsequently revised by Jer-R because the Hebrew vocabulary of ch. 52 differs from that of the remainder of Jer.[136] On the other hand, the location of ch. 52 between two sections which were both revised by Jer-R (chapters 29-51 and Bar 1:1-3:8) makes it likely that it underwent the same revision.

NOTES

CHAPTER III

1. The most frequent type of "variation" is the use of non-stereotyped renderings of a certain Hebrew word as opposed to stereotyped renditions of the same word. Some examples to this effect are discussed by G. Bertram, "Der Sprachschatz der Septuaginta und der des hebräischen Alten Testaments," *ZAW* 16 (1939) 88ff.

2. On the other hand, A. Scholz, *Der masorethische Text und die LXX. Übersetzung des Buches Jeremias* (Regensburg 1875) 14 described some of the differences between Jer a' and b' (III 9,45,47,52 IV 1,3,17,18), as follows: "Der Übersetzer wechselt gern in den Ausdrücken bei Wiedergaben der nämlichen hebräischen Wörter."

3. Gk 1 and Gk 2 are the *main* renditions of a given Hebrew word in Jer a' and b' respectively. While it is assumed that in these cases Gk 1 was the original reading of Jer b', it is not impossible that in some instances Jer b' contained a different rendition, i.e., Gk 3.

4. This assumption is corroborated by the findings of ch. VI which show that some words were rendered with Gk 1 in the OG of Jer, Ez and the MP, often to be altered by Jer-R with Gk 2.

5. The following items adduced in ch. III were mentioned by these scholars: Spohn, *Ieremias Vates*, 17: 18,49; Frankl, "Studien", 449: 13,16; Thackeray, "Gr.Tr.Jer.", 247ff.: 1,2,4, 6,7,9,10,15,23,28,29,39,42,44,45,46,47,49,51; *id.,Septuagint*, 31: 43; *id.,Grammar*, 139: 30; Baudissin, *Kyrios*, I, 191, n. 1: 37; Ziegler, *Beiträge*, IV: 32; Turner, *Syntax*, 122ff.: 27, 243: 36, 41ff.: 41; H. A. Redpath, *JThSt* 7 (1906) 608-609: 37.

6. On stereotyped renderings, see the present author's paper, "Three Dimensions of LXX Lexicography", to be published shortly.

7. J. Ziegler, "Pap. 967", 94.

8. A. Rahlfs, *Lucians Rezension der Königsbücher*, *Septuaginta-Studien* 3 (Göttingen 1911).

9. On the relationship between Lucianic and "proto-Lucianic" elements, see E. Tov, *RB* 79 (1972) 101-113 and the bibliography mentioned there.

10. See Barthélemy, *Devanciers*, 246ff.

11. See, e.g., H. J. Schoeps, "Symmachusstudien III: Symmachus und der Midrasch", *Biblica* 29 (1948) 31-51; *id.*, *Biblica* 26 (1945) 100-111.

12. Barthélemy, *Devanciers*, 48ff.

13. *Ib.*, 59-60.

14. *Ib.*, 69ff.

15. See, e.g., to the discussion on Pap.Ryl.Gr. 458 starting with its *editio princeps* by C. H. Roberts, *Two Biblical Papyri in the John Rylands Library* (Manchester 1936), as well as to the revisions described by the following scholars: P. Katz, *Philo's Bible etc.* (Cambridge 1950); D. W. Gooding, *Recensions of the Septuagint Pentateuch, Tyndale Lecture 1954* (London 1955); G. Zunz, "Der Antinoe Papyrus der Proverbia und das Prophetologion", *ZAW* NF 27 (1956) 124-184 (on which see especially P. Katz, *ZAW* NF 28 (1957) 77-84); D. Barthélemy, *Devanciers*.

16. The same rendition occurs in Sym in Ez 14:15 (LXX: ἀφανισμός).

17. Other meanings of שׁמם are rendered in Jer with ἐξίστημι (2:12 4:9 18:16) and σκυθρωπάζω (19:8 27(50):13).

18. This rendition may have been influenced by phrases like Ez 14:15 עובר מבלי שׁממה והיתה. See further Ez 33:28 Jer 9:9,10,11 and *passim*.

19. Differences between Jer a' and b' are not due to a possible differentiation between שׁממה and שׁמה, both occurring *passim* in the book.

20. See Ziegler, *Beiträge*, 49.

21. In Jer a' ταλαιπωρία further renders שׁבר (4:20) and שׁברי or שׁודי (MT שׁארי) in 28(51):35.

22. Etymologically, ταλαιπωρ- represents τλάω ('to endure') and πωρ- ('hardship' = πενθ-, see Suidas, s.v. ταλαίπωρος).

23. Rendered as such in Ob 5 Is 16:4 Job 12:6.

24. Mich 2:4 Job 15:22.

25. The number of translations of שֹׁד as 'destruction' is too large for the assumption of a variant שׁד.

26. Jer 15:8 ταλαιπωρία] λυμαινομενος σ'. 28(51):56 ταλαιπωρία] διαφθειρων σ', ταλαιπωρων α'(86), προνομευων α' (Syh). 31(48):8 ὄλεθρος] προνομευων α'.

27. For both the Heb אמן and its Greek translation, cf. S. Talmon, "*Amen* as an Introductory Oath Formula", *Textus* 7 (1969) 124-129.

28. Besides, אמן is transliterated in 1 Chr. 16:36 Neh 5:13 8:6.

29. See Ziegler, *Beiträge*, 28-29.

30. Because ἐπίχειρον is not attested to in Greek literature, Origen was unable to explain the meaning of this word. He writes: "ἐπίχειρον ἤ τὸ σκῆπτρον παρίστησιν ἤ τοὺς ὑπὸ τὴν ἀρχὴν ἤ τοὺς μισθωτούς, ἐπίχειρα γὰρ ὁ μισθός" (Ghisler, *Catenae*, 481; quoted by Schleusner, s.v.). At the end of this sentence, Origen refers to the plural form of ἐπίχειρον, denoting 'wages'.

31. Ziegler prints in 47(40):1: μετά B-S-106' C' 26 Bo Aeth Arm] υστερον 88 L-407; pr υστερον rel(to 88 L-407 add : Pap. Sorb. Inv. 2250, published by J. van Haelst, *Recherches de Papyrologie* 1 (1961) 113-120).
The evidence may be explained as following:
1. It is not impossible that μετά was the original rendition of Jer-OG (now preserved in BS...only), replaced by Jer-R with ὕστερον (only preserved in 88 L-407 Pap.Sorb.Inv. 2250). Many MSS contain a hybrid reading ὕστερον μετά resulting from Jer-R's revision. This suggestion has an advantage over one alternative explanation:
2. ὕστερον has crept into the MS tradition of 47(40):1 from 36(29):2 38(31):19,19. Such an assumed development would be awkward because only in Jer b' is (יַ)אחר rendered with ὕστερον and nothing calls for its secondary insertion in 47(40):1.
3. A third explanation seems more plausible: ὕστερον μετά is a late doublet composed of an original μετά and an Origenic or Lucianic reading ὕστερον. The lack of concordances to O and L prevents us from knowing whether they employed this rendition elsewhere as well.

32. LSJ, s.v. ὕστερον IV,1 records ὕστερον + gen. as 'behind', a meaning which might have developed easily into a temporal usage, as in Jer b'.

33. A similar usage is found in Matth. 21:32 22:27 (cf. Luc. 20:32!); see Blass-Debrunner-Funk 164,4. However, Jer-R presumably preceded Matthew (see VII, section 3).

34. See Sois.-Soin., *Infinitive*, 79 for references.

35. The non-occurrence of πρὸς τὸ μή in the LXX outside of Jer b', together with its presence in some of the books of the Apocrypha and the NT (cf. C. W. Votaw, *The Use of the Infinitive in Biblical Greek* [Chicago 1896] 20 and Kneucker, *Baruch, ad* 1:19), may suggest a late date for this rendition.

36. The genitive of τοῦ μή in 7:10 depends upon the preceding verb. Jer-LXX probably read בְּ(אֵ)נְצְלְךָ (thus Streane, *Jeremiah, ad loc.*).

37. See Sois.-Soin., *Infinitive*, 72.

38. This assumption is based on the fact that both in classical Greek and in the LXX ἐργάζομαι is used primarily as 'to carry out work'. However, neither ἐργάζομαι nor עבד occur in Jer-LXX and Jer-MT in this meaning, so that our suggestion is conjectural.

39. By this practice Jer-R enlarged the semantic range of ἐργάζομαι.

40. For yet a different view, see F. Gryglewycz, *Biblica* 37 (1956) 324.

41. Cf. C. Bertram, παρακαλέω, *ThWNT* 5, 775, n. 20.

42. ἀναπαύω and παύω are distinct "Lieblingswörter" of Jer b'. In Jer b' παύω renders not only כלה, of which the Gk is a frequent equivalent, and נחם, but also דמם (31(48):2 32: 23(25:37); cf. II 2), שבת (38(31):37(35)), דכא (51(44):10) and מוש (38(31):35). ἀναπαύω renders רגע (29(47):6), שקט (30:12 (49:23)) and שאנן (31(48):11). ἀναπαύω does not occur in Jer a'. παύω occurs only in 28(51):63 (כלה).

43. This view concurs with Giesebrecht, *Jeremia*, XXX. Streane, *Jeremiah*, 192, on the other hand, depicts Jer-R's lexical choice as euphemistic; Martin, *Syntax*, 176-77, similarly considers it anti-anthropomorphic (cf. also Fritsch, *Pentateuch*, 17). However, the latter two characterizations are not borne out by the evidence since παύομαι in 38(31):15 does not refer to God.

44. Examples of similarly incorrect etymological renderings of Aq are mentioned by Reider, *Prolegomena*, 38-39.

45. Cf., however, J. Barr, *Biblical Words for Time*[2] (London 1969) 36ff. See further below, p. 166.

46. The distinction between sections 1 and 2 is artificial, created to serve our immediate purposes.

47. In Rabbinic Hebrew נפץ thus assumed the meaning of פוץ; see Jastrow, *ad loc.*

48. דמן is not attested to in post-Biblical Hebrew (Levi).

49. A similar opinion has been expressed by Frankl, "Studien", 449-450. It seems improbable that the first translator consciously distinguished between παράδειγμα (Israel) and κόπριον (the other nations) (thus A. Geiger, *Urschrift und Übersetzungen der Bibel* (Breslau 1857) 415).

50. Cf. Aristophanes, *Thesm.*, 670: τοῖς ἄλλοις παράδειγμα ὕβρεως.

51. Likewise, in Nah 2:5 was יחוללו הרכב rendered by συγχυθήσονται τὰ ἅρματα, in accordance with the preceding καὶ οἱ ἱππεῖς θορυβηθήσονται (MT הרעלו והברשים).

52. The vocalization of יחללו may also have been founded on a deviating exegetical tradition, also reflected in the translations of Aq (ἐγκαυχῶνται) and Sym (καυχῶνται).

53. See Jastrow, s.v. גרר II. Note further that Aq and Sym frequently rendered מגור and מגורה with συστροφή ('mob').

54. Cf. בלחות ('terror', 'destruction') - ἀπώλεια in Ez 26:21 27:36 28:19.

55. מגר is attested, i.a., in Ps 89:45 and in Aramaic in Targ. Jon. to Ps 101:5,8 119:139 143:12 (MT צמח) and Ezr 6:12. A connection between מָגוֹר (to be read as מְגוֹר ?) and 'מגר' was suggested, although in a different way, by A. M. Honeyman, "Māgôr Mis-sābîb and Jeremiah's Pun", *VT* 4 (1959) 424-426.

56. ἐάν (9 x), εἰ (4 x), εἰ πῶς (3 x), ἐὰν πῶς (1 x), εἰ ἄρα (1 x), ἵνα (2 x), ὅρα μή (1 x), ὅπως (6 x).

57. μήποτε, based on a similar understanding of the Heb, occurs in Gen 24:5,39 27:12 43:12 1 Ki 18:27 Job 1:5.
It is noteworthy that אולי is rendered in Gen 18:24-32 with ἐάν (6 x) but in 24:5 - 43:12 with μήποτε and ἴσως. This discrepancy between the two parts of Gen may provide an additional criterion for the distinction between the two parts of Gen to which attention was drawn by O. J. Baab, "A Theory of Two Translators for the Greek Genesis", *JBL* 52 (1933) 239-243.

58. Cf. IV, n. 34; VII, n. 7.

59. Including כבה and כנמא. כן, כזאת etc. are not included.

60. 16:7 ἔλεγεν.

61. One of the three instances is 9:9 ἔλεγεν.

62. See also column 1a.

63. See Baumgärtel in Herrmann-Baumgärtel, *Beiträge*, 21-22.

64. Jer-R's rendition not only ousted an earlier τάδε λέγει κύριος, but it also constituted the most consistently stereotyped rendering of the Hebrew phrase found in the LXX.

65. The preserved evidence refers mainly to O and/or L, whether or not preceded by the "Three" or one of them (mostly Th). The precise numbers are: L alone 20 x; L, Aq and Sym 1 x; Aq and Sym 1 x.
The following two exceptions were noted in Jer: Jer 13:1 L' and 17:19 L'-198-538 and the "Three" οὕτως εἶπεν κύριος (LXX τάδε λέγει κύριος).

66. OL alone 1 x; OL and Th 8 x; O, Aq and Sym 1 x.
In 18:11, on the other hand, the "Three" (※), O (※) and L add: οὕτως λέγει κύριος.

67. See Sois.-Soin., *Zusätze*, 155 for O and Reider, *Index Aquila*, 167 for Aq. Ziegler's claim "sicherlich hat α' niemals ταδε λεγει übersetzt" ("Einleitung", 92) is probably correct.

68. Elsewhere ἀλλότριος generally renders נכרי and נכר, i.a. in the phrase under review θεοὶ ἀλλότριοι (e.g., Jer 2:21 5:19 8:19).

69. E.g., 34:4(27:5) δόξῃ ἐν ὀφθαλμοῖς.

70. וכישר בעיניכם - καὶ ὡς βέλτιον ὑμῖν.

71. Shenkel, *Kings*, 13-18, showed that the OG translator of Ki rendered בעיני + human with ἐν ὀφθαλμοῖς and בעיני + God with ἐνώπιον (cf. Fritsch, *Pentateuch*, 12), while the *kaige*-Th reviser limited himself to the literal rendering ἐν ὀφθαλμοῖς.

Jer-OG cannot be compared to Ki-OG because Jer a' includes only one case of בעיני + human (7:11).

While it is true that Jer-R rendered 'ה בעיני with prep. + ὀφθαλμός only (*not* merely with ἐν ὀφθαλμοῖς as *kaige*-Th), he varied the rendering of בעיני + human (33(26):14 47(40):4,5 Bar 1:12). Jer-R and *kaige*-Th are therefore not similar.

72. Also Origen rendered לפני mainly with κατὰ πρόσωπον, cf. Sois.-Soin., *Zusätze*, 146.

73. The same rendition of לקח occurs another 17 times in the LXX (including Jer 9:20 32:14(25:28)).

74. The translation of מתחרה with παροξύνῃ in 22:15 probably should be considered a translation guess similar to the rendering in 12:5.

75. See III 14.

76. For a similar employment of certain Greek words in the LXX of Is, see R. R. Ottley, *The Book of Isaiah according to the Septuagint* (Cambridge 1906) II, 270; Ziegler, *Isaias*, 13-14; Seeligmann, *Isaiah*, 57.

77. In 22:6, however, a passive form is found.

78. E.g., 17:6 לא תשב - οὐ κατοικεῖται

79. רבו משרבתינו לך חטאנו - πολλαὶ αἱ ἁμαρτίαι ἡμῶν ἐναντίον σοῦ ὅτι σοὶ ἡμάρτομεν . ἁμαρτάνω + dat. may have been used here by way of variation because the alternative rendition (ἁμαρτίαι) ἐναντίον occurred earlier in the same verse. See further Ziegler, *Beiträge*, 94-95.

80. This translation is discussed by Fritsch, *Pentateuch*, 59-60 and D. H. Gard, *The Exegetical Method of the Greek Translator of the Book of Job*, JBL Monograph Series VIII (1952) 29. Additional examples of this rendering are listed by Johannessohn, *Präpositionen*, 192, 196.

81. Cf. Helbing, *Kasussyntax*, 215-217 and Martin, *Syntax*, 122.

82. The alternative explanation admittedly uses a double standard for the reconstruction of the underlying Heb of Bar: it is not impossible that ἁμαρτάνω ἔναντι/ἐναντίον reflects חטא לפני, because this construction occurs frequently in the *later* Hebrew in which Bar was written (e.g., Sir 38:15 (LXX ἔναντι), B.T. *Ber.* 17a, 19a, *Yoma* 36b, *Meg.* 30a, 31b, *Ta'anit* 27b; cf. also 1 Sam 20:1 (LXX ἐνώπιον)).

83. This rendition is either an unrevised remnant of the OG, or a Hexaplaric addition (thus Martin, *Syntax*, 191, n. 1), or, more likely, a result of the translator's wish for variation (ἀπό + noun occurs in the same verse).

84. מבלי does not occur in the Heb of Jer b'.

85. E.g., Is 6:11 50:2 Ez 33:28 34:8 Zeph 3:6. διά/παρά + art. inf. is also the most frequent rendition of the "Three" (mainly παρά, e.g., Jer 28(51):29,37 33(26):9) and of O (usually παρά, e.g., Jer 19:11 40(33):12 51(44):22).

86. For a similar situation in Biblical Hebrew, compare, e.g., 4:7 עריך תצינה מאין יושב and 32:43 שממה היא מאין אדם להכריתו לבלתי חיות בו יושב למאדם ועד בהמה ובהמה with 51:62.

87. Jer-R's employment of ἀπό as the standard rendition of מן created a Hebraism in constructions like the present one, since ἀπό is not used in classical Greek as 'without', 'deprived of' (except in such *composita* as ἀπαγορεύω, ἀπόφονος, see LSJ, s.v. ἀπό, D 6).

88. However, this rendering quite correctly reflects only the first of the two compounds of מאין. An attempt to represent also the second component entailed renderings such as those of Jer-OG and the "Three" (see n. 85).

89. To Turner's figures for Jer b' (4:754 = 1:188; see below) we added the relevant figures for Bar.

90. Turner did not explicitly mention the *Vorlagen* of the occurrences of δέ which are included in his calculation. δέ probably mainly represented a *waw*.

91. The same tendency is visible in the following LXX revisions: (1) Aq and *kaige*-Th: see Reider, *Prolegomena*, 43; Sois.-Soin., *Zusätze*, 148-149; Ziegler, *Beiträge*, 151-157. (2) Lam (according to Barthélemy, *Devanciers*, 47, part of *kaige*-Th): cf. Ziegler, *ib.*, 167. (3) Pap. 967 of Ez: cf. Ziegler, "Pap. 967", 89. (4) O: cf. Sois.-Soin., *ib.*, 148-149; Ziegler, *ib.*, 157.

92. Cf. Ziegler, *ib.*, 127. All numbers are quoted from Ziegler, who, incidentally, does not list the verses to which the numbers refer. Ziegler's numbers refer to Jer 29-52 only, but relevant figures for Bar could not be added because Ziegler does not state to which combinations of prep. + noun + suff. he refers.

93. The article should probably be omitted here with C' (cf. also 51(44):6,17 where the article is wanting).

94. Generally an infinitive with a pron. suff., e.g. 11:4 ביום הוציאי אותם.

95. Jer 7:22 α', 11:4 α', 11:7 θ' O (✗), 48(41):4 θ' (=LXX!).

96. In the following instances θεός is secondary in MS S: 26(46):23 S ο θεος (κυριος B; κυριος ο θεος rel) 28(51):7 S θεος (κυριος rel) 44(37):17 S θεος (κυριος rel).

97. 1 Ki(11 x) 1 Chr(10 x) 2 Chr(5 x) 1 Esdr(6 x) Ps(11 x) Prov(21 x) Is(67 x). The figures are culled from H. A. Redpath, *JThSt* 7 (1906) 608. Redpath's numbers are slightly exaggerated because he also includes variants from individual MSS.

98. Cf. Baudissin, *Kyrios*, I, 191, n. 1: "Vielleicht beruht es auf Verschiedenheit der Übersetzer, dass die "Vertauschung", soviel ich siehe, nur bis 28:7 des griechischen Textes vorkommt, von da an nicht mehr".

99. Ziegler reconstructed σου<ουχι> . σου<ου> seems to be more probable.

100. Thus *passim*.

101. Cf. Blass-Debrunner-Funk, 427.

102. The data are culled from Martin, *Syntax*, 41.

103. In most of the above-mentioned instances, the translator stressed the pronoun, usually following MT. In addition, one notes that in nine instances the emph. pron. either precedes or follows another pers. pron. (2:16(17),19 7:19 12:8,9 13:25 15:16 22:16 24:7, e.g., σε ἐμέ). It may thus be suggested that the juxtaposition of the two pronouns caused the use of the emphatic forms.

104. Since the tendency to represent the Heb with a stereotyped rendition, exemplified in the previous section, is also a form of "translational consistency", this section incorporates *additional* forms of translational consistency.

105. עבד of God - δοῦλος 7:25 25:4 26(46):27 (παῖς in 26(46):28 is probably a variation after δοῦλος in the preceding verse). עבד of human is rendered with παῖς in 21:7 22:4 and with δοῦλος in 2:14. If Jer-OG indeed distinguished between the two usages of עבד, the distinction has not been carried out consistently.

106. Jer-R did not make any of the distinctions between different meanings or usages of עבד such as were made by some of the other translators, cf. n. 104 and also W. Zimmerli, παῖς θεοῦ, *ThWNT* 5, 672ff.; see further Thackeray, *Grammar*, 7-8; P. Katz, *Die Welt des Orients* 2 (1954-9) 268.

107. λέγει κύριος (om OL) in 23:29 is the non-original part of a doublet (see also Ziegler, *Beiträge*, 100).

108. Cf. Ziegler, *Beiträge*, 37-38.

109. The discussion of the translation options of נאם in נאם ה should not be separated from other combinations with נאם like נאם בלעם (Num 24:3,15). Since their number is small, they

may be mentioned here: φησί (Num 4 x; Ps 1 x) and τάδε λέγει
(Prov 1 x); the *Vorlage* of 2 Sam 23:1 has been read differently
by the Greek translator.

110. In four instances Jer-R left λέγει κύριος of the OG
unrevised. In six other places the text reads εἶπε κύριος.
These latter renditions may be remnants of the OG - cf. two
identical renditions in Jer a'. Alternatively, some of them
may reflect a variant 'ה אמר (= εἶπε κύριος in 6:15 31(48):8
37(30):3 40(33):13 51(44):26). Or, less likely, Jer-R might
have used this equivalent himself.

111. G. R. Driver, *The Hebrew Scrolls* (Oxford 1951) 41 assumed that the "ancient translators" treated נאם as a finite
verb (נָאַם) rather than a noun. His hypothesis may find support
in the Rabbinic Hebrew verb נאם/נאום (cf. Jastrow, s.v.), as
well as in the following inner-Greek evidence (*not* in the Qumran orthography נואם; see E. Y. Kutscher, *The Language and Linguistic Background of the Isaiah Scroll (1QIs^a)* [Leiden 1974]
499):
      It may be contended that the LXX translators represented
נאם with a verb rather than a noun because of syntactical difficulties (see below). However, these obstacles are lacking in
Num 24:3,15 ויאמר נאם בלעם..ונאם הגבר which is nevertheless
rendered as ...εἶπεν φησὶν Βαλααμ...φησὶν ὁ ἄνθρωπος. For
similar cases see Num 24:4,16 Prov 30:1 Ps 36(35):2.
      There are, however, strong arguments in favor of the as-
sumption that the translators read נָאַם, although treating it as
a finite verb:
      That at least Origen and Sym knew of the existence of a
noun נְאָם may be inferred from:
      1. In the second column of the Hexapla in Ps 36(35):2,
Origen transcribed נאם as νουμ, cf. G. Mercati, *Psalterii
Hexapli Reliquiae* I (Vatican 1958), while he rendered the Heb
with φησί in the fifth column. (It may, however, be argued
that the fifth column was independent of the second column
whose text presumably existed before his time).
      2. In Jer 23:31, where נאם does *not* occur in the phrase
'ה נאם, Sym rendered it with λόγος. Besides, he always rendered 'ה נאם with φησὶ κύριος
      It is further noteworthy that 'ה נאם nearly always occurs
in an extra-syntactical position which made it nearly impossible for the Greek translators and revisers to render the Heb
literally, e.g., with (ὁ) λόγος (τοῦ) κυρίου. Such a translation would have disturbed the syntax of the surrounding Greek
sentence.
      It is difficult to reconcile the two lines of argument.
Possibly some translators indeed read נָאַם, although the majority read נְאָם. On the whole, the arguments favor a נְאָם vocalization by the translators.
      The question as to whether the translators read either נָאַם
or נְאָם was first brought to my attention by Prof. S. Talmon.

112. The "Three", O and L were checked for Jer-LXX only.
A more generalizing remark for the renderings used by O and Th
is made by Sois.-Soin., *Zusätze*, 155: "in den asterisierten Zu-
sätzen und danach auch wenigstens in ϑ' ist dagegen φησὶ κύριος
die gewöhnliche Wiedergabe".

113. For the variants of the last three verses, see Ziegler, "Einleitung", 46.

114. The *Vorlage* of χρηματίζω in Job is not easily ascertainable. Cf. Helbing, *Kasussyntax*, 245 and Ziegler, "Einleitung", 46.

115. Cf. Helbing, *ib*.

116. The occurrences of נביא as 'false prophet' are listed in BDB, s.v.

117. It is no coincidence that the wish to make this distinction arose in the LXX of Jer: Jeremiah and his biographer refer to false prophets more than any other OT author. Thus Jer-R acted as an exegete, who introduced an element of precision into the terminology of the Hebrew book.

118. Thus also J. Reiling, "The Use of ΨΕΥΔΟΠΡΟΦΗΤΗΣ in the Septuagint, Philo and Josephus", *NT* 13 (1971) 148.

119. 14:14,15 20:6 23:25,25,32 34:10,14,16(27:12,17,19). The noun itself was coined after such nouns as ψευδόμαντις, ψευδομάρτυς and ψευδολόγος.

120. Cf. further 38(31):1 לכל משפחות ישראל - τῷ γένει Ισραηλ. The wording of this verse was probably influenced by 38(31):35,37(36) γένος Ισραηλ.

121. The following doubts should be raised against the relevance of ἡγεμών in 28(51):57 to the present discussion:
  1. ἡγεμών (= שר), occurring in the sequence ἡγεμόνας... σοφούς...στρατηγούς, may have been influenced by similar adjacent sequences (in which ἡγεμών renders פחה):
Jer 28(51):23 ἡγεμόνας (ηγεμονα A) καὶ στρατηγούς.
Jer 28(51):28 ἡγουμένους (ηγεμονας A)...καὶ στρατηγούς.
Cf. also Ez 23:23 ἡγουμένους (V; ηγεμονας rel) καὶ στρατηγούς.
  2. ἡγεμών is not unanimously attested by all witnesses of 28(51):57: ἡγεμόνας B-S-538 A O L'] ηγουμενους rel (cf. Ziegler, *Beiträge*, 48).
  3. It is not impossible that the translator read פחותיה שריה סגניה in his *Vorlage* in place of MT שריה וחכמיה חכמיה וסגניה. The rendering of פחה with ἡγεμών is paralleled by the examples mentioned under (1).

122. This distinction was not consistently carried out because Jer-R left 45(38):22,25 unrevised.

123. τόπος, inserted in some MSS in 27(50):44 from the parallel verse 29:20(49:19), should be omitted with MSS B-S-106' C'-613 Bo Aeth (thus Ziegler).

124. גָּוֶה(גָּוָה) is further rendered with νομή in Prov 24:15 Am 1:2 Zeph 2:6 Ez 25:5 (cf. VI 63).

125. Neither the OG nor Jer-R treated the two lexemes גָּוֶה and גָּוָה differently.

126. See BDB, s.v. שלל, 2; Rudolph, *Jeremia*, *ad* 21:9; Bright, *Jeremiah*, 184.

127. MT 30:11 is identical with 46:28 except for הפצותיך in 30:11 versus הדחתיך in 46:28. See S. Talmon, "Synonymous Readings in the Textual Traditions of the OT", *Scripta Hierosolymitana* 8 (1961) 353.

128. Dan 9:7 ϑ'; Jer 8:3 α'σ'; 23:3 <α'σ'>; 34:8(27:10) α'ϑ' O(✗) L; 36(29):14,18 ϑ' OL ✗; 50(43):5 α'ϑ' ✗ (86). See further VII 2.

129. Already at an early date διασπορά was used as a technical term denoting the Jewish diaspora, cf. Deut 28:25 Jer 15:7 41(34):17 Ep.Jac. 1:1. Note further that the renditions listed in the right column refer to the scattering of Israel (with the exception of Jer 37(30):17); in these cases διασπείρω denotes the 'bringing into the διασπορά'. Cf. K. L. Schmidt, διασπορά, *ThWNT* 2 (1935) 98-104 and Seeligmann, *Isaiah*, 113 on Is 35:8.

It is not certain whether Jer-R was influenced by the technical meaning of the verb since 30(49):5 refers to Edom and 37(30):17 has the *simplex* of the verb.

130. It is improbable that Jer-R made a distinction between גֶּבֶר - δυνατός and גב(ו)ר - ἰσχυρός: (1) δυνατός renders גֶּבֶר inadequately and the juxtaposition in 51(44):20 of τοῖς δυνατοῖς and ταῖς γυναιξί makes such an assumption unlikely. (2) In 37(30):6 and 38(31):22 גֶּבֶר is rendered with ἄνθρωπος.

131. It is noteworthy that μαχητής occurs primarily in chapters 25-32 which contain the oracles against the nations. It is also found once outside these chapters, and moreover in 26(46):5,6 ἰσχυρός is employed. As a result, no firm distribution pattern for μαχητής and ἰσχυρός in Jer a' can be formulated.

132. Some additional examples of differences between Jer a' and b', not included in chapters III and IV, could support the assumption that Jer a' embodies a revision.

133. Cf., however, εφυλαττεν in MSS AW in Job 29:2, mentioned by Thackeray, *Grammar*, 123. Thackeray refers also to Job 17:4 AC, but this reference could not be located.

134. "Sehr fraglich bleibt, ob Kap. 52 wirklich nur ein späterer Nachtrag ist" (Ziegler, "Einleitung", 128, n. 1).

135. See συνοχή in v. 5 (VI 16); στερέω in v. 6 (II 4); μετὰ κρίσεως in v. 9 (II 16).

136. See ἐπιστάτης in v. 25 (IV 9).

CHAPTER IV

ADDITIONAL DIFFERENCES BETWEEN JER A' AND B'
("SYNONYMOUS RENDITIONS")

The preceding chapter dealt with differences between Jer a'
and b' which were explained in a particular way. We have attempted to demonstrate that some renditions in the first part
of the book were replaced in the second part of the book with
renditions displaying a certain revisional tendency.

This chapter lists additional differences between the two
parts of the book which are not characterized by any particular
revisional tendency such as the ones described in the previous
chapter. We shall list here different renditions of a certain
Hebrew word which are found concurrently in the LXX, and without any grammatical or contextual condition determining the occurrence of one rather than the other. We refer, for example,
to the different renditions of הכעיס, namely παροργίζω and
παραπικραίνω (example 1). We suggest calling such renditions
"synonymous renditions" (a term which is taken from S. Talmon's
"synonymous readings"[1]) because from a translator's point of
view they are synonymous representations of one Hebrew word.
Generally, the Greek words themselves are also synonymous in
meaning, but this is not implied in the term "synonymous renditions".[2]

While the occurrence of synonymous renditions in Jer a'
and b' does not necessarily prove our thesis--indeed, several
of the examples listed below were taken by Thackeray as evidence for his two translator theory[3]--it seems to us that such
renditions are to be expected in Jer-R's revision as they are
present also in other revisions of the LXX: Revisers such as
Symmachus, Origen and Lucian--and to a lesser extent, Aquila--
inserted into their revisions also new translation equivalents
which were not more literal or consistent than the renditions
they replaced.[4] It is hard to know in every instance why the
revisers replaced the old renditions with new ones since we are
lacking thorough studies of the revision techniques employed.
Sometimes the revisers introduced new words because they simply

preferred them to the old ones. In other cases, the synonymous renditions may bear a certain revisionary trait which cannot always be ascertained. For this reason some of the examples of this chapter should perhaps be listed in the previous chapter.

Examples of renditions of Jer-OG, replaced with synonymous ones, are provided below. Unless otherwise specified, there is no significant difference between the two renditions. It should be pointed out that many of Jer-R's renditions are more rare in the LXX than those in Jer a'.

The items are presented as in ch. III. → references refer to Jer a'b' only.

(1) הכעיס

παροργίζω (5 x)	παραπικραίνω (4 x)
7:18,19 8:19 11:17 25:6; and *passim* in the LXX.	39(32):29,32 SA (πικρ. rel.) 51(44):3,8; and further Deut 32:16 B (ἐκπικρ. rel.)

The two words are close in meaning;[5] παραπικραίνω ('to embitter') is a stronger expression.

(2) שכן

κατασκηνόω (4 x)	καταλύω (3 x)[6]
7:12 17:6 23:6 28(51):13; and *passim* in the LXX.	29:17(49:16) 30:9(49:31) 32:10(25:24); and Sir (4 x).
	---→ κάθημαι Bar 3:3(?).
	Jer-R apparently cherished the root καταλυ- (see also III 48)

Jer-R's rendition is more rare in the LXX.

שמחה, ששון (3)

χαρά (3 x)

15:16 - שמחה   16:9 - ששון
25:10 - ששון;
and *passim* in the LXX.

χαρμονή, χαρμοσύνη (4 x)

31(48):33 שמחה - χαρμοσύνη
(χαρμονη S^C QV) 38(31):13 ששון
- χαρμονή (χαρμοσυνη QOC';
ευφροσυνη A) 40(33):11 שמחה -
χαρμοσύνη (χαρμονη AVL) Bar
2:23 χαρμοσύνη (cf. V18);
χαρμονή further occurs in Job
(3 x) and χαρμοσύνη in Lev 22:
29 and 1 Sam 18:6.

---> 7:34 קול שמחה - φωνὴ
χαιρόντων.

Jer-R's rendition is more rare in the LXX.

אמר ל/אל (4)[7]

a. *past tense*

εἶπον πρός (21 x)

1:7,9,12,14 3:6,11 9:13(12)
11:6,9 13:6,12 14:11,14 15:
1,2 16:10 18:11 19:1,14
21:3 24:3 28(51):61;
and frequently in the LXX.

εἶπον + dat. (4 x)

2:27 13:18 20:3
28(51):59

εἶπον + dat. (28 x)

33(26):17,18 35(28):15
42(35):13 43(36):15,19 (προς
AC') 44(37):18 45(38):4,14,
15,17,19,24,25 47(40):2,14,15
48(41):6 BAC' (om SQV),8
49(42):2,4,5,9 50(43):2
51(44):20,24,34(45:4)

εἶπον πρός (6 x)

33(26):12 35(28):5,13 36(29):
25 46(39):16 47(40):16

b. *future tense*

ἐρῶ πρός (8 x)

11:3 13:12,13 14:17 15:2
21:8 22:8 23:35 (MT על)

ἐρῶ + dat. (2 x)

32:13(25:27) 45(38):26

ἐρῶ + dat. (6 x) | ἐρῶ πρός (1 x)

4:11 10:11 16:11 (προς | 36(29):24
AVOC') 17:20 BS (προς rel)
19:3 23:33

c. *present tense*

λέγω + dat. (1 x) | λέγω πρός (3 x)

23:17 | 39(32):25 45(38):20 50(43):1

The stereotyped LXX rendition of אמר אל (in the MT of Jer
strongly prevailing over אמר ל-) is εἶπον πρός,[8] also found in
Jer-OG. Jer-R, on the other hand, preferred εἶπον + dat.,[9]
leaving eight renditions unrevised.[10] Similar differences between Jer a' and b' are visible in the translation of the imperfect of אמר.[11]

(5) יען

ἀνθ'ὧν (4 x) | ἐπειδή (3 x)

5:14 7:13 19:4 (יען אשר) | 31(48):7 36(29):31 (יען אשר)
23:38; | 42(35):18 (יען אשר);
and *passim* in the LXX. | and *passim* in the LXX.

---> ἐπειδή 25:8. | ---> δι'ἥν 36(29):23 (יען אשר).

(6) כאשר

καθώς (9 x) | καθά (6 x)

7:14,15 12:16 13:5 17:22| 39(32):42 51(44):17,30 Bar
18:4 19:11 27(50):15,18 | 1:6 2:2,28

καθάπερ (2 x) | καθάπερ (1 x)

13:11 23:27 | Bar 2:20

---> ἀνθ'ὧν 5:19. | ---> ὥσπερ 31(48):13 38(31):
                           | 28 50(43):12; ὡς 51(44):13;
                           | καθώς 33(26):11 49(42):2,18.

Jer-R preferred καθά (which is not found in Jer a') as a rendering of כאשר, in contrast to Jer-OG's καθώς. Although similar in meaning, the two conjunctions have a different background: καθώς originated only in the Hellenistic period and an Atticist such as Phrynichus condemned it in favor of καθό and καθά.[12]

(7) ל + inf. constr. (לקטֹל)[13]

art. inf. : 56 x	art. inf. : 35 x
anarthr. inf.: 16 x;	anarthr. inf.: 59 x;
the art. inf. is further	the anarthr. inf. is further
favored by the LXX of Jud	preferred by the translators
2 Chr Ez and by Aq[14] and	of the Pent and many other
Th.[15]	books, by Sym[16] and Th-Dan.[17]

The rendition favored by Jer-OG contains a formal equivalent for ל (τοῦ). The un-Greek employment of the article may have caused Jer-R and other revisers to omit it often.

(8) פשע

ἀσεβέω (3 x)	ἀφίστημι (2 x)
2:8,29 3:13;	40(33):8 Bar 3:8;[18]
further in the MP (see VI 62),	and further Ez 20:38. Cf. al-
Is 59:13 Ez 18:31.	so 2 Chr 21:8,10,10 -פשע
	מתחת יד...

(9) פקיד

καθεσταμένος (1 x)	ἐπιστάτης (2 x)
20:1 (פקיד of the temple);	36(29):26 (פקיד of the temple)
and 2 Chr 31:13. καθίστημι	52:25 (פקיד of the soldiers);
also renders פקד in the LXX	and elsewhere 2 Ki 25:19
(i.a. 2 x in Jer a' and 5 x	(// Jer 52:25). ἐφίστημι also
in Jer b').	renders פקד in the LXX (i.a.
	2 x in Jer a' and 1 x in Jer
	b').

(10) רעה + pron. suff. or in the constr. state

κακία (11 x)

1:16 2:19 3:2 4:18 6:7
7:12 8:6 11:15,17 12:4
28(51):24 (αδικια A);
and *passim* in the LXX.

κακά (5 x)

2:27 11:12 14:16 15:11
18:8;
and *passim* in the LXX.

---→ κάκωσις 2:28 (κρισις C)
11:14 28(51):2; πονηρία 23:11.

πονηρία (5 x)

31(48):16 39(32):32 40(33):5
51(44):3 Bar 2:26;
and *passim* in the LXX.

κακά (2 x = 5 x)

51(44):5,9 (4 x)

As in the remainder of the LXX, רעה is rendered in Jer a'
and b' by κακά, both when used absolutely and when containing
a pron. suff. or occurring in the constr. state. In the latter
two conditions, however, Jer-OG more strongly favored κακία,
while Jer-R preferred πονηρία.

(11) לכד

ἁλίσκομαι (7 x)[19]

8:9 27(50):2,9,24 28(51):31,
41,56;
and *passim* in the LXX.

---→ συλλαμβάνω 5:26 6:11.

λαμβάνω (6 x)

31(48):1,41 39(32):3,28
41(34):22 Bar 1:2;
and *passim* in the LXX.

συλλαμβάνω (7 x)

31(48):7,44 39(32):24
41(34):2 (not in MT) 44(37):8
45(38):3,28;
and *passim* in the LXX.

(12) רפא (*qal* and *pi'el*)

ἰάομαι (7 x)	ἰατρεύω (3 x)
3:22 6:14 15:18 17:14,14	37(30):13 (MT רפאות),17
19:11 28(51):8;	40(33):6;
and *passim* in the LXX.	and further 2 Ki 8:29 9:15
	2 Chr 22:6 (all רפא *hithpa'el*),
---→ ἰατρεύω 28(51):9.[20]	9 (MT מתחבא).

Jer-R's rendition is more rare in the LXX.

(13) קצה

ἄκρον (3 x)	μέρος (3 x)
12:12,12 25:16(49:36);	32:17,19,19(25:31,33,33);
and *passim* in the LXX.	and *passim* in the LXX.[21]

ἔσχατον (3 x)

10:13 28(51):16,32;
and *passim* in the LXX.

(14) יצת

ἀνάπτω (6 x / 5 x)	καίω (3 x)
9:12(11) (11:16)[22] 17:27	30:16(49:27) 39(32):29 (κατακ.
21:12,14 (MT הַצַּתִּי) 27(50):32;	OC) 50(43):12;
and *passim* in the LXX.	and *passim* in the LXX.
---→ καίω 26(46):19 Wutz	---→ κατακαίω 30(49):2;
καυθήσεται] MSS κληθησεται	ἀνάπτω 31(48):9 (ἅπτω BS).
ουαι; ἐμπυρίζω 4:26 (MT	
נְצְתָּה) 28(51):30,58.	

(15) נתץ

κατασκάπτω (2 x)[23]	καθαιρέω (3 x)
1:10 2:15;	38:28(31:27) 40(33):4 (κάθ-
and *passim* in the LXX.	ημαι AC') 52:14;
	and *passim* in the LXX.

הרס

κατασκάπτω (1 x)	καθαιρέω (3 x)
27(50):15;	38(31):40 49(42):10 51:34
and *passim* in the LXX.	(45:4);
	and *passim* in the LXX.
καθαιρέω (1 x)	
24:6	

Jer-OG preferred to render verbs of destruction with κατασκάπτω, while Jer-R opted for καθαιρέω.

(16) מלט

ἀνασῴζω (2 x)	σῴζω (9 x)
26(46):6 28(51):6;	31(48):6,8,19 (ἀνασῴζω Q)
and *passim* in the LXX.	39(32):4 41(34):3 45(38):18,
	23 46(39):18 48(41):15;
	and *passim* in the LXX.

פלט, פליט

ἀνασῴζομαι (3 x)	σῴζομαι (3 x)
27(50):28,29 28(51):50;	49(42):17 51(44):14,28;
and *passim* in the LXX.	and *passim* in the LXX.
	---→ ἀνασῴζομαι 51(44):14.[24]

(17) רֵעַ

πλησίον (13 x)	πολίτης (2 x)[25]
5:8 6:21 7:5 9:4,8,20(3,7,	36(29):23 38(31):34 BS (αδελ-
19) 19:9 22:8,13 23:27,30,	φος AO; πλησιον rel);[26]
35 26(46):16;	and further Prov 11:9,12
and *passim* in the LXX.	24:43(28).
	---→ πλησίον 41(34):15,17
	43(36):16.

πολίτης (Jer-R) occurs only rarely in the LXX[27] and its occurrence in Jer b' is therefore noteworthy even though πλησίον is more frequent in Jer b' (3 x) than πολίτης.

(18) נבלה

νέκρος (3 x)	θνησιμαῖον (2 x)[28]
7:33 9:22(21) 19:7;	41(34):20 43(36):30;
and Deut 28:26.	and *passim* in the LXX.

---→ θνησιμαῖον 16:18.

(19) נטויה (ביד/זרוע)

(ἐν χειρὶ) ἐκτεταμένῃ ! (1 x)	(ἐν βραχίονι/ἐπιχείρῳ) ὑψηλῷ (4 x)
21:5;	34:4(27:5) 39(32):17,21 Bar 2:11;
cf. נטה - ἐκτείνω *passim* in the LXX.	and *passim* in the LXX.
	This rendition may have been influenced by the similar rendering of the parallel phrase יד רמה with χεὶρ ὑψηλή.[29]

(20) נתך (subject חמה)

χέω ! (1 x)	στάζω (3 x)
7:20	49(42):18,18 51(44):6;
	and elsewhere in the LXX, also with other subjects.

(21) חרב

μάχαιρα (35 x)	ῥομφαία (12 x)
2:30 4:10 5:12 9:16(15) 11:22 12:12 14:12,13,15,16, 18 (ρομφαια AOL') 15:2,2,3,9 16:4 18:21,21 19:7 20:4,4 21:7,9 24:10 25:17(49:37) 26(46):10,14,16	45(38):2 46(39):18 49(42):16, 17,22 50(43):11 51(44):12, 13,18,27,28 Bar 2:25; and *passim* in the LXX.

102

27(50):16,21,35,36,36,37,37; | μάχαιρα (13 x)
and *passim* in the LXX.

29(47):6   31(48):2,10   32:2,

ῥομφαία (2 x)

13,15,17,24(25:16,27,30,31,38)
33(26):23   34:6(27:8)   38(31):

5:17   6:25

2   39(32):24,36   41(34):17

Though predominant in Jer a', μάχαιρα is used in Jer b'
only in half of the verses. It may thus be assumed that in
some instances[30] Jer-R replaced μάχαιρα with ῥομφαία.

(22) צוה

ἐντέλλομαι (16 x) | συντάσσω (9 x)

1:7,17   7:22,23,23,31   11:4,4 | 33(26):2,8   34(27):3(4)
13:5,6   14:14   17:22   19:5 | 36(29):23   39(32):13,35
23:32   27(50):21   28(51):59; | 41(34):22   44(37):21   Bar 1:20;
and *passim* in the LXX. | and elsewhere in the LXX.

ἐντέλλομαι (13 x)

29(47):7   39(32):23   42(35):6,
10,14,18   43(36):5,8,26
45(38):10,27   Bar 2:9,28

ἐντέλλομαι, the only rendition of the Heb in Jer a', occurs also in Jer b', possibly as an unrevised remnant of the OG
of that section. Jer-R also changed ἐντέλλομαι to συντάσσω (9
x). συντάσσω does not occur in Jer a', nor does it frequently
render צוה in any other part of the LXX except Ex and Num.

(23) רעש (subject הארץ)

σείω (3 x) | φοβέομαι (1 x)

8:16   27(50):46   28(51):29; | 29:22(49:21) BS (σείω rel);[31]
and further Ez (4 x), with dif- | and Ez 27:28.
ferent subjects.

(24) הָמָה

ἤχω ! (3 x)

5:22 (waves)   27(50):42 (sea)
28(51):55 (waves);
and 5 x in the LXX.

κυμαίνω (1 x)

6:23 (sea);
and Is 17:12.

μαιμάσσω ! (1 x)

4:19 (heart)

βομβέω ! (2 x)[32]

31(48):36,36 (heart)   38(31):
36 (waves)

σπεύδω ! (1 x)

38(31):20 (intestines)

APPENDIX

The exact dividing line between Jer a' and b'

As part of the working hypothesis for chapters III and IV,
it was postulated that Jer b' is preserved from 29(47):1. This
assumption is verified here.

Listed below are the characteristic renditions of Jer a'
(OG) and Jer b' (Jer-R) on both sides of the imaginary dividing
line. The list contains characteristic renditions of Jer a'
(OG) in 28(51):41-64, whereas characteristic renditions of Jer-
R which occur in this section are underlined. The same method
is applied to renditions peculiar to Jer-R in the section on
the other side of the imaginary dividing line, viz. 29:1-23(47:
1-7; 49:7-22).

1. Jer 28(51):41-64

41	לכד - ἁλίσκομαι	IV	11
41	שמה - ἀφανισμός	III	1
43	שמה - ἄβατος, adj.	III	1
50	פלטים - ἀνασφζομαι	IV	16
52,53	נאם ה' - λέγει κύριος	III	43
54	שבר - συντριβή	III	35
55	המה - ἦχω	IV	24
56	שודד - ταλαιπωρία	III	2
56	לכד - ἁλίσκομαι	IV	11
56	גבור - μαχητής	III	51
57	שרים - ἡγεμόνας BSAOL'] ηγουμενους rel	III	47
58	כה אמר ה' - τάδε λέγει κύριος	III	18
58	ערער - κατασκάπτω	IV n. 23
62	שממה - ἀφανισμός	III	1
62	לבלתי היות - τοῦ μὴ εἶναι	III	6

2. Jer 29:1-23(47:1-7, 49:7-22)

2	כה אמר ה' - τάδε λέγει κύριος	III	18
4	שדד - ἀπόλλυμι	III	2
8	כה אמר ה' - τάδε λέγει κύριος	III	18
9	עת - χρόνος	III	10

106

11	שדד - ὄλλυμι	III 2
11	זרע - ἐπίχειρον	III 4
13	כה אמר ה' - <u>τάδε λέγει κύριος</u>	III 18
14	נאם ה' - <u>λέγει κύριος</u>	III 43
14,18	שמה - ἄβατος	III 1
20	נוה - τόπος	III 48
20	לפני - κατὰ πρόσωπον	III 22
21	שמם - ἀβατόω	III 1
21	נוה - κατάλυσις	III 48
22	רעש - φοβέομαι	IV 23

Since the hand of Jer-R can be detected from 29(47):4 onwards,[33] it is reasonable to assume that the MSS of Jer-LXX display his revision from 29(47):1 onwards.[34] See further VII, section 2.

The likelihood that Jer b' starts at the beginning of chapter 29 rather than after 29:15(49:14) (after the last "exception" in v. 14) is increased by an additional factor: V. 3 contains six pairs of prepositions + (double) noun + pron. suff. In four cases the LXX, conforming with the Heb, lacks articles. In one instance it has one article, and in another it has two. This trend of conforming with the Heb points to Jer-R rather than to the OG (see III 32).

NOTES

CHAPTER IV

1. S. Talmon, "Synonymous Readings in the Textual Traditions of the OT," *Scripta Hierosolymitana* 8 (1961) 335-383.
For a discussion of some synonymous renditions in the LXX, see
Hatch, *Essays*, 22ff. "Synonymous renditions" in the LXX de-
serve to be studied in a separate monograph.

2. Many of these synonymous renditions appear elsewhere
as variants in the MSS of the LXX or as variants between the
LXX and the text quoted from the LXX in the NT and Church
Fathers.

3. The following items adduced in this chapter are mentioned by Thackeray, "Gr.Tr.Jer.", 247ff.: 1,2,3,6,7,8,10,12,
14,17,22,24; Martin, *Syntax*, 117ff.: 4; Köhler, "Beobachtungen,"
25:20.

4. See Hatch, *Essays*, 27 for Sym; Sois.-Soin., *Zusätze*,
155 and Johnson, *Samuel*, 42ff. and J. Ziegler, *Festschrift G.
R. Driver* (Oxford 1963) 176ff. for O; for L: J. Ziegler, *Biblica* 40 (1959) 224-227 (where earlier literature is mentioned)
and B. M. Metzger, *Chapters in the History of NT Textual Criticism* (Leiden 1963) 25; and for Aq: Reider, *Prolegomena*, 34ff.

5. Hesychius explains παραπικραίνειν with παροργίζειν.
For παραπικραίνω see especially Walters, *Text*, 150-154.

6. See further 44(37):13 בְּעַל פְּקִדָת - ἄνθρωπος παρ'ᾧ κατέ-
λυσε, probably read as פְּקִדֹת, cf. 52:11 בבית הַפְּקֻדֹת and BDB, s.v.
פְּקֻדָּה.

7. No similar discrepancy between Jer a' and b' is recognizable for λαλέω (usually reflecting דִּבֶּר):

Jer a'		Jer b'	
λαλέω πρός	12 x	λαλέω πρός	9 x
λαλέω + dat.	1 x	λαλέω + dat.	4 x

Cf. Helbing, *Kasussyntax*, 238-239.

8. Jer-OG's renditions, almost exclusively reflecting אֶל,
conform with the general picture of εἶπον in the LXX:

אמר אל - εἶπον πρός	812 x	ל- אמר - εἶπον + dat.	459 x
אמר -ל - εἶπον πρός	49 x	אמר אל - εἶπον + dat.	333 x

The figures are culled from Helbing, *Kasussyntax*, 218.

9. The reviser might have avoided εἶπον πρός because he
preferred to limit πρός to the local sense of אֶל. However,
probably neither the OG nor the reviser had a clear intention
when using either εἶπον πρός or εἶπον + dat., both good Greek
expressions (see LSJ, s.v.). Some books of the LXX prefer one
of the two renderings, but in such cases the other one is not
excluded; see Helbing, *Kasussyntax*, 217-220.

108

Martin, *Syntax*, 118-119, distinguished in Jer between
cases in which God is the subject of εῖπον, and those in which
εῖπον has a human as its subject. However, since examples of
the first group are confined to the Heb of Jer a', the distinction does not seem to be justified.

The differentiation between the two renditions is not determined by the occurrence of personal names after the verb
which might have caused the use of πρός rather than the dative.
Among the occurrences of εῖπον in Jer a' one finds one p.n.
(personal name) rendered by εῖπον πρός and one by εῖπον with
the dative. In Jer b' nine of the 29 cases of εῖπον with the
dative are followed by a p.n., and likewise five of the six
cases of εῖπον πρός are followed by a p.n. This picture makes
Jer-R's preferences for εῖπον with the dative more evident.
Jer-R rendered nine occurrences of אמר with a p.n. by εῖπον +
dat. although in these cases one would have expected πρός according to the above-mentioned statistics.

10. A similar opposition between Ez a' and b' was noticed
by Turner, "Ezekiel", 13.

11. The evidence for the present tense of the verb, although scanty, is at variance with that for the past and future
tenses.

12. *Eclogae*, 397, quoted by LSJ, s.v. See further Swete,
Introduction, 297, and Turner, *Syntax*, 320.

13. The figures are culled from Sois.-Soin., *Infinitive*,
173 ("ein sehr deutlicher Unterschied" between the two parts of
Jer). To the figures for Jer we have added those for Bar (35 =
34 + 1; 59 = 52 + 7).

14. See Reider, *Prolegomena*, 50.

15. See Schmitt, *Theodotion*, 83-84.

16. Sois.-Soin., *Infinitive*, 201.

17. See Schmitt, *ib*.

18. The reconstruction of Bar is based upon Jer 33:8 MT
(*contra* Kneucker, *Baruch*, *ad loc*.).

19. See further 2:26 נמצא - ἁλίσκομαι.

20. This rendition was probably introduced as a variation
after 28(51):8 ἰάομαι.

21. μέρος in the meaning of 'side' is not attested in the
available dictionaries, but the relevant evidence is supplied
by J. A. L. Lee, "A Neglected Sense of μέρος," *Antichton* 6
(1972) 39-42.

22. גדלה הצית אש עליה... - ἀνήφθη πῦρ ἐπ'αὐτήν μεγάλη ἡ
θλῖψις ἐπὶ σέ (om ἀνήφθη πῦρ ἐπ'αὐτήν O). ἀνάπτω belongs to
the non-original part of the doublet, see Ziegler, *Beiträge*,
100.

23. κατασκάπτω renders further in Jer a' שחת (5:10) and ערער (28(51):58). It does not occur in Jer b'.

24. This rendition was probably introduced as a variation after σώζω, occurring at the beginning of the sentence.

25. In the listed passages πολίτης undoubtedly means 'fellow man', a meaning which is not quoted in the lexica. Only Hesychius records a meaning close to 'fellow man': πολίτης ὁ συμπολιτευόμενός τινι καὶ συνών (cf. 3:20 רֵעַ - συνών).

26. See Ziegler, "Einleitung", 45.

27. πολίτης further renders עמית in Zach 13:7 and בני עמי in Gen 23:11.

28. See further 40(33):5 פגר - νεκρός.

29. Ex 14:8 Num 33:3 Deut 32:27 Is 26:11. Cf. also Is 3:16 נטויות גרון - ὑψηλῷ τραχήλῳ.

30. Especially chapters 45-51, cf. VII, n. 7.

31. See Ziegler, "Einleitung", 45.

32. βομβέω occurs elsewhere only in 1 Chr 16:32 (רעם); βόμβησις is found only in Bar 2:29 (המון), cf. V 19.

33. For a possible reading of Jer-R in 28(51):57 see III, n. 121.

34. In 29:2,8,13,14(47:2 49:7,12,13) four renditions of the phrases כה אמר ה' and נאם ה' were left unrevised possibly because of their formulaic character. The fact that all four instances occur immediately after the imaginary dividing line is intriguing (cf. VII, n. 7).

CHAPTER V

THE RELATIONSHIP BETWEEN BARUCH AND JER-LXX

There can be no doubt that the first part of Bar (Bar 1:1-
3:8), extant in Greek and in several secondary translations,
was originally composed in Hebrew,[1] but opinions are divided
whether the second part was written either in Greek or in Hebrew. Although our main interest lies in the first part of Bar,
relevant data from Bar 3:9 ff. are not excluded *a priori*.

In considering the textual status of Bar, scholars have
been preoccupied with two major problems: first, the number of
documents composing Bar, a question which has both textual and
literary aspects;[2] second, the question of the relationship between Bar, Jer and Dan: Bar, like the bulk of Qumran literature
and several apocryphal books, comprises a mosaic of Biblical
passages. The two books most frequently quoted and elaborated
upon in this mosaic are Dan and Jer and it has been recognized
that there exists a special relationship between Bar on the one
hand and Jer and Dan on the other.[3]

This chapter is devoted to an examination of the relationship between the two translations of Bar and Jer, omitting consideration of their Hebrew *Vorlagen*.[3] Previous discussions of
the issue have not distinguished consistently between the primary (Hebrew) and secondary (Greek) level, and this inaccuracy
has led to misunderstandings.

The discussion of the translation equivalents of Bar is
based on a reconstruction of its Hebrew *Vorlage* which is found
in the appendix to this chapter. Like all reconstructions, also this one is tentative, but it should be stressed that two
factors render many details in the reconstruction rather stable:
(1) Bar was translated with literal accuracy by a relatively
consistent translator;[4] (2) the reconstruction can be supported
by many Biblical parallels which the author of the Hebrew Bar
most likely had in mind. These parallels are provided in the
study mentioned on p. 127.

111

112

In Bar's mosaic of Biblical verses, quotations from Jer,
often phrased like the LXX of Jer, are prominent. Some scholars asserted that this resemblance between Bar and Jer-LXX resulted from Bar's use of the Greek of Jer.[5] Elaborating upon
this theory, Kneucker stated that Bar was so well acquainted
with Jer "dass er bei seiner Arbeit unwillkührlich--gedächtniss-
mässig--hebräische Worte und Satzverbindungen in ähnlicher und
gleicher Weise griechisch wiedergab" (*Baruch*, 85). Schürer[6]
and Thackeray (at one time)[7] even assumed that Bar deliberately
imitated the style of Jer.

The majority of scholars, however, explained the resemblance between Bar and Jer-LXX as resulting from an identical
translator for both books,[8] or for Jer-LXX and the first part
of Bar.[9] Thackeray explained the similarities in a more satis-
factory manner; for, while working on the problem of the different translators of Jer, he found that the first part of Bar
(1:1-3:8) was actually rendered by the second translator of Jer,
Jer. β'.[10]

Thackeray's view of the relationship between Jer b' and
Bar is basically correct. We hope to prove the correctness of
Thackeray's preliminary statement which was appended to his article on Jer.[11] It is of interest to note that Thackeray re-
luctantly abandoned this view at a later stage,[12] but finally
returned to his original opinion.[13]

While according to Thackeray the second part of Jer and
the first chapters of Bar were produced by the second translator of Jer, in our opinion they contain the work of Jer-R. It
is our intention to show that both Bar 1:1-3:8 and Jer 29-52
were finally formulated by one person (Jer-R). In this way we
hope to prove one of the presuppositions on which some of the
examples in chapters II-IV are based. It should be pointed out
that this chapter provides no additional proof that Jer b' is a
revision rather than a second translation. Relevant data concerning the revisional elements included in Jer 29-52 and Bar
were provided in ch. III.

Our discussion of the relationship between Bar and Jer is
rather complicated because the examples have to be subdivided
into many categories. This system has been chosen because we
want to be able to dismiss alternative explanations before

reaching our own conclusion that Jer-R's hand is also visible
in Bar. As a result, similarities between Bar and Jer-R are
subdivided into two groups, with three additional groups of
items further exemplifying Bar's relation to Jer-LXX (see n. 1
below):

1. Bar = Jer-R in quotations from Jer b' (items 1-5)
2. Bar = Jer-R outside quotations from Jer b'
   α. Bar = Jer-R ≠ Jer-OG (items 6-19)
   β. Bar = Jer-R = *LXX* ≠ Jer-OG (see n. 2 below) (items
      20-27)
3. Bar = Jer a'b' (items 28-30)
4. Bar ≠ Jer b' (items 31-33)
5. Bar ≠ Jer a' (items 34-35)

A further distinction is made in groups 1 and 2 between:

a. Agreements between Bar and Jer b' in some isolated
renditions;

b. Similarities between Bar and Jer-R in recurring renditions which distinguish Jer b' as a whole from Jer a' (and the
remainder of the LXX). See below, n. 3.

Note 1: The examples below refer to significant (dis)agree-
        ments only, excluding disagreements which involve dif-
        ferent *Vorlagen*. Thus, one should not expect to find
        references to all the passages of Jer which are quoted
        in Bar.

Note 2: The translation vocabulary of Jer-R and Bar often
        agrees with that of the other LXX books, while the
        corresponding translation option of Jer-OG is isolated
        within the LXX (2α). In contrast to the examples of
        group 2α, the items of group 2β indicate that Bar
        could have been rendered by any one of the LXX trans-
        lators, with the exception of Jer-OG.

Note 3: The distinction between category (a) and (b) is made
        to counter the claim that agreements between Bar and
        Jer-R in given phrases result either from Bar's use of
        Jer b' or from a reworking of Bar according to Jer b'.
        We maintain that this argument cannot be held against
        evidence gathered in category (b), especially when
        words characteristic of Jer-R are found within quota-
        tions from Jer a'.

Note 4: It is important to stress that no example of Bar = Jer
OG ≠ Jer-R could be found.

In the following, "Jer b'" and "Jer-R" denote Jer 29-52
only, and do not include Bar as they do in the remainder of
this study. ! and * refer to renditions and words occurring in
Jer b' and Bar only. Reference is made to the relevant discussions in chapters II-IV where some of the below-mentioned renditions are discussed in full.[14]

1. *Bar = Jer-R in Quotations from Jer b'*

The following examples could be taken as proof that Bar
was retouched according to the LXX of Jer b'. However, the
data adduced in section (2) refute such an assumption.

a. *Agreements between Bar and Jer b' in some
isolated renditions*

(1) לזועה - ὑποχείριος !

Bar 2:4 καὶ ἔδωκεν αὐτοὺς ὑποχειρίους πάσαις ταῖς βασιλεί-
αις ταῖς κύκλῳ ἡμῶν εἰς ὀνειδισμὸν καὶ εἰς ἄβατον;
Jer 49(42):18 καὶ ἔσεσθε εἰς ἄβατον καὶ ὑποχείριοι καὶ εἰς
ἀρὰν καὶ εἰς ὀνειδισμόν (והייתם לאלה ולשמה ולקללה ולחרפה).

The Heb Bar paraphrased Jer 29:18 ונתחים לזועה לכל ממלכות
הארץ לאלה ולשמה ולשרקה ולחרפה בכל הגוים (not in the LXX), but
the Greek Bar's use of ὑποχείριος is related to the LXX of Jer
49(42):18, whose wording is close to Jer 29:18. Kneucker's
assumption (*Baruch*, ad loc.) that in both cases ὑποχείριος[15]
reflects לזועה is probably correct.[16]

(2) קרח - παγετός

Bar 2:25 ἐξερριμένα τῷ καύματι τῆς ἡμέρας καὶ τῷ παγετῷ
τῆς νυκτός ; Jer 43(36):30 ἐρριμένον ἐν τῷ καύματι τῆς ἡμέρας
καὶ ἐν τῷ παγετῷ τῆς νυκτός (משלכת לחרב ביום ולקרח בלילה).

Both translations appear to be based upon the LXX of Gen
31:40.[17] παγετός occurs elsewhere only in Sir 3:15 (כפור).

(3) דֶּבֶר - ἀποστολή !

Bar 2:25 καὶ ἀπεθάνοσαν ἐν πόνοις πονηροῖς ἐν λιμῷ καὶ ἐν
ῥομφαίᾳ καὶ ἐν ἀποστολῇ ; Jer 39(32):36 ἐν μαχαίρᾳ καὶ ἐν λιμῷ
καὶ ἐν ἀποστολῇ (בחרב וברעב ובדבר).

ἀποστολή should probably be explained with Schleusner,
s.v., as 'pestilentia a Deo immissa'[18] and not with LSJ, *Suppl.*,
as 'exile'.[19] דֶּבֶר does not occur elsewhere in Jer b'; in Jer
a' it is rendered by θάνατος, as in the remainder of the LXX.

(4) ירש - κυριεύω !

Bar 2:34 quotes Jer 37(30):3. Only in these two places is
ירש rendered by κυριεύω (cf. Ex 15:9 הוריש - κυριεύω and Num
21:24 ירש - κατακυριεύω).[20]

b. *Similarities between Bar and Jer-R in recurring renditions*
which distinguish Jer b' as a whole from Jer a'
(and the remainder of the LXX)

(5) שמה - ἄβατος !

Bar 2:4 = Jer 49(42):18 (quoted in item 1). The rendering
of שמה with ἄβατος is discussed in item 15 below.

2. *Bar = Jer-R Outside Quotations from Jer b'*
α. *Bar = Jer-R ≠ Jer-OG*

The below-mentioned examples provide reasonable proof that
Jer-R and Bar are identical.

a. *Agreements between Bar and Jer b' in some isolated renditions*

(6) לאיש יהודה ולישבי ירושלם

Bar 1:15 = Dan 9:7. Bar's translation differs from both
Dan-LXX and Dan-Th, but concurs with Jer 42(35):13:
Bar 1:15

= Jer 42(35):13	ἀνθρώπῳ	Ιουδα καὶ	τοῖς κατοικοῦσιν		Ιερου-σαλημ
Dan-LXX 9:7	ἀνθρώποις	Ιουδα καὶ		καθημένοις	ἐν Ιερου-σαλημ
Dan-Th 9:7	ἀνδρὶ	Ιουδα καὶ	τοῖς ἐνοικοῦσιν		ἐν Ιερου-σαλημ

116

Note the different renderings of לְאִישׁ[21] and of וְלִישְׁבֵי.

(7) תורה - πρόσταγμα

Bar 1:18 and 2:10 = Dan 9:10. While Dan-LXX and Dan-Th rendered תורה by its usual equivalent (νόμος), Bar used πρόσταγμα, a rendition which recurs only in Jer 39(32):23, 51(44): 10 and 2 Chr 19:10 - thus very rare when compared to the numerous occurrences of νόμος.[22]

(8) דאב - πεινάω !

Bar 2:18 = Deut 28:65. Instead of the rendition of דאבון נפש in Deut (τηκομένη ψυχή), Bar rendered the Heb by ἡ ψυχὴ ἡ πεινῶσα. Elsewhere in the LXX is דאב rendered by πεινάω only in Jer 38(31):25 (נפש דאבה - ψυχὴ πεινῶσα) and 38(31):12. It seems as if this translation reflects רעב (interchanges of ר/ד and א/ע) but it should, in fact, be considered a "pseudo-variant" (cf. II, n. 9), resulting from the translator's ignorance of דאב.

(9) שבת - ἐκλείπω

Bar 2:23 = Jer 7:34 (Jer a'). The first word of the quotation (השבית - καταλύω) appears in Bar as ἐκλείψειν ποιέω. The rendering of שבת by ἐκλείπω recurs only in Jer 43(36):29 and Jos 5:11.

(10) מעללים - πράγματα !

Bar 2:33 = Jer 25:5 (Jer a'). In Jer מעללים is rendered with ἐπιτηδεύματα, as in the remainder of the LXX. Bar's rendition (πράγματα) recurs only in Jer 51(44):22.

b. *Similarities between Bar and Jer-R in recurring*
renditions which distinguish Jer b' as a whole
from Jer a' (and the remainder of the LXX)

(11) לבלתי - πρὸς τὸ μή ! (III 6)

Bar 1:19 καὶ ἐσχεδιάζομεν πρὸς τὸ μή ἀκούειν τῆς φωνῆς αὐτοῦ ; cf. Bar 2:5 πρὸς τὸ μή ἀκούειν τῆς φωνῆς αὐτοῦ.

Bar 1:19 = Dan 9:11 בקלך שמוע לבלתי וסור, Dan-LXX καὶ ἀπέστησαν
τοῦ μὴ ἀκοῦσαι τῆς φωνῆς σου, Dan-Th καὶ ἐξέκλιναν τοῦ μὴ
ἀκοῦσαι τῆς φωνῆς σου.

The usual LXX rendition of לבלתי is τοῦ μή, occurring also
in the LXX and Th translations of Dan. Bar's rendition πρὸς τὸ
μή, on the other hand, recurs only in Jer b'; more precisely,
the use of the art. inf. with πρός + acc. (rendering both לבלתי
and למען) is confined to Jer b' (III 6,7). Therefore, the
identical rendition of לבלתי with πρὸς τὸ μή in Bar and Jer b'
strongly suggests the identity of Bar and Jer-R, especially
since the similarity is found within a quotation from Dan.

(12) עבד ('to serve someone') -
ἐργάζομαι ! (III 8)

This rendition occurs only in Jer 34:5 - 47:9 (11 x) Bar
1:22 2:21,22,24.

(13) הדיח - διασπείρω (III 50)

Bar 2:13 and 2:29 resemble Jer's style, but do not elaborate upon any particular passage. Bar 2:4 and 3:8, on the other
hand, paraphrase Jer 24:9 (Jer a'). In all four verses Bar
agrees with Jer-R in translating הדיח by διασπείρω and not by
ἐξωθέω, a rendition which characterizes Jer a' (it occurs, e.g.,
in the above-mentioned 24:9; cf. further III 50).

(14) כה אמר ה' - οὕτως εἶπε κύριος (III 18)

Bar 2:21 οὕτως εἶπε κύριος. Since Jer-R's rendition of
the Heb, οὕτως εἶπε κύριος (replacing an earlier τάδε λέγει
κύριος) occurs only rarely outside Jer b', the agreement between Bar and Jer-R is all the more significant.

(15) שמה - ἄβατος ! (III 1)

Bar 2:23 quotes Jer 7:34 (Jer a') and the end of the verse
uses one of the characteristic expressions of Jer, היתה...לשמה.
Unlike the LXX of Jer a' (ἀφανισμός), Bar rendered שמה with
ἄβατος, a rendition which is confined to Jer b'.

. The same rendition occurs in Bar 2:4, quoting Jer 49(42): 18 (see item 5).

(16) מאין + noun - ἀπό + noun (III 28)

Bar 2:23 καί ἔσται πᾶσα ἡ γῆ εἰς ἄβατον ἀπὸ ἐνοικούντων. The first part of the phrase quotes Jer 7:34 (Jer a'), while the last two words have many parallels in Jer and Zeph, but not in Jer 7:34. Like Jer-R, and unlike Jer-OG, Bar rendered מאין + noun literally with ἀπό + noun.

(17) בעיני - prep. + ὀφθαλμός (III 21)

Bar 1:22 ποιῆσαι τὰ κακὰ κατ'ὀφθαλμοὺς κυρίου θεοῦ ἡμῶν; cf. Jer 39(32):30 ποιοῦντες τὸ πονηρὸν κατ'ὀφθαλμούς μου ; 18:10 ποιήσωσι τὰ πονηρὰ ἐναντίον μου.

Bar's treatment of בעיני conforms with that of Jer-R (see III 21). However, the evidence for Bar is scanty, especially since Bar 1:12 εὑρήσομεν χάριν ἐναντίον αὐτῶν probably also re-flects בעיני.[23]

(18) שמחה - χαρμοσύνη (IV 3)

Bar 2:23 = Jer 7:34 (Jer a'). Instead of Jer's קול שמחה - φωνὴ χαιρόντων, Bar translated שמחה with χαρμοσύνη. χαρμοσύνη occurs elsewhere only in Lev 22:29 1 Sam 18:6 Jer 31(48):33 40(33):11 and Bar 4:23.

(19) βομβ- (IV 24)

Bar 2:29 βόμβησις ('buzzing'), probably translating המון, is a hapax for the LXX. The cognate verb βομβέω occurs only in Jer 31(48):36 - המה, 38(31):36 - המה and 1 Chr 16:32 - רעם.

β. Bar = Jer-R = LXX ≠ Jer-OG[24]

The items of this group indicate that Bar could have been rendered by any one of the LXX translators with the exception of Jer-OG.

(20) עבד - παῖς (III 42)

This rendition occurs in Jer 32:5 - 52:8 (14 x), Bar 1:20
2:20,24,28 3:37 and *passim* in the LXX. Jer-OG rendered the
Heb both with δοῦλος (4 x) and with παῖς (3 x). However, עבד
appears in Bar in its religious use, and Jer-OG rendered such
instances mainly by δοῦλος.

(21) אלהים אחרים - θεοὶ ἕτεροι (III 19)

This rendition occurs in Jer 39:29 - 51:15 (6 x), Bar 1:22
and *passim* in the LXX. Jer-OG rendered the Heb mainly with
θεοὶ ἀλλότριοι (12 x).

(22) הטה אזן - κλίνω τὸ οὖς (III 20)

Bar 2:16 = Dan 9:18. Bar's rendition הטה אזנך - κλῖνον τὸ
οὖς σου conforms with Dan-Th, Jer b' (4 x) and the remainder of
the LXX, and differs from that of Dan-LXX and Jer-OG (see III
20).

(23) גִּבֹּר - δυνατός (III 51)

This rendition occurs in Jer b' (3 x), Bar 1:4,9 (גְּבָרִים
read as גִּבֹּרִים) and *passim* in the LXX. Jer-OG rendered the Heb
mainly with μαχητής (8 x).

(24) כאשר - καθά (IV 6)

This rendition occurs in Jer b' (3 x), in Bar 1:6 2:2,28
and *passim* in the LXX. καθά does not occur in Jer a'.

(25) צוה - συντάσσω (IV 22)

Bar 1:20 συντάσσω occurs within a quotation from Jer 11:4
(Jer a'). This common LXX rendition occurs also 8 times in Jer
b', but never in Jer a'.

(26) ל + inf. constr. rendered by the Greek
anarthr. inf. (IV 7)

Bar's preference for the anarthr. inf. (7 x; art. inf. 1
x) conforms with Jer-R (anarthr. inf. 52 x; art. inf. 34 x).

Jer-OG, on the other hand, usually rendered the *lamed* with the
art. inf. (56 x; anarthr. inf. 16 x).

(27) יׁשב - ἐνοικέω

This rendition occurs in Jer b' (8 x), Bar 2:23 and *passim*
in the LXX. ἐνοικέω does not occur in Jer a'.

3. *Bar = Jer a'b'*

Bar shares with Jer a'b' three renditions, two of which
are mistranslations. These examples are considered as possible
proofs that Bar was part of the OG translation of Jer (see below).

(28) מַסְגֵּר - δεσμώτης [!] (II 27)

Bar 1:9 quotes Jer 24:1 (Jer a') and differs slightly from
Jer 36(29):2 (Jer b'). In all three places מַסְגֵּר has been read
as מְסְגָּר or מְסֻגָּר and rendered with δεσμώτης, a word which recurs
but once in the LXX.

(29) חֻצוֹת ('streets') - ἔξωθεν [!] (II 14)

Bar 2:23 = Jer 7:34 (Jer a'). Instead of Jer's ἐκ
πόλεων Ιουδα καὶ <u>ἐκ διόδων</u> Ιερουσαλημ, Bar rendered מערי יהודה
ומחצות ירושלם with ἐκ πόλεων Ιουδα καὶ <u>ἔξωθεν</u> Ιερουσαλημ. The
mistranslation of חֻצוֹת with ἔξωθεν occurs only in Jer a'b' and
Bar. Cf. II 14.

(30) <u>ἀποικισμός</u> * (II 42)

This word occurs only in Jer a' (1 x), Jer b' (3 x) and
Bar (2 x).

4. *Bar ≠ Jer b'*

Thus far the discussion has focused upon agreements between Bar and Jer b', pointing out only one minor discrepancy.
This item and two additional differences are listed here.

(31)

Jer 43(36):30 ῥίπτω, Bar 2:25 ἐκρίπτω (see item 2).

(32)

Jer 39(32):40 καὶ τὸν φόβον μου δώσω <u>εἰς</u> τὴν καρδίαν αὐτῶν
(ואת יראתי אתן בלבבם); Bar 3:7 ἐπί.

(33)

Jer 34:10(27:12) εἰσαγάγετε τὸν <u>τράχηλον</u> ὑμῶν (הביאו את
צואריכם); Bar 2:21 κλίνατε τὸν <u>ὦμον</u> ὑμῶν (הטו צואריכם).

5. *Bar ≠ Jer a'*

Many important differences between Bar and Jer a' were
noted above, namely, those cases in which Bar agreed with the
vocabulary of Jer-R while quoting from Jer a'. These examples
are summarized on pp. 122-24. The following two items represent additional points of difference between Bar and Jer a':

(34)

Bar 1:21-22 = Jer 7:24. Instead of Jer's πορεύομαι
(הלך), Bar used οἴχομαι (cf. II 25), and instead of τοῖς
ἐνθυμήμασι τῆς καρδίας αὐτῶν τῆς κακῆς (בשררות לבם הרע), he
rendered ἐν διανοίᾳ καρδίας αὐτοῦ τῆς πονηρᾶς.

(35)

Bar 2:26 διὰ πονηρίαν οἴκου Ισραηλ differs from Jer 11:17
ἀντὶ τῆς κακίας οἴκου Ισραηλ (בגלל רעת בית ישראל); cf. also IV
10.

6. *Conclusions*

The following chart summarizes the important agreements
between Bar and Jer-R:

Bar	quoting from	identical with LXX of	supposed *Vorlage* of Bar = MT of Jer, etc.	translation of Bar = Jer-R	parallel transl. of Jer-OG, if any
(1) 2:4	Jer 29:18	Jer 49(42):18	לזועה	ὑποχείριος !	
(2) 2:25	Gen 31:40 and	Gen 31:40 and	קרח	παγετός	
	Jer 36:30	Jer 43(36):30			
(3) 2:25	Jer 32:36	Jer 39(32):36	דבר	ἀποστολή !	θάνατος
(4) 2:34	Jer 30:3	Jer 37(30):3	ר' שם	κυριεύω	
(5) 2:4	Jer 42:18	Jer 49(42):18	שמה	ἄβατος !	ἀφανισμός
(6) 1:15	Dan 9:7	Jer 42(35):13	הזאת ו ר' ל' ושכני ירושלם	ἀνθρώπῳ Ιουδα καὶ τοῖς κατοι- κοῦσιν Ιερουσαλημ	
(7) 1:18 2:10	Dan 9:10	Jer 39(32):23 and 51(44):10	תורה	πρόσταγμα	
(8) 2:18	Deut 28:65	Jer 38(31):25	דאב	πεινάω !	
(9) 2:23	Jer 7:34(Jer a')	Jer 43(36):29	שבת	ἐκλείπω	
(10) 2:33	Jer 25:5(Jer a')	Jer 51(44):22	מעלליכם	πράγματα !	
(11) 1:19	Dan 9:11	Jer-R	לבלתי	πρὸς τὸ μή !	τοῦ μή
(20) 1:20	Dan 9:11	Dan 9:11 and Jer-R = LXX	עבד	παῖς	δοῦλος
(20) 2:20,24,28	-	Jer-R	עבד	παῖς	δοῦλος
(20) 3:37	-	Jer-R	עבד (?)	παῖς	δοῦλος
(12) 1:22	-	Jer-R	עבד	ἐργάζομαι !	δουλεύω
(12) 2:21	Jer 27:12	Jer-R	עבד	ἐργάζομαι !	δουλεύω
(12) 2:22,24	Jer 27:9	Jer-R	עבד	ἐργάζομαι !	δουλεύω
(13) 2:13,29	-	Jer-R	חדר	διασπείρω	ἐξωθέω

Bar	quoting from	identical with LXX of	supposed *Vorlage* of Bar = MT of Jer, etc.	translation of Bar = Jer-R	parallel transl. of Jer-OG, if any
(13) 2:4 3:8	Jer 24:9 (Jer a')	Jer-R	הֱיֵה	διασπείρω	ἐξωθέω
(14) 2:21	–	Jer-R	כֹּה אָמַר יְה	οὕτως εἶπε κύριος	τάδε λέγει κύριος
(15) 2:23	Jer 7:34 (Jer a')	Jer-R	שְׁמָמָה	ἄβατος !	ἀφανισμός
(16) 2:23	Jer 7:34 (Jer a')	Jer-R	מֵאֵין + noun	ἀπό + noun	verbal form
(17) 1:22	–	Jer-R	לְעֵינֵי	κατ' ὀφθαλμούς	ἐναντίον
(18) 2:23	Jer 7:34 (Jer a')	Jer-R	שִׂמְחָה	χαρμοσύνη	
(19) 2:29	–	Jer-R	חֵטְא	βόμβησις	
(21) 1:22	–	Jer-R = LXX	אֱלֹהִים אֲחֵרִים	θεοὶ ἕτεροι	θεοὶ ἀλλότριοι
(22) 2:16	Dan 9:18	Dan-Th and	אֶת אֹזֶן	κλίνω τὸ οὖς	προσέχω τὸ οὖς
(23) 1:4	–	Jer-R = LXX	גִּבּוֹר	δυνατός	μαχητής
(24) 1:6 2:8,28	–	Jer-R = LXX	כַּאֲשֶׁר	καθά	
(25) 1:20	Jer 11:4 (Jer a')	Jer-R = LXX	בְּרִית	συντάσσω	
(26) 10 x	–	Jer-R = LXX	לְ + inf. constr.	anarthrous inf.	articular inf.
(27) 2:23	–	Jer-R = LXX	אֲשֶׁר	ἐνοικέω	
(28) 1:9	Jer 24:1 (Jer a')	Jer-R = Jer-OG	מַסְגֵּר	δεσμώτης !	δεσμώτης !

Bar	quoting from	identical with LXX of	supposed *Vorlage* of Bar = MT of Jer, etc.	translation of Bar = Jer-R	parallel transl. of Jer-OG, if any
(29) 2:23	Jer 7:34 (Jer a')	Jer-R = Jer-OG	הַרְבֵּה	ἔξωθεν !	ἔξωθεν !
(30) 2:30,32	–	Jer-R = Jer-OG	שֶׁבֶר	ἀποικισμός *	ἀποικισμός *

The agreements between Bar and Jer-R were divided into two groups: agreements occurring within quotations from Jer b' and agreements found outside such quotations. Similarities outside quotations were found to outnumber those within. It is therefore incorrect to assume that the similarities in vocabulary resulted from Bar's borrowing from Jer-LXX because, if they occur outside quotations from Jer, they cannot be considered as borrowings. For the same reason it cannot be assumed either that the quotations from Jer in Bar were revised according to Jer-LXX. It is further inconceivable that the translator of Bar either imitated Jer or was influenced by his style, because the agreements are limited to the *second* part of Jer.

The large number of agreements clearly prove that Jer-R revised Bar. Some of the agreements occur between isolated renditions found in both Bar and Jer b' (1a, 2a), while others reflect characteristic recurring renditions, some of which occur only in Jer b' and Bar (1b; 2α, b). Nearly all the examples were taken from the vocabulary of Jer-R and Bar; in addition, four agreements in the rendering of syntactical features were listed (11,16,24,26).

Two facts reinforce the similarity between Bar and Jer-R:

1. Bar does not significantly agree with any translation other than Jer b' and the Pentateuch.[25] Since the translators of many books of the LXX often relied upon the earlier-translated Pentateuch, renditions peculiar to the Pent and Bar (and Jer b') only are to be expected.

2. Some of the similarities between Bar and the technique of Jer-R are found within verses identical with verses in Dan (6,7,11,22).

The thirty important agreements between Jer-R and Bar are more striking when one considers the complete lack of similarity between Jer a' and Bar. In fact, the two often disagree:

1. Various words in passages quoted from Jer a' were rendered in Bar according to the technique of Jer-R whenever that technique differed from Jer-OG (9,10,13,15,16,18,25). Cf. further items 34-35.

2. Several of Bar's renditions conform with the usual LXX technique, including Jer-R, while disagreeing with Jer-OG's (unusual) renditions (group 2β).

Thus the hand which we have detected in Bar and Jer b' cannot be recognized in Jer a'.

The few--but important--similarities between Bar, Jer a' and Jer b' listed in items 28-30 may bear witness to the stage of the first translation of Jer and Bar evidenced in Jer a' and in the substratum of Jer b' and Bar. However, evidence connecting Bar with the OG of Jer is not as strong as the links between Bar and Jer-R. The reason for this discrepancy is the difficulty in documenting examples of the former group.[26]

It should be noted that the results of the investigation of the textual relationship between Jer and Bar are conclusive for Bar 1:1-3:8 only. Except for one less important similarity between Bar 4:23 and Jer-R (item 18), there is no indication that the relationship of Bar 3:9 ff. to Jer-R is the same as that of Bar 1:1-3:8 to Jer-R. In fact, it is as yet uncertain whether Bar 3:9 ff. was translated at all.

However, any conclusion on the relationship between Bar 3:9 ff. and Jer based on an *argumentum ex silentio* may be misleading, since Bar 3:9 ff. provides no data for a suitable comparison with the LXX of Jer: In contrast to Bar 1:1-3:8, Bar 3:9 ff. never quotes Jer. Since its contents differ both from Jer and the first part of Bar, it is very difficult to prove any possible equation of Jer-R and Bar 1:1-3:8 with Bar 3:9 ff. by comparing their respective vocabularies. Such a comparison is further hampered by the uncertainty concerning the original language of Bar 3:9 ff. If one could successfully demonstrate the linguistic unity of the two (three?) parts of Bar, it could be assumed that Bar 3:9 ff. was revised by Jer-R; however, the linguistic unity of Bar remains to be examined. The linguistic pilot studies known to me tend to disprove such a unity.[27]

The Hebrew Vorlage of Bar 1:1-3:8

The discussion of the translation options in Bar is based
on our reconstruction of the Hebrew *Vorlage* of 1:1-3:8. This
reconstruction is presented here without any annotation. A
full list of Biblical parallels which the author of Bar most
likely hand in mind--and which thus support our reconstruction
--as well as some notes are found in the present author's *The
Book of Baruch (Greek and Hebrew), Texts and Translations*,
Pseudepigrapha Series 6, *Society of Biblical Literature* (1975).
The reader will also find there an analysis of the tentative
nature of our reconstruction.

The reconstruction presented below is based upon Ziegler's
printed text, reflecting his view of the original form of Bar,
of which MS B generally is the most faithful representative.[28]

While the entire Hebrew reconstruction must remain tentative, a few particularly doubtful retroversions are noted by
underlining, e.g., 2:25 בתחלאים. At times alternative possibilities are suggested in parentheses, e.g. (ל)מקטן, i.e., מקטן
or למקטן. The relatively defective orthography[29] makes no claim
to represent the actual *Vorlage* of the translator.

ואלה דברי הספר אשר כתב ברוך בן נריה בן מחסיה בן צדקיה בן	1
חסדיה בן חלקיה בבבל : בשנה החמישית בשבעה לחדש בעת אשר לכדו	2
הכשדים את ירושלם וישרפוה באש :	
ויקרא ברוך את דברי הספר הזה באזני יכניה בן יהויקים מלך יהודה	3
ובאזני כל העם הבאים אל הספר : ובאזני הגברים ובני המלכים ובאזני	4
הזקנים ובאזני כל העם (ל)מקטן (ו)עד גדול כל הישבים בבבל על נהר	
סוד : ויבכו ויצומו ויתפללו לפני ה' : ויקבצי כסף <u>איש כאשר השיגה</u>	6-5
<u>ידו</u> : וישלחו ירושלם אל יהויקים בן חלקיה בן שלוח הכהן ואל הכהנים	7
ואל כל העם הנמצאים עמו בירושלם : בקחתו את כלי בית ה' המוצאים מן	8
ההיכל להשיב אל ארץ יהודה בעשרה לסיון כלי כסף אשר עשה צדקיה בן	
יאשיה מלך יהודה : אחרי הגלות נבוכדנאצר מלך בבל את יכניה ואת	9
השרים ואת המסגר ואת הגברים ואת עם הארץ מירושלם ויבאם בבל :	
ויאמרו הנה שלחנו אליכם כסף וקנו בכסף עולות וחטאת ולבונה	10

127

ועשר מנחה והעלו על מזבח ה׳ אלהינו : והתפללו בעד חיי נבוכדנאצר	11
מלך בבל ובעד (ואל) חיי בלשאצר בנו למען יהיו ימיהם כימי השמים על	
הארץ : ויתן ה׳ עז לנו ויאר את עינינו ונחי(ה) בצל נבוכדנאצר מלך	12
בבל ובצל בלשאצר בנו ונעבד אתם ימים רבים ונמצא חן בעיניהם :	
והתפללו בעדנו אל ה׳ אלהינו כי חטאנו לה׳ אלהינו ולא שב אף ה׳	13
וחמתו ממנו עד היום הזה : וקראו את הספר הזה אשר שלחנו אליכם	14
להתודות בבית ה׳ ביום חג וביומי מועד :	
ואמרו לה׳ אלהינו הצדקה ולנו בשת הפנים כיום הזה לאיש יהודה	15
ולישבי ירושלם : ולמלכינו ולשרינו ולכהנינו ולנביאינו ולאבותינו :	16-17
אשר חטאנו לה׳ (לפני ה׳) : ומרדנו בו ולא שמענו בקול ה׳ אלהינו	18
ללכת בתורת ה׳ אשר נתן לפנינו : (ל)מן היום אשר הוציא ה׳ את	19
אבותינו מארץ מצרים ועד היום הזה ממרים היינו עם ה׳ אלהינו וסור	
לבלתי שמוע בקולו : ותדבק בנו הרעה והאלה אשר צוה ה׳ למשה עבדו	20
ביום הוציא את אבותינו מארץ מצרים לתת לנו ארץ זבת חלב ודבש כיום	
הזה : ולא שמענו בקול ה׳ אלהינו ככל דברי הנבאים אשר שלח אלינו :	21-22
ונלך איש בשרדות לבו הרע לעבוד אלהים אחרים לעשות את הרע בעיני ה׳	23
אלהינו :	
$\frac{2}{1}$	
ויקם ה׳ את דברו אשר דבר עלינו ועל שפטינו השפטים את ישראל	
ועל מלכינו ועל שרינו ועל איש ישראל ויהודה : לא נעשתה תחת כל	2
השמים כאשר נעשתה בירושלם ככתוב בתורת משה : לאכל איש (את) בשר	3
בנו ואיש (את) בשר בתו : ויתן אתם לזועה (לזעוה) לכל הממלכות אשר	4
סביבתינו לחרפה ולשמה בכל הגוים (אשר) סביבתינו אשר הדיחם ה׳ שם :	
ויהיו למטה ולא למעלה כי חטאנו לה׳ אלהינו לבלתי שמוע בקולו :	5
לה׳ אלהינו הצדקה ולנו ולאבותינו בשת הפנים כיום הזה : אשר	6-7
דבר ה׳ עלינו כל הרעה הזאת באה עלינו : ולא הלינו את פני ה׳ לשוב	8
איש ממחשבות (ממרעצות) לבם הרע : וישקד ה׳ על הרעה ויביאה עלינו	9
כי צדיק ה׳ על כל מעשיו אשר צוה אתנו (לנו) : ולא שמענו בקולו	10
ללכת בתורת ה׳ אשר נתן לפנינו :	
ועתה ה׳ אלהי ישראל אשר הוצאת את עמך מארץ מצרים ביד חזקה	11
ובאתות ובמופתים (ר)בכח גדול ובזרע נטויה ותעש לך שם כיום הזה :	
חטאנו (ה)עוינו (ה)רשענו : ה׳ אלהינו ככל צדקתיך ישב אפך ממנו כי	12-13
בשארנו מעט בגוים אשר הדזחתנו שם : שמע ה׳ אל תפלתנו ואל תחנונינו	14
והצילנו למענך ותן לנו חן לפני שוברינו : למען ידע כל הארץ כי אתה	15
ה׳ אלהינו כי שמך נקרא על ישראל ועל עמו : ה׳ השקיפה ממעון קדשך	16
רשיח לבך (והבט) אלינו הטה ה׳ אזנך תשמע : פקח עיניך וראה כי לא	17
המתים בשאול אשר לקחה רוחם מקרבם יתנו כבוד צדקה לה׳ : כי לב	18
רגז ורגל ההלכת כפופה ו(נ)כשלה וכליון עינים ונפש הדאבון יתנו לך	
כבוד צדקה ה׳ :	
כי לא על צדקות אבותינו ומלכינו אנחנו מפילים תחנונינו לפניך	19

ה' אלהינו : כי שלחת אפך וחמתך בנו כאשר דברת ביד עבדיך הנבאים   20

לאמר : כה אמר ה' הטו צואריכם ועבדו את מלך בבל ושבו על הארץ אשר   21

נתתי לאבותיכם : ואך לא תשמעו בקול ה' לעבד את מלך בבל : (ו)השבתי   22-23
מערי יהודה ומחצות ירושלם קול ששון וקול שמחה קול חתן וקול כלה
וחיתה כל הארץ לשמה מאין יושב :

ולא שמענו בקולך לעבד את מלך בבל ותקם את דבריך אשר דברת ביד   24
עבדיך הנבאים להרציא את עצמתו מלכינו ואת עצמת אבותינו

ממקומם(ן) : והנן משלכות לחרב ביום ולקרח בלילה וימתו בתחלאים   25

(בנגעים) רעים ברעב בחרב ובדבר : ותתן את הבית אשר נקרא שמך עליו   26
לחרבה(לשממה) כיום הזה בגלל רעת בית ישראל ובית יהודה :

ותעש עמנו ה' אלהינו ככל חסדך וככל רחמיך הרבים : כאשר דברת   27
ביד עבדך משה ביום צוותך אתו לכתב את תורתך לפני בני ישראל לאמר :   28

אם לא תשמעו בקולי כי ישמעו אלי כי עם קשה ערף הוא וישיבר אל   29

אדיחם שם : כי ידעתי כי לא ישמעו אלי כי עם קשה ערף הוא וישיבו אל   30
לבבם בארץ שבים : וידעו כי אני ה' אלהיהם ונתתי להם לב ואזן שמעה   31

(קשובה) : וירודו לי בארץ שבים ויזכרו שמי : וישבו מערפם הקשה   32
(מקשי ערפם) ומרע מעלליהם כי יזכרו את דרך אבותם החטאים לה' (לפני   33
ה') : והשיבתיב אל הארץ אשר נשבעתי לאבותם לאברהם (ר)ליצחק וליעקב   34
וירשוה והרביתים ולא ימעטו : וכרתי להם ברית עולם להיות להם   35
לאלהים והמה יהיו לי לעם ולא אתוש עוד את עמי ישראל מעל האדמה אשר
נתתי להם :

ה' צבאות אלהי ישראל נפש בצרה ורוח עטופה קראה (צעקה) אליך :   3
                                                                          1

שמע ה' וחננו כי חטאנו לך (לפניך) : כי אתה שכן עד ואנחנו אבדי   2-3

עד : ה' צבאות אלהי ישראל שמע נא אל תפלת מתי ישראל ובני החטאים   4

לך (לפניך) אשר לא שמעו בקול ה' אלהיהם ותדבק בנו הרעה : אל תזכר   5

עונות אבותינו כי זכר ידך ושמך בעת הזאת : כי אתה ה' אלהינו ונודך   6

ה' : כי על כן נתת (את) יראתך על לבבנו לקרא בשמך ונודך בשביגנו כי   7

השיבנר אל לבבנו כל עון אבותינו החטאיר לך (לפניך) : הנה אנחנו   8
היום בשביננו אשר הדחתנו שם לחרפה ולאלה ולאלה (ולזועה) ככל עונות
אבותינו אשר פשעו בה' אלהינו :

NOTES

CHAPTER V

1. For a detailed proof of what appears to be the *communis opinio* on the original language of Bar 1:1-3:8, see J. J. Kneucker, *Das Buch Baruch, Geschichte und Kritik, Übersetzung und Erklärung auf Grund des wiederhergestellten hebräischen Urtextes* (Leipzig 1879) 20ff. Prof. J. Strugnell has kindly informed me that he has not identified any fragments of the lost Hebrew text of Bar among the Qumran fragments from cave IV.

2. See the various commentaries, and especially A. Penna, *Baruch, La Sacra Bibbia* (Roma-Torino 1956) where earlier literature is quoted.

3. Cf. E. Tov, "The Relation between the Greek Versions of Baruch and Daniel" in: M. E. Stone, ed., *Studies in the Bible and Armenian Philology* (Jerusalem 1975).

4. On the literalness of Bar's translation, see Kneucker, *Baruch*, 24ff., 82. His consistency is exemplified by several recurring phrases which are translated identically: 1:18 = 2:10; 1:15 = 2:6 ; 1:19 = 2:5.

5. L. Bertholdt, *Historische Einleitung etc.* (Erlangen 1814) IV, 1752; H. Hävernick, *De Libro Baruchi Commentatio Critica* (Königsberg 1843) 9 (not accessible to me); O. C. Whitehouse *apud* Charles, *Apocrypha*, I, 557.

6. E. Schürer *apud* J. Herzog (ed.), "Apokryphen des AT," *Realencyklopädie für protestantische Theologie und Kirche*[3] (Leipzig 1896) I, 642.

7. Thackeray, *Septuagint*, 87. See below, n. 12.

8. F. Hitzig, *Die Psalmen* (Heidelberg 1836) II, 119-120; A. Dillmann, *Jahrbücher für Deutsche Theologie* 3 (1858) 480; D. Zündel, *Kritische Untersuchungen über die Abfassungszeit des Buches Daniel* (Basel 1861) 190.

9. O. F. Fritzsche, *Kurzgefasstes Exegetisches Handbuch etc.* (Leipzig 1851) I, 173; H. Ewald, *Die jüngsten Propheten des Alten Bundes*[2] (Göttingen 1868) III, 255; J. T. Marshall in J. Hastings (ed.), *Dictionary of the Bible* (Edinborough 1898-1904) I, 252. See also n. 12.

10. Thackeray, "Gr.Tr.Jer." (1903) 261-266. See also his article "Septuagint" *apud* J. Orr *et alii* (edd.), *The International Standard Bible Encyclopaedia* IV (Chicago 1915) 2730.

11. Thackeray's evidence, for Bar 1-2 only, is provided in three pages of examples, many irrelevant to the issue.

12.   Thackeray, *Septuagint* (1920) 87.   At this time
Thackeray was convinced that the translator of Bar imitated
Jer's style.

13.   See his commentary on Bar *apud* C. Gore, *A New Commentary on Holy Scripture* (London 1928) II, 105.   To the best of
my knowledge, four scholars have expressed their agreement with
Thackeray's views: E. Nestle, *Septuaginta Studien* 4 (Stuttgart
1903) 15-16; Harwell, *Baruch*, 65-66 (according to Harwell, Jer.
β' translated the *whole* book of Bar); A. Penna, *op. cit.*, 16;
B. N. Wambacq, "l'Unité littéraire de Bar., I-III,8" in J. Cop-
pens (ed.), *Sacra Pagina* I = *Bibl. Ephem.Theol.Lovar.* XII-XIII
(Paris 1959) 455-460.

14.   The following of the items mentioned below were noted
by Thackeray, "Gr.Tr.Jer.", 262ff.: 1,3,5,8,9,11,12,14,15,18,
19,22,23,24,28,29,30.

15.   ὑποχείριος ('subject to...') generally governs a noun
in the dative.   Therefore it would seem that the wording of Jer
49(42):18 depends upon Bar 2:4.   However, ὑποχείριος is also
used absolutely, both in the LXX (Num 21:2 Jos 6:2) and in
classical Greek (LSJ, s.v.).

16.   The reconstructed *Vorlage* of Bar, ויתנח לזועה לכל
הממלכות, may be compared to identical phrases in Jer 15:4   24:9
29:18   34:17 (in all Q: זעוה).   Cf. further Deut 28:25 where
the same word is constructed with a different verb (והיית
לזעוה).   On the basis of this evidence one is inclined to re-
construct the *Vorlage* of the LXX of Jer 49:18 as היתם לשמה
ולזועה ולקללה ולחרפה (cf. 2 Chr 29:8 MT).
   The reconstruction of ὑποχείριος as לזועה is not without
problems since the two words have a different meaning.   However, the retroversion is sustained by the quoted parallels of
the *whole* phrase and by the fact that the majority of the
translators of the LXX were apparently unfamiliar with
זעוה/זועה and thus guessed its meaning: all six occurrences of
זעוה/זועה are rendered differently, and only two approach our
understanding of the Heb.   Cf. further Bar 3:8 ὀφλησις which
is also tentatively reconstructed as לזועה.

17.   היתי ביום חרב וקרח בלילה - ἐγενόμην τῆς ἡμέρας
συγκαιόμενος τῷ καύματι (καυσωνι A...) καὶ παγετῷ τῆς νυκτός.

18.   Thus also E. Nestle *Septuaginta Studien* 4 (Stuttgart
1903) 16.   The only parallel for a passive meaning of ἀποστολή
is provided by its use as 'expedition' in Thuc. 8:8 (LSJ, s.v.;
cf. also ἀπόστολος - 'messenger').
   The translation of דבר by ἀποστολή may be viewed as a eu-
phemism or a Midrashic rendition: According to several passages
in the OT, pestilence is "sent" by God, see especially Jer 24:
10 ושלחתי בם את החרב את הרעב ואת הדבר--note that the same three
punishments are mentioned in Jer 39(32):36--and, further, Lev
26:25 Is 9:8 Ez 14:19 and 2 Chr 7:13, in all of which the expression שלח דבר occurs.   Cf. also Ps 78:49 where משלחת מלאכי
רעים, specified in the next verse i.a. as דבר, was rendered in
the LXX (77:49) by ἀποστολὴν δι'ἀγγέλων πονηρῶν.

19. LSJ, *Suppl.* does not quote any evidence in support of its explanation of ἀποστολή in Jer and Bar.

20. R. Polzin, *HThR* 60 (1967) 469-470 and esp. n. 9 (brought to my attention by Prof. J. Strugnell) explained the 11QPs^a form ירשׁו (col. XVIII 1.16) from רשׁה (to rule) rather than ירשׁ. Along the same lines he suggested that the LXX translators who rendered ירשׁ in Num 21:24 and Jer 37(30):3 with κατακυριεύω and κυριεύω respectively, derived the Heb from רשׁה, since the Greek verbs primarily render verbs denoting 'to rule'. Polzin's suggestion, which may be extended to the LXX of Ex 15: 9, is attractive; however, the mentioned renditions may also be viewed as *ad hoc* exegesis.

21. In the phrase under consideration, לאישׁ is rendered in the plural throughout Jer: 4:4 11:2 12:9 17:25 18:11 39(32):32.

22. Although generally reflecting מצוה and חק, *this* πρόσταγμα in Bar and Jer b' should not be considered to presuppose either one because of the parallel in Dan 9:10. S. H. Blank, "The LXX renderings of OT Terms for Law", *HUCA* 7 (1930) 276 holds a different view.

23. It appears that Bar 2:14 δὸς ἡμῖν χάριν κατὰ πρόσωπον τῶν ἀποικισάντων ἡμᾶς does not reflect the preposition בעיני (thus Kneucker, *ad loc.*), but לפני; cf. the rendering of לפני with κατὰ πρόσωπον in Bar 2:19 and the MT of Esth 2:17 and 8:5.

24. See p. 113, n. 2.

25. Bar 2:5 = Deut 28:13   ὑποκάτω .
    Bar 2:16 = Deut 26:15   καθοράω .
    Bar 2:18 = Deut 28:65   ὀφθαλμοὶ ἐκλείποντες .
    Bar 2:25 and Jer 43(36):30 = Gen 31:40 παγετός (cf.
       item 2).

26. Likewise, the examples of chapters III and IV outnumber those of ch. II.

27. A. Wifstrand, "Die Stellung der enklitischen Personalpronomina bei den Septuaginta", *Bulletin de la Société Royale des Lettres de Lund* (1949-50) 64; R. A. Martin, "Some Syntactical Criteria of Translation Greek", *VT* 10 (1960) 297-306, 309-310. See also Martin's forthcoming syntactical study of Bar.

28. Cf. also Kneucker, *Baruch*, 97.

29. Cf. *ib.*, 29.

CHAPTER VI

THE RELATIONSHIP BETWEEN THE LXX OF JER, EZ AND THE MP

The investigation of the vocabulary of Jer a' and b' has
often referred to the LXX of MP and Ez. Relevant data are
listed here in detail (with references to chapters III-IV), together with much material not included in the preceding chapters.

It is important to deal here separately with the relationship between Jer, Ez and the MP because the data listed below
shed some light on the nature of the OG of Jer. Furthermore,
an analysis of the data will provide some support for the working hypothesis presented in this study: Important similarities
between Jer a', Ez and the MP regarding renditions and rare
words suggest that the three are closely related. Jer b' is
excluded from this group because it normally presents other
translation equivalents. Although the majority of the new
translation equivalents of Jer-R are revisional, the examples
themselves do not provide additional proof that the second part
of Jer contains a revision rather than a different translation.
It should be added, however, that if we are correct in assuming
that Jer a', the MP and Ez a' (see below) were produced by one '
person, it is unlikely that this translator embarked upon the
translation of one complete book (the MP), one half book (Jer),
and either another half book (Ez a') or another whole book
(Ez). Rather, it stands to reason that this translator embarked on the translation of the *whole* of these three books. If
this reasoning is correct, some of the conclusions of this
chapter may be taken as additional support for the working hypothesis concerning the nature of Jer b'.

This chapter lists important agreements (common renditions
and rare words) between (1) Jer and the MP; (2) Jer and Ez; (3)
Jer and both the MP and Ez.

As in chapter II, a distinctive agreement is defined as a
rendition or word which is common to two or more LXX books and
which distinguishes them from the remainder of the LXX. Such
an agreement is more significant if the particular rendition is

135

the only one or the main one utilized in the books under discussion. Information of this kind is provided below.

Since the discussion of the relationship between Jer, Ez and the MP requires the use of unbiased terminology, the renditions occurring in the two parts of Jer are referred to as Jer a' and b' rather than Jer-OG and Jer-R.

The ---→ references relate to additional renditions of the Heb in the remainder of the LXX. If these data are listed in chapters III-IV, reference is made to the relevant items.[1]

As a rule, we shall not repeat detailed references or descriptions of translation options which are provided in chapters III-IV. A reference like (III 2) at the beginning of an item refers the reader to the relevant discussion for further information.

1. *Jer and the MP*

a. *Jer a' and the MP*

α. *Common renditions*

(1) שדד - ταλαιπωρέω (III 2)

The main rendition of Jer a' (6 x) and the MP (Hos 10:2 Mich 2:4 Joel 1:10,10 Zach 11:2,3,3); elsewhere 2 x (Jer b': (ἀπ)όλλυμι).

---→ See III 2.

שְׁדוֹד, שֹׁד - ταλαιπωρία (III 2)

A characteristic rendition of Jer a' (3 x) and Mich 2:4 שָׁדוֹד נשדנו - ταλαιπωρίᾳ ἐταλαιπωρήσαμεν (Jer b': ὄλεθρος).

---→ See III 2.

(2) אלהים אחרים - θεοὶ ἀλλότριοι (III 19)

The main rendition of Jer a' (12 x) and of the MP (Hos 3: 1); elsewhere 6 x (Jer b': θεοὶ ἕτεροι).

(3) נָחַם - μετανοέω (III 9)

The main rendition of Jer a' (4 x), and the only rendition of the MP (Am 7:3,6   Joel 2:13,14   Jon 3:9,10   4:2   Zach 8:14); elsewhere 3 x (of which once in Jer b'). In Jer b' (ἀνα)παύο- μαι is used.

---→ See III 9.

(4) עָשַׁק - καταδυναστεύω

One of the two renditions used in Jer a' (7:6   27(50):33) and the main rendition of the MP (Hos 5:11   12:7(8)   Am 4:1 Zach 7:10); elsewhere 1 x.   Cf. עֹשֶׁק - καταδυναστεία in Am 3:9 Jer 6:6   Ez 22:12 (elsewhere the word occurs only twice).

---→ Especially συκοφαντέω and ἀδικέω.

(5) יַעֲנָה - σειρήν !

Jer 27(50):39   Mich 1:8; cf. Is 13:21 בת יענה - σειρήν.

---→ (בת)יענה - στρουθός.

(6) מַשָּׂא - λῆμμα

Jer a' 7 x (23:33(ρημα S*),33,34,36,36,38,38), MP 5 x (Nah 1:1   Hab 1:1   Zach 9:1   12:1   Mal 1:1); elsewhere 1 x.

---→ Is: ὅρασις, ὅραμα, ῥῆμα.

(7) גִּבּוֹר - μαχητής (III 51)

Jer a' 8 x and the MP 8 x (Am 2:14   Joel 2:7   3(4):9,11 Ob 9   Zach 9:13   10:5,7); elsewhere 2 x.

---→ See III 51.

(8) נִלְוָה אֶל ה' - καταφεύγω ἐπί/πρὸς (τὸν) κύριον !

Jer 27(50):5 and Zach 2:11(15) only.

---→ προστίθημι, συμπαραγίνομαι, also when לוה is used with reference to God (Is 56:3,6).

138

(9) אדיר - μεγιστάν !

Jer 14:3   Nah 2:6   Zach 11:2.

---→ Variously.

(10) דרש - ἀντέχω !

Jer 8:2   Zeph 1:6.

---→ Mainly ζητέω or one of its *composita* (also in Jer and the
MP).

(11) פוש - σκιρτάω !

Jer 27(50):11   Mal 4:2(3:20).

---→ ἐξιππάζομαι Hab 1:8.   The Heb does not occur elsewhere.

(12) מש(ו)בה - κατοικία !

Jer 3:6,8,12   Hos 11:7   14:5. This rendition should be
considered as an etymological translation of מש(ו)בה on the
basis of ישב.

---→ In Jer: ἀποστροφή Jer 5:6   8:5 (*ex* שוב); ἀποστασία 2:19
(*ex* שבב); σύντριμμα 3:22, ἀμαρτία 14:7, both in accordance with
their context.

(13) תהלה - καύχημα

Jer 13:11   17:14   28(51):41 and Zeph 3:19,20; elsewhere
Deut 10:21.   Cf. הלל - (κατα)καυχάομαι (especially Jer-LXX).

---→ Especially αἴνεσις.

(14) הלך - συνέρχομαι !

Jer 3:18   Zach 8:21.

---→ ἔρχομαι and its *composita*.

(15) מצור - συνοχή !

Jer 52:5 Mich 5:1(4:14); cf. צרר - συνέχω (2 Sam 20:3)
and צור - συνέχω (1 Sam 23:8).

---→ Especially περιοχή.

(16) התפלש - καταπάσσω !

Jer 6:26 Mich 1:10.

---→ Elsewhere the Heb word occurs only twice.

(17) הלך אחר - ἐξακολουθέω

Jer 2:2 Am 2:4; elsewhere Sir 5:2.

---→ Stereotyped two word renditions.

(18) בתולה- חפמּטע !

Jer 2:32 Joel 1:8.

---→ Especially παρθένος (also in Jer and the MP)

β. *Rare words*

All words listed below are rare in the LXX. Some of them
are infrequently used *composita* or compound words, while the
simplex form or other *composita* of the simplex form may be frequent LXX words. E.g., ἀναξηραίνω (item 24) is rare in the
LXX, while ξηραίνω (rendering חרב and יבשׁ similar to its *com-
positum* ἀναξηραίνω) occurs in the whole LXX (including Jer and
the MP).

(19) κατακαυχάομαι *

Jer 27(50):11 - עלז; 27(50):38 - יתחללו (MT יתהללו, cf.
III 14); Zach 10:12 - יתחללו (MT יתהלכו).

(20) חבור - 'Ιταβύριον *

Jer 26(46):18 Hos 5:1.[2]

---→ Θαβωρ.

(21) χρεμετισμός * (II 35)

Jer 8:6 - מלחמה (?); 8:16 13:27 - מצהלה; Am 6:7 - מרזח.

(22) χερσόομαι

Jer 2:31 - מאפליה; Nah 1:10 - MT סבכים; elsewhere Prov
24:46(31).

(23) σχοῖνος

Jer 8:8 - עט; 18:15 - שביל; Mich 6:5 Joel 3(4):18 - השטים;
elsewhere Ps 138(139):3 - רבעי.

(24) ἀναξηραίνω

Jer 27(50):27 - חרב; Hos 13:15 - יבש; elsewhere Sir 43:3 -
הרתיח, 14:9 (=?).

(25) ἱππασία *

Jer 8:16 - אבירים; Hab 3:8 - מרכבות.

(26) πνευματοφορ- *

Jer 2:24 שאפה רוח - ἐπνευματοφορεῖτο; Hos 9:7 איש הרוח -
ἄνθρωπος ὁ πνευματοφόρος; Zeph 3:4 - פחז.

According to the *Thesaurus*, πνευματοφορ- is not attested
to before the time of the LXX.

(27) σμῖλαξ *

Jer 26(46):14 - סבך (MT סביביך); Nah 1:10 - סבך (MT
aliter).

---→ סבך - φυτόν, δάσος, ὑψηλοί, μάνδρα.

(28) שַׁעֲרוּרָה, שַׁעֲרוּרִיָה - φρικτός ! , φρικώδης *

Jer 5:30 18:13 23:14: φρικτός. Hos 6:10 φρικώδης; cf.
Jer 2:12 שֹׁעַר - φρίττω (MT שֹׂעַר).

(29) συντριμμός

Jer 4:20 - שבר; Am 5:9 - שד; Zeph 1:10 - שבר; Mich 2:8 - שבר (?; MT שובי); elsewhere 2 Sam 22:5 - משבר.

---→ שבר - Especially σύντριμμα, συντριβή.

(30) καταδύω/δύνω

Jer 28(51):64 - שקע; Am 9:3 - נסתר; Mich 7:19 - כבש; elsewhere Ex 15:5 - ירד.

(31) διόρυγμα

Jer 2:34 - מחתרת; Zeph 2:14 - חלון; elsewhere Ex 22:2(1) - מחתרת. Note further that διορυγή occurs only in Jer 38(31):9 (נחל) and that διορύσσω is limited to Ez 12:5,7,12 Job 24:16.

b. *Jer a'b' and the MP*[3]

(32) דמם, דמה - ἀπορρίπτω ! (II 2)

A characteristic rendition found only in Jer a' (3 x), b' (1 x), Hos 10:7 11:1(10:15) (2 x) Ob 5.

(33) ה' צבאות - κύριος παντοκράτωρ (II 26)

The only rendition of Jer a' (7 x), b' (9 x), the MP (100 x);[4] elsewhere 10 x.

---→ See II 26.

(34) חמדה - ἐκλεκτός ! (II 3)

Jer a' 1 x, b' 1 x, the MP 2 x.

---→ See II 3.

(35) ἐκλείπω (various *Vorlagen*) (II 17)[5]

ἐκλείπω is much more frequent in Jer a'b' and the MP than in other parts of the LXX. We noticed in II 17 that the translator of Jer a'b' sometimes used this verb as a "stopgap" translation when experiencing difficulties. The same holds

true for the MP: Hos 4:3 - אסף; 13:2 - נשק; Am 8:13 - עלף; Jon
2:8 - עטף; Nah 1:4 - אמלל; Hab 2:13 - יגע; 3:17 - גזר; Zeph
1:2,3 - סוף; 2:9 - חדל (? MT חרול); 3:6 - צדה; Zach 11:9 - כחד;
13:8 - גרע (ἐκθλίβω C).

(36) σύλλημψις (II 44)

Jer a' 2 x, b' 1 x, the MP 1 x; elsewhere 1 x.

---→ See II 44.

c. *Jer b' and the MP*

(37) <u>במה - ἄλσος</u> !

Jer 33(26):18 Mich 3:12 (parall).

---→ Especially ὑψηλόν and βωμός, also in Jer and the MP.

(38) <u>פחד - ἐξίστημι</u> !

Jer 43(36):24[6] Hos 3:5 Mich 7:17.

---→ Especially φοβέομαι.

2. *Jer and Ez*
a. *Jer a' and Ez*
α. *Common renditions*

Because it is important to determine which section of Ez
agrees with the renditions of Jer a'(b'), the below-mentioned
examples are arranged in the sequence Ez a', b', c' (Ez 1-27,
28-39, 40-48).

(39) <u>נקע, יקע - ἀφίστημι</u> ! (Ez a')

Jer 6:8 Ez 23:17,18,18,22,28.

---→ The Heb word occurs rarely elsewhere.

(40) רפה (ידים) - παραλύομαι ¹ (Ez a')

Jer 6:24 27(50):43 Ez 21:7(12).

---→ Especially ἐκλύω.

(41) צוּר - Σορ ¹ (Ez a')

Jer 21:13 (MT צֻּר) and 10 times in Ez 26-27.

---→ Τύρος *passim*, including Jer b', Ez b' and the MP.

(42) שכן - ὀμορέω ¹ (Ez a')

Jer 27(50):40 Ez 16:26. Elsewhere the Greek verb occurs only once.

---→ Variously; cf. also IV 2 for Jer.

(43) שלט - φαρέτρα ¹ (Ez a')

Jer 28(51):11 Ez 27:11.

---→ Variously.

(44) חרר - ἐκλείπω ¹ (Ez a')

Jer 6:29 Ez 15:4. See also VI 35.

---→ Variously.

(45) כלמה - ἀτιμία (Ez a'b'c')

Jer 3:25 6:15 (MT הכלים) 20:11 23:40 (כלמות) 28(51):51 Ez 16:52,63 36:7,15 39:26 44:13.

---→ αἰσχύνη, βάσανος, ὀνειδισμός, ἐντροπή, ὄνειδος.

(46) עריץ - λοιμός ¹ (Ez b')

Jer 15:21 Ez 28:7 30:11 31:12 32:12.

---→ Variously.

(47) πολυανδρεῖον - גאי,גיא,המון * (Ez b')

Jer 2:23, 19:2,6,6 - גיא; Ez 39:11 - גאי; Ez 39:11,15,16 - המון.

The rendering of גאי,גיא in both Jer and Ez with πολυανδρεῖον indicates a close connection between the two books. The background of this rendition is adequately explained by Walters.[7]

---→ גיא, גאי mainly φάραγξ, also in Jer and Ez.

β. *Rare words*

(48) κόλασις ! (Ez a'c')

Jer 18:20 (= ?); Ez 14:3,4,7 18:30 44:12 - מכשול.

(49) διασκορπισμός * (Ez a')

Jer 24:9 - זועה (Q: זעוה); Ez 6:8 - זרה; 13:20 - פרחות.

(50) βελόστασις * (Ez a')

Jer 28(51):27 - טפסר; Ez 4:2 - כר; 17:17 21:22(27) - דיק.

(51) πέλυξ * (Ez a')

Jer 23:29 - פטיש; Ez 9:2 - כלי מפץ.

(52) רכב - ἱππάζομαι * (Ez a')

Jer 27(50):42 Ez 23:6,12.

---→ Variously.

(53) ποίκιλμα * (Ez a')

Jer 13:23 - חברברת; Ez 23:15 (MT אזור); 27:16 - רקמה.

(54) κατακεντέω * (Ez a')

Jer 28(51):4 - דקר; Ez 23:47 - ברא.

(55) προμαχών * (Ez a') (cf. II 38)

Jer 5:10 - שור (MT שרותיה); 40(33):4 - חרב (cf. II, n. 39); Ez 4:2 - דיק.

(56) חוֹתָם - ἀποσφράγισμα * (Ez b')

Jer 22:24 Ez 28:12 (MT חוֹתָם).

---→ σφράγις, δακτύλιος.

b. *Jer b' and Ez*

(57) סללה - χάραξ (Ez a')

Jer 40(33):4 Ez 4:2 26:8; elsewhere Is 37:33. Cf. further Ez 17:17 שפך סללה - χαρακοβολία.

---→ πρόσχωμα, χῶμα.

(58) רעש - φοβέομαι ! (Ez a')

Jer 29:22(49:21) BS (σείω rel; cf. IV 23) Ez 27:28

---→ Cf. IV 23.

(59) ὑγρασία * (Ez a')

Jer 31(48):18 - צמא; Ez 7:17, 21:7(12) - מים.

(60) שממה - ἀπώλεια ! (Ez b')

Jer 30(49):2 51(44):12 Ez 29:8,9,12 32:15.

---→ Cf. III 1.

3. *Jer a', the MP and Ez*
α. *Common renditions*

(61) שמה, שממה - ἀφανισμός (Ez a') (III 1)

The main rendition of Jer a' (18 x), the MP (15 x),[8] and Ez a' (9 x);[9] elsewhere 2 x (Jer b': ἄβατος).

---→ Cf. III 1.

146

שמם - ἀφανίζω (Ez a'b') (III l)

One of the renditions of Jer a' (3 x),[10] the only rendition of the MP[11] and the main rendition of Ez[12] (Jer b': ἀβατόω).

(62) פשׁע - ἀσεβέω (Ez a')

The only rendition of Jer a' (3 x; cf. IV 8), Ez (18:31), and the main rendition of the MP (Hos 7:13 8:1 Am 4:4 Zeph 3:11; Hos 14:10 פֶּשַׁע - ἀσεβής);[13] elsewhere Is 59:13.

---→ Especially νομ-.

פֶּשַׁע - ἀσέβεια (Ez a')

The only rendition of Jer a' (5:6) and the MP (19 x),[14] and the main rendition of Ez;[15] elsewhere 5 x.

---→ Especially nouns derived from νομ- and ἁμαρτ-.

(63) נוה , נוה - νομή (Ez a') (III 48)

The main rendition of Jer a' (6 x) and the MP (Am 1:2 Zeph 2:6), further Ez 25:5; elsewhere 1 x (Jer b': τόπος, κατάλυσις, κατάλυμα).

(64) צרר - συστρέφω, συστροφή (Ez a')

Jer 4:16 נצרים - συστροφαί (derived from צרר); Hos 4:19, 13:12 צרר - συστροφή; Ez 13:20 צרר - συστρέφω; elsewhere 1 x.

(65) קדים - καύσων (Ez a')

Jer 18:17 (cf. 28(51):1; not in MT) Hos 12:1(2) 13:15 Jon 4:8 Ez 17:10 19:12; elsewhere 1 x.

---→ Especially νότος, also in Ez a'c'.

(66) חץ - βόλις (Ez a')

Jer 9:8(7) 27(50):9 Hab 3:11 Zach 9:14 Ez 5:16; elsewhere 1 x.

---→ Especially βέλος (not in Jer, the MP and Ez).

(67) עבר - διοδεύω (Ez a')

Jer 2:6 9:12(11) 27(50):13 Zeph 3:6 Zach 7:14 Ez 5:14
14:5 (36:34 AL'); elsewhere 2 x.

---→ Variously.

(68) שיח - στηρίζω (Ez a'b') (III 11)

Jer a' 3 x, Am 9:4, Ez 9 x (6:2 13:17 15:7 20:46(21:2)
21:2(7) 25:2 28:21 29:2 38:2).

---→ Variously.

(69) ישב - κατοικέομαι (Ez a'b') (III 26)

A free rendition of Jer a' (10 x), the MP (Joel 3(4):20
Zach 1:11 2:4(8) 7:7 9:5) and Ez (26:20 29:11 35:9 39:6);
elsewhere 5 x.

(70) כי - διότι (Ez a'c') (III 30)

Jer a' 25 x, the MP 123 x,[16] Ez a' 62 x,[17] Ez c' 5 x;[17]
only one occurrence in Ez b'[17] and none in Jer b'; elsewhere
not frequent.[18]

Jer a', the MP and Ez a' share a rendition which is not
very frequent in the LXX.[18] The above numbers are important
for the understanding of the relationship between the different
sections of Ez; see below, p. 150.

---→ Cf. III 30.

(71) תורה - νόμιμα (Ez c')

Jer 33(26):4 (νομοι AVOL') Hos 8:12 Ez 43:11 44:5,24;
elsewhere 1 x.

---→ Especially νόμος (also in Jer, Ez and the MP).

148

β. *Rare words*

(72) λῃστής * (Ez a')

Jer 7:11 - פרץ; 18:22 - גדוד; Hos 7:1 - גדוד; Ob 5 - שודד;
Ez 22:9 אנשי רכיל - ἄνδρες λῃσταί.

(73) גאון - φρύαγμα * (Ez a')

Jer 12:5 Hos 4:18 Zach 11:3 Ez 7:24 24:21.

---→ Especially ὕβρις (also in Jer a'b', Ez b' and the MP).

(74) קבץ (mainly *pi'el*) - εἰσδέχομαι * (Ez a')

Jer 23:3, the MP (Hos 8:10 Mich 4:6 Hab 2:5 Zeph 3:8,
19,20 Zach 10:8,10), Ez (11:17 20:34,41 22:19,20,20).

---→ Especially συνάγω (also in Ez and the MP).[19]

(75) κατάσκιος * (Ez a')

Jer 2:20 - רענן; Hab 3:3 - פארן (?); Zach 1:8 - מצלה;
Ez 20:28 - עבות.

(76) אָהַב - ἐραστής (Ez a')

Jer a' (22:20,22), the MP (Hos 2:5,7,10,12,13(7,9,12,14,
15)) and Ez 16:33,36,37 23:5,9,22; elsewhere 1 x. Cf. further Jer 4:30 עֲגָב - ἐραστής.

---→ The Heb occurs elsewhere only twice.

(77) τέσσαρα ! (Ez a')

Jer 15:3 (SAQ τεσσερα) Zach 1:18 6:1 Ez 1:6,8.

---→ τέσσερα. The LXX translators generally changed the first
alpha of τέσσαρα to an *epsilon* because of the ensuing *rho*
(Thackeray, *Grammar*, 73). The original *alpha* has been preserved only in the above-mentioned cases.

(78) ὑποκαίω (Ez a')

Jer 1:13 סיר נפוח סירות דונה Am 4:2 - λέβης ὑποκαιόμενος; Am 4:2
- λέβητες ὑποκαιόμενοι; Ez 24:5 (MT דהר); elsewhere 2 x.

The LXX of Am manifestly depends upon Jer-LXX.

(79) ἐνθύμημα (Ez a'c')

Jer 3:17, 7:24 - שררות; Mal 2:16 - לבוש (but cf. Ziegler);
Ez a'c' - גלולים (15 x);[20] Ez 14:22,23 24:14 - עלילה; elsewhere 6 x (Sir 4 x).

(80) τὸ παράπαν (Ez a'c')

Jer 7:4 (not in MT), Zeph 3:6 - מבלי; Ez 20:9,14,15,22,
41:6 (not in MT) 46:20 - לבלתי; elsewhere 1 x.

(81) διεκβολή * (Ez c')

Jer 12:12 - שפי; Ob 14 - פרק; Zach 9:10 - אפס; Ez 47:8 -
מוצאים; 47:11 - צאה; 48:30 - תוצאה.

4. *Conclusions*

Many important similarities between Jer a', Ez(a') and
the MP in renditions and rare words suggest that the three are
closely related. This relationship is apparent both between
Jer a' and the MP; Jer a' and Ez(a'); Jer a', the MP and Ez
(a'); and between the MP and Ez a'c'.[21] According to Thackeray,
the positive evidence mentioned above may be supplemented by a
certain amount of negative evidence, namely the absence of certain common words from this group of books.[22] Few important
disagreements between Jer a', Ez and the MP can be discovered.[23]

The similarities between Jer a', Ez and the MP are so
striking that we postulate with Thackeray that the three
books[24] were translated by one individual or otherwise by one
group.[25] Since this translator produced a translation which
we describe as the OG of Jer, it follows by implication that
the extant translations of Ez and the MP also exhibit the OG
version.[26]

One should be aware of the tentative character of our
conclusions, which are based upon significant similarities
collected in the course of the study of Jer-LXX only. It is,
however, important to stress that we did not encounter any differences between Jer a', Ez a' and the MP[27] with regard to
their characteristic renditions described in chapters II-VI.[28]

While significant agreements between Jer a', the MP and Ez
are rather numerous, few significant agreements between these
books and Jer b' are discernible. Furthermore, in nearly all
instances of special agreements between Jer a', the MP and Ez,
Jer b' stands apart with his own translation equivalents. The
majority of the latter are revisions, such as the ones described in ch. III. For example, שממה is rendered in Jer a',
the MP and Ez by ἀφανισμός, but in Jer b' by ἄβατος (item 61).
In this case, Jer-R probably substituted an earlier ἀφανισμός
with ἄβατος as suggested in ch. III. Also, for other examples,
such as 1,2,3,7,57,58,61,62,63,65,67, it is assumed that Jer-R
replaced earlier renderings of Jer a', Ez and the MP. As indicated on p. 135, the data listed in this chapter provide scant
independent support for the assumption that Jer b' is a revision rather than a second translation.

Similarities between Ez and the OG of Jer are distributed
in Ez in an interesting way: 30 are limited to Ez a', 2 to
a'b', 4 to a'c', 4 to b', 2 to c' and one is found in a'b'c'.
The considerable agreement of the OG of Jer and the MP with
only the first part of Ez can hardly be coincidental. Hence,
it stands to reason that Ez a' reflects the OG of Ez, while the
other two sections contain a different text type, possibly a
revision. For example, in the OG of Jer a', the MP and Ez a',
כי is represented by both ὅτι (passim) and διότι (respectively
25, 123 and 62 times), while in Jer b' it is represented only
by ὅτι. It may thus be assumed that the reviser of that section preferred to render the Heb with ὅτι only; the same
applies to Ez b' (only one instance of διότι) and to Ez c' (5
cases of διότι). Precise data are listed in item 70; see also
items 41, 61 and 62.

The assumption that Ez b' represents a later revision may
further be corroborated by the following:

1. Thackeray, "Ezekiel", and Herrmann[29] listed differences between the two (three) different "translators" Ez a'c'
and b' (Ez a', b' and c'). Yet, at the same time, Thackeray
(*ib.*, 406) acknowledged the existence of important similarities
between Ez a' and b'.

2. Approaching the question from a different angle,
Barthélemy, *Devanciers*, 47, assigned Ez b' to a *kaige*-like revision.

The correctness of this hypothesis has yet to be verified
by a minute inner-Greek analysis of Ez-LXX.

NOTES

CHAPTER VI

1. The following items adduced in this chapter were mentioned by Thackeray, "Proph.", 580ff.: 6,7,20,24,25,26,27,41,
43,50,51,52,55,59,70,72,74,76,80,81; Thackeray, *Grammar*, 73:
77.

2. חבור is transliterated in the same way in Eusebius'
Onomasticon (P. de Lagarde, *Onomastica Sacra* (Gottingae 1870)
268) and Josephus, *Ant. Jud.* V,1,22 XIII,15,4; *Bell. Jud.* IV,
1,8. Cf. also Ἀταβύριον in Polybius V,70,6.
The ending of Ἰταβύριον may be compared to that of כרמל,
transliterated as Καρμήλιος in 1 Ki 18:19,20 2 Ki 2:25 4:25.
The prothetic *iota*, on the other hand, is hard to account for--
Thackeray, *Grammar*, 170, n. 4 refers to Ἀταβύριον ("heights
in Rhodes and at Agrigentum") as a possible source of influence on the present spelling of Ἰταβύριον.

3. Sections 1bc and 2b are not subdivided into (α) common
renditions and (β) common rare words since the examples are too
few.

4. Some or all of the MSS of Am 6:14 Zeph 2:9 Zach 1:3,
3 7:4 read κύριος τῶν δυνάμεων, which is generally Hexaplaric.
Further, in Zach 13:2, MSS B..read Σαβαωθ. Ziegler correctly
refers both readings to the apparatus. Cf. J. Ziegler, *Duode-
cim Prophetae, Septuaginta...Vol.XIII* (Göttingen 1943) 122-123.

5. Cf. also item 44 for Ez.

6. ἐξέστησαν Schleusner] εξεζητησαν AQ*, εξεζησαν C,
εζητησαν rel.

7. According to P. Walters, *Text*, 179, the unexpected
translation of גיא with πολυανδρεῖον derived from Ez 39:11,15,
16 where גוג המרן גיא is literally rendered with τὸ Γαι τὸ
πολυανδρεῖον τοῦ Γωγ. Since Γαι and πολυανδρεῖον are used here
synonymously, the translators of Ez also rendered elsewhere
גיא(גאי) with πολυανδρεῖον. In these translations, Walters
perceived influence from Ez-LXX on Jer-LXX. However, it is
probable that identity of translator rather than influence lies
at the source of the mentioned similarity.

8. Hos 5:9 Mich 1:7 6:16 7:13 Joel 1:7 2:3 3(4):19,
19 Zeph 1:13,15 2:4,13 3:1(2:15) Zach 7:14 Mal 1:3.

9. Ez 4:16 (שממון) 6:14 7:27 12:19 (שממון) 12:20
14:8,15 15:8 23:33.
Additional renditions of שממה in Ez were listed by Herrmann in Herrmann-Baumgärtel, *Beiträge*, 11. The different renditions of שממה were assigned by him to the three assumed
translators of Ez. E.g., Ez a' always used ἀφανισμός, with the
exception of 14:16 (ὄλεθρος).

153

10. See also ἐρημόω in 10:25.

11. Hos 2:12(14) Am 7:9 9:14 Mich 6:13 Joel 1:17
2:20 (שממה) Hab 1:5 Zeph 2:9 (שממה) 3:6 7:14.

12. Ez 4:17 6:6 12:19 19:7 20:26 25:3 36:4,34,35,
35,36. שמם is further represented by συντρίβω (6:4), ἐρημόω
(29:12 30:7,7 32:15 33:28,29 35:3,7) and ἀπόλλυμι (30:12,
14). The various renditions of שמם were assigned by Herrmann
(ib.) to the three translators of Ez. See further n. 9.

13. See also Am 4:4 ἀνομέω W(vid.)] ἀσεβέω B-V l Γ'-613
C'-68-239.

14. Am 1:3,6,9,11,13 2:1,4,6 3:14 5:12 Mich 1:5,5,13
3:8 6:7 7:18.

15. Ez 18:28,30,31 21:24(29).

16. Hos 1:2,4,6,9 3:4 4:1,1,10,14 5:1,3,14 6:7(6)
7:6 8:6,13 9:1,4,12,12,16 10:3 11:1,9 13:13,15 14:2,5,10
Am 3:7,14 4:2,13 5:3,4,17,22 6:8,11,14 7:11 9:9 Mich 1:3,
7,9 2:1 3:7 4:4,10 5:4(3) 6:4 7:6,8 Joel 2:1,11,23
3(4):1,12,13,17 Ob 15,16,18 Jon 1:10,12 4:2 Nah 1:15(2:1)
2:2(3),2(3) 3:19 Hab 1:5,6 2:3,8,11,17 3:17 Zeph 1:7,18
2:4,9,10,14 3:8,8,13,20 Hag 2:5(4),7(6),24(23) Zach 2:6,8,
8,9,10,13(10,12,12,13,14,17) 3:9,9,10(8,8,9) 4:9,10 5:3
6:15 8:6,10,14,17,23 9:1,2,8,13,16 10:2,2,5,6,8 11:2,11,16.
Both in this note and the next one Ziegler's text is
quoted without the variants listed in the apparatus.

17. Ez 1:20 2:5,6,6 3:5,7,9,20,26,27 5:6,13 6:10,13
7:8,8,9(4,4,5),13,19,23 8:12,17 10:17 11:12 12:2,3,6,15,20,
25 13:9,14,21 14:7,23,23 16:14 17:21,24 18:32 20:12,20,
38,40,42,44 21:5,7,21,32(10,12,26,37) 22:16,22 23:28,34,49
24:24,27 25:5,6,7,11,17 34:11 40:4 42:6,13,14 47:12.

18. According to Thackeray, Grammar, 139, the books of
the LXX contain 358 instances of διότι, of which 250 occur in
the MP, Ez a' and Jer a'. Even though Thackeray's statistics
include too much evidence for our purpose (he includes not only
doubtful readings but also occurrences of διότι reflecting a
Vorlage other than כי), they show that the translators of Ez
a', Jer a' and the MP used διότι more than the other LXX translators (cf. further III 30).

19. Ez 16:37,37 28:25 29:13 34:13 37:21 38:8 39:17,
27 Hos 1:11(2:2) Mich 1:7 4:12 Joel 3(4):2,11. One notes
that εἰσδέχομαι occurs more frequently in Ez a', while συνάγω
prevails in Ez b'.

20. Ez 14:5,7 16:36 18:6,15 20:16,24,31 22:3,4
23:7,30,37,49 44:10.

21. Cf. Thackeray, "Proph.", 580ff.; Septuagint, 29.

22. Thackeray, "Proph.", 582, mentions the following
words "καθά (one doubtful instance in Ez. α and one in Jonah),
οὖν, παιδίον, πάλιν (one instance in Jer. α), παραγίνεσθαι,

παύειν (one instance at the end of Jer. α), ποτέ, συναντᾶν, συντάσσειν". Some of Thackeray's examples are convincing (οὖν versus Ø; συντάσσειν versus ἐντέλλεσθαι), while others are less powerful.

23. In one instance, however, Jer-LXX differs rather significantly from the MP and Ez: ὅν τρόπον, generally rendering כאשר, occurs frequently in the whole LXX, including the MP (18 x), Ez a' (15 x) and Ez c' (7 x), but never in Jer-LXX (cf. further Johannessohn, *Kasus*, 81).

24. Baumgärtel in Herrmann-Baumgärtel, *Beiträge*, 32-38, S.E. Johnson, *The Septuagint Translators of Amos*, diss. Univ. of Chicago (Chicago 1938) and G. Howard, *VT* 20 (1970) 108-112, advocate multiple authorship for the MP as a whole or for Amos. However, such claims were convincingly refuted by Thackeray, *Septuagint*, 29; Kaminka, *Studien*, 8-9; J. Ziegler, *Die Einheit der Septuaginta zum Zwölfprophetenbuch, Beilage zum Vorlesungsverzeichnis der Staatl. Akademie zu Braunsberg* (1934-1935) 1-16; T. Muraoka, *VT* 20 (1970) 496-500.

25. Thackeray, *Septuagint*, 39, tentatively suggested that one translator rendered both the Prophetical Books and Reigns c'c'.

26. Similarly Thackeray, "Proph.", 578-579 and *Septuagint*, 29, 117. While according to Thackeray Jer a', Ez a'c' and the MP formed part of one large unit, distinct from the *translators* Jer b' and Ez b', we tentatively suggest to assign the three books to one primary unit which was subsequently revised in two of its sections (Jer b' and Ez b'; see below). Cf. also M. L. Margolis, *JAOS* 30 (1910) 304, T. Muraoka, *Textus* 8 (1973) 22-23, and J. A. Arieti, *JBL* 93 (1974) 343.

27. The differences mentioned by Thackeray, "Proph.", 582, are not significant. Likewise, we are not convinced by the examples which Kaminka, *Studien*, 14-15, used in attempting to prove that the translator of the MP "did not know Jer and Ez"; moreover, the majority of them refer to Jer b'.

28. Thus differences in the rendering of isolated words, phrases and verses should be disregarded since similar differences occur within any book of the LXX. Cf. especially J. Ziegler, *Biblica* 34 (1953) 399ff.

29. Herrmann-Baumgärtel, *Beiträge*, 1-19.

CHAPTER VII

SOME CONCLUSIONS

1. *A Characterization of Jer-R*

In the course of our discussion several characteristics of
Jer-R became evident. On the basis of the data listed above
and some additional criteria, we shall attempt here to characterize Jer-R's revision as a whole.

Jer-R must have used a Hebrew text for his revision. His
tendencies run parallel to those of other revisers as indicated
in the footnotes. While retouching the OG according to this
Hebrew text, he introduced several new translation options;
some of these were merely synonymous (ch. IV);[1] as a rule, however, the reviser inserted renditions which in his opinion better expressed the meaning of the Heb (III, section 1),[2] he corrected some erroneous renditions (section 2), introduced stereotyped and more consistent renditions of the Heb (sections 3
and 4),[3] and corrected the OG in other ways (section 5). That
Jer-R was a revision is further made probable by a few important agreements with the "Three", discussed in the appendix to
this section.

It is evident that at times Jer-R's aims were incompatible. Thus his distinction between προφήτης and ψευδοπροφήτης
(III 45) as well as between λαλέω and χρηματίζω (III 44) is
contrary to the tendency toward the stereotyped rendering of
individual Hebrew words (III, sections 3 and 4). In addition,
many of the examples of synonymous renditions (ch. IV) are not
literal reflections of the Heb, and other renditions are imprecise (e.g., III 9,49,50,51).

Jer-R employed renditions which had been used before him
as well as renditions which are not found in other parts of the
LXX, the majority of which preceded his revision (see below):
III 1,2(partly),3,5,6,7,8,9,10,14,18(rarely elsewhere),44(rarely elsewhere),49. Jer-R apparently also coined new words which

are not attested to in other Greek sources: ἀβατόω (III 1),
ἐπίχειρον (III 4).[4]

Chapters III and IV list many examples of renditions which
were revised by Jer-R. Since the items discussed comprise only
a small percentage of the translation of Jer b', it is of interest to consider Jer-R's approach to the whole of the OG.
Because objective data for the determination of the extent of
Jer-R's revision are lacking--the OG of Jer b' is lost--we must
content ourselves with conclusions drawn from inference:

1. Since Jer-R dealt with *minutiae* such as the article
and various prepositions,[5] it is reasonable to assume that his
revision was at times thorough.

2. Recognition of a relatively large number of agreements
between Jer a', Ez and the MP suggests the same conclusion.
Many of these renditions were altered by Jer-R, as can often be
shown.

On the other hand, several facts suggest that Jer-R's revision was neither thorough nor consistent:

1. Several free and erroneous renditions common to both
Jer a' and b' were not revised by Jer-R (II 1,2,14,15,16,17,18,
26,27,28,30).

2. Numerous free or "inconsistent" renditions were left
as such in Jer b' and revised only by the "Three", O and L.

3. Certain renditions were in some cases revised but in
others left untouched. Such unrevised readings are listed
amongst the data provided in ch. III and IV.[6] The appearance
in Jer b' of both the revised and the unrevised renditions can
be ascribed to no other factor but inconsistency.[7]

4. In the following instances, Jer-R changed the Greek
lexemes only, without modifying Jer-OG's understanding of the
Hebrew words:

a. The OG rendering of שֹׁד, ταλαιπωρία, was changed by
Jer-R to ὄλεθρος, both reflecting the Hebrew *nomen agentis* as a
nomen actionis (III 2, see p. 48).

b. Both λέγει κύριος (Jer-OG) and φησὶ κύριος (Jer-R)
represent נְאֻם as a verb (III 43).

c. In 29:21(49:20), Jer-R altered an earlier ἀφανίζω (also found in the parallel 27(50):45) to ἀβατόω. In both verses the form of נְשִׁים was understood similarly.

It thus appears that Jer-R seriously intended to make the OG conform to his idea of a more literal and stereotyped translation, but he was not at all consistent in carrying out his intention. Jer-R's inconsistency is discussed above, pp. 44-45.

The majority of the examples in chapters III and IV are qualitative revisions, i.e., renditions which replace earlier translation options. In a few instances, Jer-R's quantitative revisions omit or add elements in accord with MT, e.g., III 24, 32,33. Thus it stands to reason that Jer-R paid the same attention to quantitative and qualitative differences between the OG and his Hebrew *Vorlage*. This assumption cannot be substantiated, however, since we have no access to the OG of Jer b' or to the Hebrew *Vorlage* of Jer-R.

Our characterization of Jer-R is founded upon a comparison of renditions of the same Hebrew words in both Jer a' and b'. Since this is the only objective method, we refrain from commenting on non-comparative evidence, i.e., a comparison of translation techniques referring to different Hebrew *Vorlagen*.[8]

No data are available for comparing the translational skills of Jer-OG and Jer-R. According to our working hypothesis, Jer-R had the advantage of possessing the OG translation which he tried to improve, and the data described in ch. III indeed indicate that Jer-R's translation was more precise and stereotyped than that of the OG.[9] Hence Thackeray's suggestion that Jer. β' (for him the second *translator*) was "unskilled"[10] and "the weaker scholar of the two"[11] is not borne out by the data collected by us nor are his own examples convincing (see n. 10). Further, it seems to us that Thackeray's group of "literal or unintelligent versions" in which he includes Jer. β'[12] is based on a wrong assumption: "literal" versions are not necessarily "unintelligent" and *vice versa*.

Nothing is known about the literary background and geographical origin of the reviser.

APPENDIX

Jer-R and the "Three"

Only a few characteristic renditions of Jer-R not retouched by Th and Aq have been transmitted as ϑ' or α' (see pp.
165ff.). As a rule, the "Three" altered renditions found in
Jer a' and b' in accordance with their own translation technique: e.g., Jer-OG's rendition of שׁדד, ταλαιπωρέω, was changed
by Jer-R to (ἀπ)όλλυμι (III 2). Aq,[13] on the other hand, generally rendered the Heb with προνομεύω (or προνομή), Sym used
mainly διαφθείρω, while Th, like Jer-OG, used ταλαιπωρέω
(ταλαίπωρος).

The following examples of renditions common to Jer-R and
the "Three" in their translations of the whole OT undoubtedly
indicate a close relationship--if not interdependence--between
them. It seems to us that the first example is rather important.

1. The most common LXX rendition of נאם 'ה is λέγει
κύριος, changed by Jer-R to φησὶ κύριος, occurring only three
times outside Jer b' (III 43). It is noteworthy, therefore,
that φησὶ κύριος is also the standard rendition of the "Three".
It is very hard to determine with whom this rendition originated.[14]

2. Jer-R changed Jer-OG's rendition of נדד (ἐξωθέω) to
διασπείρω (6 x) and σπείρω (1 x) (III 50). Since the rendition
of the Heb with διασπείρω recurs only once in the LXX (cf. also
three occurrences of διασπορά), it is significant that the
"Three", Dan-Th, O and L employ this rendition *passim*.[15]

3. Jer-OG's rendering of שׁממה, ἀφανισμός, was revised by
Jer-R to ἄβατος (III 1). This rendering occurs only in Jer-R
and in Sym in Ez 14:15 (LXX ἀφανισμός).

4. Jer-R revised μετά as a rendition of אחר(י) to ὕστερον
+ gen. (III 5). While this rendition does not occur elsewhere
in the LXX, it is found in Sym in Ps 72(73):24 and in the late
revision Ndpt in Num 31:2.[16]

162

2. *Why is Jer-R's Revision Preserved Only in Jer b'?*

To postulate a revision of Jer 29ff. only cannot be justified because it is hard to understand why a reviser would start
at 29:1, leaving aside the whole first part of the book. It is
assumed, therefore, that Jer a' has also undergone revision by
Jer-R, although such a revised text has not been preserved and
no vestige of this revision can be traced.[17]

It must be admitted that neither internal nor external
evidence known to us provides a reasonable clue as to why the
revision of Jer-R is found only in Jer b'. Therefore, we shall
have to turn to an irrational solution based on an assumption
that a mistake was made sometime between the preparation of the
original translation and the writing of our present manuscripts.
A calculation of the respective lengths of Jer a' and b'
presents the key to the solution of the problem: Both in their
Greek form[18] and in their Hebrew *Vorlagen*[19] the two are nearly
identical in length (if Bar 1:1-3:8 is included).[20,21] The
fact that the lengths of both Jer a' and b' equal half of Jer-
LXX leads to the assumption that Jer-LXX was divided into two
scrolls of approximately equal length, a rather common practice
in antiquity.[22] Hence it can be assumed that there were two
sets of scrolls of Jeremiah--one set of two scrolls of the OG
and another set of two scrolls containing an early revision of
the OG, namely Jer-R. For some reason, a scroll containing the
first half of the text type of the OG was combined with one of
the type of Jer-R, and this combination became the archetype of
the present text of Jer.

The redactor of the archetype probably did not realize
that he used two different text types or else was unable to ob-
tain two scrolls of the same kind since scrolls were scarce at
that time.[23] Even the improbable assumption that the redactor
purposely chose a revised scroll for Jer b' can be accommodated
in our hypothesis.

This description necessitates two additional presuppositions:

1. All the extant manuscripts of Jer-LXX are based on one
archetype, not necessarily identical in all details with the
first translation of Jeremiah. It should be noted that the

character of the MSS easily allows for the assumption of such
an archetype, of which MSS ABS are the best representatives.[24]

  2. The dividing line in both text types occurred at the
same point. It seems reasonable that, once the precedent of
breaking up Jer-LXX at a certain point was established, it was
perpetuated in later manuscripts. Moreover, the dividing line
between Jer a' and b' marks a clear contextual division which
can easily be remembered (cf. also n. 20).

  Our explanation of the present text of Jer is best sustained by referring to parallel phenomena in other books of the
LXX:

  1. In all the MSS of 1-4 Reigns, OG sections alternate
with sections of the *kaige*-Th revision in the following sequence:[25]

Reigns a'	(1 Sam)	OG
Reigns b'b'	(2 Sam 1 - 11:1)	OG
Reigns b'c'	(2 Sam 11:2 - 1 Ki 2:11)	*kaige*-Th
Reigns c'c'	(1 Ki 2:12 - 1 Ki 21)	OG
Reigns c'd'	(1 Ki 22 - 2 Ki)	*kaige*-Th

Thackeray's[26] and Barthélemy's[27] assumption that the alternation between Reigns b'b' and b'c' had a theological basis has
been refuted by Shenkel.[28] However, in starting Reigns b'c' at
2 Sam 10:1 rather than 11:1, Shenkel unfortunately had to admit
that "the reason for beginning the KR [= *kaige*-Th] at 10:1 is
not yet apparent" (*ib.*, 118).

  Similarly, no plausible solution has been suggested for
the alternation between Reigns c'c' and c'd'. Thackeray again
ascribed this alternation to theological factors,[29] while
Barthélemy (*ib.*, 142) followed by Shenkel (*ib.*, 63), suggested
that the *kaige*-Th section started at 1 Ki 22 because the LXX
arranged the preceding two chapters in an inverted order.[30]

  An attractive alternative solution was suggested by R. A.
Kraft.[31] As in our hypothesis for Jer, Kraft suggested that
the archetype of Reigns was composed of scrolls of different
text types, probably accidentally juxtaposed. The advantage of
this view over previous assumptions is that it considers the
alternation as unintentional, while the plausibility of the

intricate intentions, set forth by other scholars, is at best
dubious.

    2. The problem of the relationship between the two
(three) parts of Ez has yet to be investigated in detail.
While Thackeray distinguished two different translators,[32] and
Herrmann three,[33] Barthélemy[34] and Kase[35] differentiated between parts of the original translation and a later revision.
It is noteworthy for our discussion that Kase ascribed the
change of text type to a combination of two different scrolls.[36]

    3. There are important agreements and differences be-
tween the two parts of Is. Scholars who stressed the differences suggested that Is was rendered by two different translators (Is a' = 1-39; Is b' = 40-66).[37] On the other hand, those
who emphasized the similarities supported the unity of the
book.[38] Of them, Ziegler[39] and Seeligmann[40] were aware that
both the differences and the agreements should be explained
adequately and thus postulated either an earlier partial translation which was used by the translator, or a subsequent partial revision of Is. It is not impossible that the present
text of Is, too, resulted from a juxtaposition of two different scrolls.

    The suggestion that revised and unrevised scrolls were
juxtaposed in the archetypes of Jer, Reigns and Ez receives
further corroboration from the following facts:

    1. The whole LXX is a heterogeneous collection of differ-
ent text types, early and late, unrevised and revised.[41] Probable revisions are Eccl (= Aq?),[42] Dan(Th),[43] Lam (= *kaige*-
Th?),[44] 2 Chr.[45] Taking into consideration the fact that the
individual books of the LXX were either written on one scroll
or were composed of various scrolls, we may assume that some of
these scrolls happened to contain revisions. The fact that
there is no rational explanation of the situation that certain
books are of a mixed text type is thus paralleled by the inex-
plicable situation in which certain LXX books as a whole contain revisions.

    2. Various uncial MSS of the LXX contain early revisions
in certain books only, e.g., MSS AFM... in Ex.-Deut.[46]

3. Some uncial and minuscule MSS shift in a single book from one text type to another,[47] a situation which resulted from the scribes' using scrolls of different text types.

3. *The Date of Jer-R's Revision*

The date of Jer-R's anonymous revision cannot be determined with the aid of external evidence. Internal evidence is scanty, but nevertheless enables a reasonable determination of the revision. When adducing below data relating to the *terminus a quo* and *terminus ad quem* of Jer-R, we shall provide several alternative criteria since some of the data are problematic either by themselves or as a means for dating.

The date of the composition of Jer-OG serves as the sole *terminus a quo* for Jer-R. Since Sirach's grandson testifies[48] that he knew the προφῆται in Greek and since it can be shown that he actually used their text,[49] it may be presumed that Jer and Bar 1:1-3:8[50] were translated before 116 B.C.[51]

The following data may be used in fixing the *terminus ad quem* for Jer-R:

1. In three cases *kaige*-Th probably presupposes Jer-R: Within the LXX the rendition of נביא with ψευδοπροφήτης occurs eight times in Jer b', once in Jer a', and once in the MP (III 45). Thus from an occasional occurrence of ψευδοπροφήτης Jer-R developed a tendency to make it the main rendition of נביא when denoting a 'false prophet'.

Outside the LXX, ψευδοπροφήτης occurs a few times in Th (*sub* ✕), O (*sub* ✕) and L in Jer b'.[52] Because no additional ψευδοπροφήτης readings are transmitted for Th (O and L cannot be checked), it stands to reason that Th's readings in Jer b' presuppose the present text of Jer-R. Moreover, Th's use of ψευδοπροφήτης in 35(28):5 with reference to Hananiah depends upon 35(28):1, where the same prophet is named ψευδοπροφήτης (Jer-R).

The OG rendering of לבלתי, τοῦ μή, was revised by Jer-R to πρὸς τὸ μή (III 6), not found elsewhere in the LXX. Outside the LXX it occurs in two asterized passages in Jer 34:15(27:18)

Th, O, L and 41(34):10 O, L' (probably based upon an earlier
rendition of Th--Origen's main source in asterized passages--
which has not been preserved). The latter reading is doubtless
influenced by an identical reading of Jer-R in the same verse.

Since this rendition is not attested to elsewhere in Th[53]
and since it is limited within the LXX to Jer b', Th in Jer
necessarily depends upon the present text of Jer-R.

Jer-R's rendition of עת with χρόνος (III 10) is shared by
O in Esth 5:13 and α'θ' in Jer 37(30):7 καὶ χρόνος θλιψέως
(LXX καὶ χρόνος στενός). Since this rendition is not found
elsewhere in the LXX nor in Aq or Th, the α'θ' reading may
have depended upon the text of Jer-R. It is, however, also
possible that the marginal reading providing this information
is imprecise.[54]

It is thus safe to assume that Th in Jer presupposes the
present text of Jer-R. This assumption gains some support from
various renditions common to Jer-R and the "Three" (see p. 161)
since Th presumably preceded the other two revisers.[55] On
this basis it can be determined that Jer-R preceded the *kaige*-
Th group, of which the readings of Th in Jer formed part.[56]
However, at the present state of research, not only the precise
date of *kaige*-Th has yet to be determined (on the basis of the
leather scroll of the MP the date of *kaige*-Th is now ascribed
to the period preceding 50 A.D.,[57] or to the end of the first
pre-Christian century[58]); moreover, the number of strata of
which *kaige*-Th is composed[59] must also be ascertained and it
must also be determined whether Th in Jer can be assigned to
the probably pre-Christian stratum.

2. The quotations from Jer 38(31):31-34 in Hebr. 8:8-12
10:16 contain two renditions which are characteristic of Jer-R:
Hebr. 8:11 = Jer 38(31):34(33) πολίτης (IV 17).
Hebr. 8:9 = Jer 38(31):32 ἐν ἡμέρᾳ ἐπιβουλομένου μου (III 33).
Also other agreements in the same verses between Jer and Hebr.
permit the assumption that the author of Hebrews (80-90 A.D.)
knew the present text of Jer-R.

3. Within Greek literature the word ψευδοπροφήτης is nearly exclusively limited to the LXX of Jer b' (III 45; see also p. 165). Thus Josephus' employment of ψευδοπροφήτης (*Ant. Iud.* X, 111; based upon Jer 44(37), where this word is not used) is clearly based on the present text of Jer-R. Although the LXX text reflected in Josephus does not contain any other *characteristic* reading of Jer-R, it is so close to that of Jer b',[60] that Josephus must have known Jer b' in its revised form. The date of the *Ant. Iud.* is 93/94 A.D.

4. The text of Jer-R is reflected in the Vetus Latina,[61] dated in the middle[62] or toward the end[63] of the second century A.D.

On the basis of a synopsis of the above data, Jer-R's revision may be dated in general terms only--between approximately 116 B.C. and ca. 50 A.D. The following may suggest that Jer-R should be dated in the earlier part of this period:

(1) Since no traces of the OG of Jer b' could be found (see n. 17), it is reasonable to assume that only a short time lapsed between the writing of the OG and the composition of the archetype in which the OG of Jer b' was replaced.

(2) Jer-R's revision is remote from the slavish literalness of *kaige*-Th and Aquila. Since the general development of LXX revisions is towards greater literalness and consistency, Jer-R antedates the other revisions from a typological point of view. Also the other little-known revisions (such as Pap.Ryl. Gk. 458 of Deut, 4Q LXX Num, 7Q LXX Ex, Pap.Chester-Beatty-Scheide 967 of Ez) are dated before the turn of the eras, some as early as 100 or 150 B.C.

4. *Some Criteria for the Reconstruction of the OG of Jer b'*

The OG of Jer b' has been lost. However, in the course of chapters II-VI we have developed a few criteria for its reconstruction:

1. Whenever Jer a' and b' significantly agree in a rendition which distinguishes both from the other LXX books, the rendition in Jer b' belongs to the OG substratum of that section (ch. II).

168

2. Whenever Jer b' agrees in a characteristic rendition
with the MP and/or Ez, this rendition belongs to the OG substratum of Jer b' (ch. VI).

3. Whenever the relationship between two renditions of
the same Heb in Jer a' and b' is that of an original rendition
to its revision (ch. III), the rendition in Jer b' is secondary
and originated with Jer-R. The OG of Jer b' was presumably
identical to the rendition found in Jer a'.

4. The same may hold true when the renditions of Jer a'
and b' are merely synonymous (ch. IV).

5. Whenever Jer a'--in contrast with Jer b'--significant-
ly agrees with the OG of the MP and/or Ez, the former is the
original rendition, while that of Jer b' is probably secondary
(ch. VI). The OG of Jer b' was probably identical with Jer a'
= MP and/or Ez.

5. *Some Implications of the Present Study for the Understanding and Use of the "LXX"*

Our study presents a certain view of the relationship between the two sections of Jer as well as on the character of
the book of Bar. We cannot claim that our suggestion is without difficulty. There are too many gaps in our knowledge.
However, if we pause for a moment and assume that the theory is
correct, there are a few implications for LXX scholarship:

It is important for the understanding of the essence of
the LXX canon that an additional section of the "LXX" has been
described as a revision rather than the OG translation. This
shows once more that the "LXX" is a heterogeneous collection of
translations, original and revised, early and late, free and
literal.

For OT scholarship, the main importance of the LXX lies in
its Hebrew *Vorlage*, which at times may be superior to MT. The
retroversion of the LXX of Jer is of particular importance in
this respect, since we believe that its underlying text is generally older than the MT. More precisely, we have attempted to
show elsewhere that the two are recensionally different, the

LXX reflecting an early edition of the book of Jeremiah, and MT containing a later edition of that book.[64] Since a detailed retroversion of the LXX of Jer is of importance for this purpose and since it utilizes an investigation of translation options, one must constantly keep in mind that the second part of the book does not contain the original translation.

If our view of the nature of the Greek translation of Bar is correct, some tentative conclusions need to be drawn with reference to the study of the LXX in general, Bar's canonical status and its date.

1. It seems that the now apocryphal book of Bar was once joined with Jer, and was translated into Greek by the translator of the latter and revised by the same reviser who retouched the second part of Jer. This means that in the text-critical study of the LXX, the book of Bar must be taken into consideration in the same manner as Jer. Evidence from the LXX of Bar may be as important for solving textual problems as similar evidence from Jer.

2. Several Church Fathers of the second century and onwards quoted parts of Bar as "Jeremiah says..."[65] We thus know that for the readers of the canon of the LXX, Bar was considered either an appendix to Jer or part of it. We may assume the same status for Bar at an even earlier date, since both the translator and the reviser of Bar referred to Bar in the same way as they did to Jer.

3. The problem of the canonical status of Bar is raised not only by the anonymous revision of the book, but also by the other LXX revisions. Ziegler's edition of Bar contains several references to renderings by *kaige*-Th[66] as well as one reference to a rendering of Aquila.[67] This one reference seems insufficient proof that Aquila revised Bar as late as 130 A.D. But *kaige*-Th undoubtedly considered Bar as part of the canon.

It is noteworthy that this situation is quite unique with regard to the books of the Apocrypha. Of the Apocrypha only Bar and the additions to Dan are known to have been revised by *kaige*-Th, or, for that matter, by any of the "Three".[68]

4. The Hebrew text of Bar, now lost, was still extant at the time of the anonymous reviser. Otherwise he could not have performed his task. The same is true for the time of *kaige*-Th

170

as well as for Origen. For at two places in Bar marginal Hexaplaric notes state οὐ κεῖται (τοῦτο) παρὰ τῷ Ἐβραίῳ, i.e.,
"this word (these words) is (are) not found in the Hebrew."[69]
Also the occurrence in the Hexaplaric manuscripts of asterisks
and obeluses shows that Origen made use of a Hebrew text. On
the other hand, in the fourth century A.D. the Hebrew was unknown to Jerome.

NOTES

CHAPTER VII

1. For similar tendencies in other LXX revisions, see IV, n. 4.

2. See Reider, *Prolegomena*, 20ff. and Rahlfs-Lütkemann, 10-11 for Aq. For *kaige*-Th see Barthélemy, *Devanciers*, *passim*; Shenkel, *Kings*, 13ff., 113ff.; M. Smith, *Biblica* 48 (1967) 443-445 and J. A. Grindel, *CBQ* 31 (1969) 499-513.

3. See Reider, *Prolegomena*, 26ff. and Sois.-Soin., *Zusätze*, 151 for Aq. For *kaige*-Th, see Sois.-Soin., *ib.* and Schmitt, *Theodotion*, 61.

4. See Reider, *Prolegomena*, 16, 33 and App. I for Aq. For O, see Sois.-Soin., *Zusätze*, 155.

5. Jer-R altered the renderings of the following prepositions and conjunctions: לבלתי III 6; למען III 7; בעיני III 21; לפני III 22; מאין III 28; כי III 30; יען IV 5. He revised previous renditions of the Hebrew article (III 32) and of the *lamed* + inf. (IV 7). Jer-R also eliminated δέ as a rendering of the *waw* (III 31).

6. E.g., in 69 instances an earlier τάδε λέγει κύριος was revised by Jer-R to οὕτως εἶπε κύριος, while in three places it was left unrevised (cf. III 18). For further examples, see III 4,5,6,7,8,9,21,22,27,28,32(?),38,41,44,45,46(?),51,52(?) IV 4, 6,7(?),10,14,16,17,22,23.

7. In a few instances the revised and unrevised renditions are found in different parts of Jer (III 4,6,7,18 IV 17, 22), but their different distribution patterns cannot be coordinated into one coherent pattern. E.g., the assumption that Jer-R was less consistent in the beginning of Jer 29-52 holds for III 1 and 18 only.

8. One may, for example, investigate the word order praed./subj./obj. in relation to its *Vorlage* in both Jer a' and b'. Various aspects of this problem were examined by Martin, *Syntax*, 52,81. Neither Martin's investigation nor a pilot study of us carried out in several chapters of Jer a' and b' reveal significant differences between Jer a' and b'.

9. That Jer b' also gives the impression of a more literal translation than Jer a', is due to the fact that Jer b' contains more prose sections than Jer a'. The prose of Jer contains few problematic words and, as a rule, is easily translatable with stereotyped renditions.

10. Thus "Gr.Tr.Jer.", 256, where Thackeray also referred to Streane, *Jeremiah*, 194. Thackeray also noted that Jer. β' "contains the most glaring instances in the LXX of a translator

172

who was ignorant of the meaning of the Hebrew, having recourse
to Greek words of similar sound" (*Grammar*, 14). This characterization of Jer b' was repeated by Martin, *Syntax*, 312.
    Neither Streane's example (23:19-20 // 37(30):23-24) nor
those of Thackeray seem to justify their assertions. Thackeray's evidence merely consists of a few Greek transliterations
of difficult words and of exclamations which developed in the
MS tradition into similar Greek words, e.g., 38(31):21 תמרורים
- τιμωρίαν ex τιμρωριμ; 41(34):5 הורי אדרן - ἕως ᾅδου ex Ω αδων.
Moreover, even if the examples had been convincing, the transliterations might have been remnants of the OG translation of
Jer b', since similar ones are found in Jer a', e.g., 8:7 עגור
- ἀγροῦ ex αγουρ. On the transliterations, see Ziegler, *Beiträge*, 83-86 and E. Tov, *Textus* 8 (1973) 82ff.

    11. *Septuagint*, 32. Since Thackeray did not compare the
skill of Jer. β' with that of Jer. α', this description is ill-
founded.

    12. Thackeray, *Grammar*, 13.

    13. Cf. Reider, *Index Aquila*; J. Ziegler, *VT* 8 (1958)
277.

    14. An interesting, albeit naive, solution to this prob-
lem was suggested by H. P. Smith, *Hebraica* 3 (1887) 195, n. 1
and repeated by F. Schwally, *ZAW* 8 (1888) 199, n. 3 and Giesebrecht, *Jeremia*, xxxiv: According to these scholars, the φησὶ
κύριος readings in Jer b' derived from the Hexapla. However, it
should be argued that these readings are too numerous for such
an assumption and this suggestion does not account for the
other characteristic renditions of Jer-R.

    15. Jer 8:3 α'σ'; 23:3 α'σ'; 34:8(27:10) α'ϑ' OL; 36(29):
14,18 ϑ' OL; 50(43):5 α'ϑ' (acc. to MS 86).
    Since Aq generally rendered the Heb with ἐξωθέω (9 x), the
four renditions with διασπείρω probably originated with either
kaige-Th or Sym. Sym also rendered the Heb once with ἐξωθέω
(37(30):17).

    16. ὕστερον also renders קֶב in Prov 22:4 (Sym), Am 4:12
(Aq) and Gen 49:19 (anonymous note in Cod. Ambros.).

    17. We have been unable to trace vestiges of the OG text
of Jer b' or of a revision of Jer a'. In Tov, *Diss. Jeremiah*,
pp. 202-208, evidence was furnished which *could* be explained as
such; however, none of the examples is conclusive, since all
have alternative explanations. Our investigation was based
upon internal evidence in MSS and early papyri of Jer-LXX, as
well as quotations in Church Fathers, in the NT, the text of
Josephus and that of the secondary versions. For details and
bibliographical references, see *ib.*, 202-203.

    18. In MS A the relation between the two parts is 66-1/2:
62-1/2 columns.

    19. The MT of Jer a' comprises 48-2/3 pp. in the edition
of M. H. Letteris (London 1953), while that of Jer b' includes
49-1/4 pp. The number of pages for the *Vorlage* of Bar 1:1-3:8

is computed as follows: Jer-LXX (ed. Swete) : Jer-MT = Bar(Gk)
: x.

The Hebrew MS used by the Greek translators was one eighth
shorter than MT (see I, n. 1). Since both parts of the Greek
Jer are shorter than MT by the same ratio (see, e.g., the "con-
spectus" in Workman, *Jeremiah*, 283-398), the Hebrew *Vorlagen* of
Jer a' and b' must have related to each other as Jer a' and b'
in the MT.

20. The assumed dividing line (28:64-29:1 according to
the sequence of the LXX) divides the book into two equal parts
and at the same time it is suitable from a contextual point of
view: the oracles against two great powers, Egypt and Babylon,
occur on one side of the dividing line (26-28), while those
against the smaller nations (29-31) occur on the other. One
notes, however, that the oracles against Egypt and Babylon are
preceded in the LXX by an oracle against Elam (25:14-19(49:34-
39)). According to some scholars (see Rudolph, *Jeremia*, 245,
274), this situation indicates that the Greek translator considered Elam as a representative of a third great power, viz.
Persia. The same may be true for the Hebrew *Vorlage* of the LXX.

21. Attention should be drawn here to the fact that the
scribe of MS A left some space in the last line of ch. 28
(i.e., at the dividing line between Jer a' and b') which he
filled with nine arabesques (>). Similarly shaped arabesques
(>·, >I, >———) are also inserted after 41(34):7,11 and at
the end of chapters 42(35) and 46(39). The evidence suggests
that the scribe(s ?) of MS A often employed these arabesques in
empty spaces at the ends of lines so that the next unit would
start at the beginning of a new line. Indeed, in 29(47):1 and
41(34):12 (the lines after the arabesques) the new unit starts
with a capital letter, and in the other three instances the
next line, which contains the "title" of a new unit, is narrow-
er than the adjacent lines. See H.J.M. Milne and T. C. Skeat,
Scribes and Correctors of the Codex Sinaiticus (London 1938)
20-21 (where a similar use of arabesques in MS S is described)
and V. Gardthausen, *Griechische Palaeographie* (Leipzig 1879)
292.

Thackeray's suggestion ("Gr.Tr.Jer.", 260), followed by
Duval, "Jer", 401, that the arabesques after 28:64 in the LXX
show that the scribe of MS A knew of the bipartition of Jer-
LXX is not convincing. Thackeray (*ib.*) misrepresents the facts
since the arabesques are *not* "usually inserted only at the end
of a book".

22. That large units were divided in antiquity into different scrolls by authors, redactors and scribes was established by Th. Birt, *Das antike Buchwesen* (Berlin 1882) *passim*; *id.*,
Die Buchrolle in der Kunst (Leipzig 1907) 215ff.; L. Blau, *Studien zum althebräischen Buchwesen und zur biblischen Literatur-
geschichte* (Strassburg 1902) 46ff.; W. Schubart, *Das Buch bei
den Griechen und Römern* (Berlin 1907) 35ff.; M.St.J. Thackeray,
"The Bisection of Books in Primitive Septuagint MSS", *JThSt* 9
(1907-08) 88-98; F. W. Hall, *A Companion to Classical Texts*
(Oxford 1913) 8ff.; K. Huber, *Untersuchungen über den Sprach-
charakter des griechischen Leviticus* (Giessen 1916) 95-99.

The following data may be added to the ancient sources and evidence cited by the scholars mentioned above:
1. That 1QIs[a] was bisected by its scribes was suggested by P. Kahle, *Die hebräische Handschriften aus der Höhle* (Stuttgart 1951) 72-77; M. Noth, *VT* 1 (1951) 224-226; C. Kuhl, *VT* 2 (1952) 332-333; M. Martin, *The Scribal Character of the Dead Sea Scrolls* (Louvain 1958), 65-70.
2. The same holds true for 1QH, see E. L. Sukenik, אוצר המגילות הגנוזות (Jerusalem 5713) 33; M. E. Del Medico, *l'Énigme des manuscrits de la Mer Morte* (Paris 1957) 207-208, 483-484; Martin, *op. cit.*, 59-64.
3. Barthélemy, *Devanciers*, 167-168, showed that the leather scroll of the Greek MP was written by two scribes.
4. It is generally assumed that 1-2 Sam, 1-2 Ki, 1-2 Chr each originally formed one book (cf. Eissfeldt, *Introduction*, 268-269, 530) whose unity was first interrupted by the LXX translators.

23. The importance of the scrolls for the understanding of early deviating text types has been well described by Bickerman, "Transmission". Among other things, he stressed that there did not exist two identical or nearly identical scrolls of any Biblical book because of the many changes inserted in the individual scrolls.

24. See Ziegler, "Einleitung", 56-60.

25. See Thackeray, "Kings" and Barthélemy, *Devanciers*, 36 and *passim*.

26. According to Thackeray, "Kings", 263, the OG translator purposely omitted the unedifying section Reigns b'c' ("the story of David's sin and the subsequent disasters of his reign"), while a later *translator* filled in the gap.

27. According to Barthélemy, *Devanciers*, 140-141, the *kaige*-Th *reviser* of Reigns revised only that section which most urgently needed it, viz. "<le> récit de la faute et des malheurs de famille de David" (Reigns b'c'), especially since this section has no parallel in Chr.

28. Since Shenkel, *Kings*, 117-120 showed that Reigns b'c' did not start with 11:1, he undermined the basis for the assumptions of Thackeray and Barthélemy.

29. According to Thackeray, *ib.*, the OG translator omitted Reigns c'd' because of its contents ("the story of growing degeneracy under the later Monarchy culminating in the captivity"), while a later translator undertook the translation of the missing section.

30. According to Shenkel, the *kaige*-Th reviser originally retouched only 2 Ki, revising merely the chronology of 1 Ki since he did not wish to engage himself in a complete revision of that section. This partial revision involved the reworking öf the end of 1 Ki 22, while the remainder of the chapter was submitted to an even more superficial correction. However, Shenkel's complicated suggestion can not be supported by any evidence.

31. R. A. Kraft, *Gnomon* 37 (1965) 482: "Prior to the development of the codex in the early centuries of our era (especially 3rd-4th), it must have been an extremely difficult matter to retain a consistent text type throughout a work like
Samuel-Kings, which would require several scrolls for its
transcription. We do not know exactly what kind of MSS Origen
consulted in his text-critical labors, but it is safe to assume
that he had access both to scrolls and at least to small-scale
codices. Origen would have had little control over the integ-
rity of the text that came into his hands, especially if it ar-
rived in the form of a codex in which sections of originally
different textual nature had been juxtaposed through the transcription of older and shorter scrolls." Kraft's assumption
necessarily implies that the books 1-4 Reigns were written on
at least five scrolls, roughly corresponding with 1 Sam, 2 Sam
a', 2 Sam b', 1 Ki and 2 Ki (starting at 1 Ki 22).

32. Thackeray, "Ezekiel", distinguished between Ez a' (1-
27) + c' (40-48) and b' (28-39). Cf. also J. Schäfer, *Theologie und Glaube* 1 (1909) 289-291; E. H. Kase *apud* Johnson,
Scheide, 64; Turner, "Ezekiel", 17ff.

33. Herrmann in Herrmann-Baumgärtel, *Beiträge*, 1ff., distinguished between Ez a', b' and c'. This assumption was accepted with a slight change by Turner, "Ezekiel" (1956), although earlier it had been refuted convincingly by Kase, *ib.*,
52-73 (1938).

34. Barthélemy, *Devanciers*, 47, tentatively characterized
Ez a'c' as the OG, while ascribing Ez b' to a *kaige*-like revision. Cf. also pp. 150-51 above.

35. According to Kase, *ib.*, Ez a' reflects a revision,
while Ez a'b' contain the OG.

36. "The fact that this revision has made its influence
permanently felt only in I-XXVII is to be connected once more
with the practice of bisecting Scriptural books. The origin
of the type of text with which we are familiar would be sufficiently accounted for by a combination of two rolls, the first
of which contained the text of I-XXVII in its revised form, the
second containing the text of XVIII [read: XXVIII; E.T.] -
XLVIII in an unrevised form" (*ib.*, 73).

37. G. B. Gray, "The Greek Version of Isaiah, Is It the
Work of a Single Translator?", *JThSt* 12 (1911) 286-293; F.
Baumgärtel in Herrmann-Baumgärtel, *Beiträge*, 20-31.

38. J. Fischer, *In welcher Schrift lag das Buch Isaias
den LXX vor ?* BZAW 56 (Giessen 1930) 2-5; Ziegler, *Isaias*,
31ff.; Seeligmann, *Isaiah*, 39ff.

39. *Isaias*, 45-46.

40. *Isaiah*, 42.

41. The heterogeneous nature of the canon of the LXX cannot sufficiently be stressed; see especially R. A. Kraft, *IDBS*,
s.v. "Septuagint" (in press).

42. See G. A. Barton, *Ecclesiastes*, *ICC* (N.Y. 1908) 8-11, where earlier literature is mentioned; Thackeray, *Grammar*, 13, 60; Barthélemy, *Devanciers*, 21-33.

43. All MSS with the exception of 88-Syh(=O) and Pap.967 contain the text of "Th"; cf. Schmitt, *Theodotion*, where earlier literature is mentioned.

44. Barthélemy, *Devanciers*, 47. According to Barthélemy, Cant and Ruth are also "probably" part of the *kaige*-Th revision.

45. Barthélemy, *ib.*, mentions also 2 Chr as belonging to a *kaige*-like revision. Previously, 2 Chr was thought to have been revised by Th (H. Howorth and C. Torrey; for precise references, see Jellicoe, *SMS*, 290ff.), but this suggestion was refuted convincingly by B. Walde, *Die Esdrasbücher der Septuaginta*, *Biblische Studien* XVIII (Freiburg im Breisgau 1913) 37ff.; G. Gerleman, *Studies in the Septuagint, II: Chronicles* (Lund 1946) 1-7; R. W. Klein, *Studies in the Greek Text of the Chronicler*, unpubl. diss. Harvard Univ. (Cambridge, Mass. 1966) 311ff.

46. See D. W. Gooding, *Recensions of the Septuagint Pentateuch, Tyndale Lecture 1954* (London 1955). For additional examples, see P. Katz, "Rezensionen", 78ff. and Wevers, "Forschungen", 45ff.

47. Relevant examples are mentioned by Thackeray, *Septuagint*, 131 and G. F. Moore, *AJSLL* 29 (1912) 50-51; see further the introductions to the various volumes of the Göttingen Septuagint. MS 54 may serve as an example: In Gen 1-22:21 it reflects a mixed text according to J. Wevers (1974) or a Lucianic text according to Rahlfs (1926), while from 22:22 onwards it contains the text-type of the *Catenae*.

48. Prologue, 1.9.

49. See J. Ziegler, *BZAW* 77 (1958) 280-281.

50. As for the date of Bar, "all attempts to fix the date of the first part of the book--nay, of the book as a whole--have failed because no definite clues are available" (R. H. Pfeiffer, *History of N.T. Times* (N.Y. 1949) 415). The main criterion for the dating of Bar is the dependence of the prayer of repentance in 1:15-2:9 on Dan 9:4-19. Even though Dan 9 was added to the book of Dan at a later stage, its date is probably close to that of the bulk of Dan (167-164 B.C.). Thus nothing prohibits the dating of Bar in the period preceding 116 B.C., as was indeed done by Harwell, *Baruch*, 66; Pfeiffer, *op. cit.*, 413-416; T. André, *Les Apocryphes de l'A.T.* (Florence 1903) 257; Penna, *Baruch*, 13.

51. This is the generally accepted date of the Greek translation of Sirach. See U. Wilcken, *Archiv für Papyrusforschung* III (1906) 321; Eissfeldt, *Introduction*, 597.

52. Jer 35(28):5ϑ'(✗) O(✗)-233 L' Arm
     35(28):10π'(✗ Q; προφητης 86) L'-233 Chr
     35(28):12 L'-233
     35(28):15 L'-233 Arm^p Tht
     35(28):17 L'-233 Chr
            ψευδοπροφήτης occurs further in:
     20:1 כהן - ἱερεύς] ψευδοπροφητης 86^{txt}-710 233
     23:14 כהנים - προφήταις] ψευδοπροφηταις Chr
     34:13(27:16) נביאיכם - προφητῶν] ψευδοπροφητων Arab.

53. Ex 8:22(18) ὥστε μή   2 Sam 14:13 τοῦ μή
     2 Ki 23:10 ut non(Syh)   Ez 3:21 ἵνα μή
     Ez 13:22 τοῦ<καθόλου μή>α'ϑ'   Ez 17:4 τοῦ μή α'ϑ'.

54. The scribe who noted the variant reading of α'ϑ' in
the margin of MS 86 might have wished to record the difference
between LXX στενός and α'ϑ' ϑλιψέως only, while being imprecise
with regard to the preceding noun which he copied from the LXX.

55. Barthélemy, *Devanciers*, 246-253, 261-265, and O'Connell, *Theodotion*, have made it plausible that Aq and Sym did
not revise the OG, but rather improved upon the *kaige*-Th revision. If proved correct, this opinion may pinpoint the origin
of many, if not all, of the collective readings of the "Three"
as *kaige*-Th.

56. Barthélemy, *Devanciers*, 47, mentioned as belonging to
the *kaige* revision readings both from the Theodotion column and
"celles <sc. ajoutes Theodotion> souvent anonymes à la Septante
de Jérémie". Even though Barthélemy was intentionally vague
(on p. 44 he mentioned "ajoutes" without any classification,
thus including anonymous "ajoutes" and those which derived from
Aq), his conclusion on the character of Th in Jer is doubtless
correct. Barthélemy's characterization of Th is based mainly
upon the translation of כן with καίγε, which also characterizes
other members of the *kaige*-Th group; cf. Barthélemy, *ib.*, 31ff.;
Schmitt, *Theodotion*, 88; O'Connell, *Theodotion*, 275.
     One should note the following shortcomings of Barthélemy's
list of καίγε readings in asterized passages in Jer:
1. The list should not have included readings of Aq, such as
34:5(27:6) and 38(31):19.
2. 28(51):44 o' (ϑ' sec. Syh) ✗ (cf. the marginal note in the
Syh) is erroneously omitted from the list.
3. Not all the listed readings are "ajoutes"; the readings in
14:5 34:5(27:6) are mere corrections.
4. Since Barthélemy did not record the readings from the Syh,
he wrote, e.g., "VIII 12 καίγε ... 88 233, la marge de Q et
l'ensemble des manuscrits 'lucianiques'". However, the source
of these readings, viz. α'σ'ϑ' (✗), is not listed by Barthélemy, since it is mentioned in the Syh.

57. Barthélemy, *ib.*, 167ff.

58. Cross, *ALQ*, 171, n. 13.

59. Since Schmitt, *Theodotion*, has shown convincingly
that Th and Dan-Th are not to be identified as one reviser, the

178

kaige-Th group must be composed of at least two layers. Cf. also J. A. Grindel, *CBQ* 31 (1969) 511 and K. Koch, *VT* 23 (1973) 362-5.

    60. *Ant. Iud.* Χ,121 λάκκον βορβόρου πλήρη = Jer 45(38):6. Χ,137 διεσπάρησαν = 52:8.   ὄψεται... Χ,141 συλληφθεὶς ἀχθήσεται...καὶ λαλήσει αὐτῷ κατὰ στόμα καὶ/ τοὺς ὀφθαλμοὺς αὐτοῦ = 41(34):3 (the text of Jos. is not based on the reading of B-S-106'-538 Bo Aeth Arab all of which omit καὶ...στόμα), or does Jos. reflect 39(32):4? Χ,145 λυχνίας = 52:19. Χ,149 = 52:24,25. Χ,175 νήπια = 48:16 Syh^mg (B-S^C(τας λοιπας*)-130-239-538 A-106 O τα λοιπα; L-407 τους λοιπους; τα νηπια και τα λοιπα 449; τα καταλοιπα rel. Does Josephus here reflect the tradition found in Syh^mg, or rather is his text influenced by the LXX of 50(43):6, where the same expression occurs?

    61. 29:14(49:13) ὅτι εἰς ἄβατον - quia nemo pertransiet (cf. III 1). 29:18(49:17) ἔσται...εἰς ἄβατον - erit...sine vestigio (cf. III 1); both examples are quoted from F. C. Burkitt, *The Old Latin and the Itala, Texts and Studies* IV, 3 (Cambridge 1896) 81-92. 31(48):1 (and *passim*) οὕτως εἶπε κύριος - sic dicit Dominus (cf. III 18); quoted from F. C. Burkitt, *The Book of the Rules of Tyconius, Texts and Studies* III, 1 (Cambridge 1895) 53 and *passim*. Elsewhere in Tyconius τάδε λέγει κύριος is rendered with haec dicit Dominus (e.g., p. 79). 37(30):8,9 ἐργῶνται - operabuntur (cf. III 8); quoted from Huglo, "Fragments de Jérémie selon la Vetus Latina", *Vigiliae Christianae* 8 (1954) 83-86--as opposed to δουλεύω - servio in 13:10, quoted from E. Ranke, *Par Palimpsestorum Wirceburgensium Antiquissimae Veteris Testamenti Versionis Latinae Fragmenta* (Vindobonae 1871). 46(39):18 ἔσται ἡ ψυχή σου εἰς εὕρεμα - erit anima tua in inventione (cf. III 49); quoted from Ranke, *op. cit.*

    62. F. Stummer, *Einführung in die Lateinische Bibel* (Paderborn 1928) 8.

    63. Roberts, *Text and Versions*, 237.

    64. Cf. E. Tov, "L'incidence de la critique textuelle sur la critique littéraire dans le livre de Jérémie", *RB* 79 (1972) 189-199.

    65. The quotations are listed by Hoberg, *Baruch*, 7-19, while Harwell, *Baruch*, 61, cites some additional data to show that Bar was appended to Jer.

    66. 1:1,2 2:2,11,29 4:13.

    67. 2:13.

    68. We may disregard the one reference to Sym in Susanna 43 where σ' probably is a mistake for ο'.

    69. 1:17 2:3.

BIBLIOGRAPHY

AG   W.F. Arndt and F.W. Gingrich, *A Greek-
                          English Lexicon of the NT* (Cambridge
                          1957).

                          O.J. Baab, "A Theory of Two Translators
                          for the Greek Genesis", *JBL* 52 (1933)
                          239-243.

Barthélemy,   D. Barthélemy, *Les Devanciers d'Aquila*,
  Devanciers   *Suppl. to VT* 10 (Leiden 1963).

Baudissin, *Kyrios*   W.W. Graf von Baudissin, *Kyrios als Got-
                          tesname im Judentum und seine Stelle in
                          der Religionsgeschichte* (Giessen 1929).

BDB   F. Brown, S.R. Driver and Ch.A. Briggs,
                          A Hebrew and English Lexicon of the OT
                          (Oxford 1959).

BH   R. Kittel and P. Kahle, *Biblia Hebraica*[3]
                          (Stuttgart 1966).

Bickerman,   E.J. Bickerman, "Some Notes on the Trans-
  "Transmission"   mission of the Septuagint", *A. Marx
                          Jubilee Volume* (N.Y. 1950) 149-178.

Blass-Debrunner-Funk   F. Blass and A. Debrunner, *A Greek Gram-
                          mar of the NT*, translated and revised by
                          R.W. Funk (Chicago 1961).

Bright, *Jeremiah*   J. Bright, *Jeremiah*, *Anchor Bible* (N.Y.
                          1965).

                          S. Brock, *The Recensions of the Septua-
                          gint Version of I Samuel*, unpubl. diss.
                          Oxford Univ. (Oxford 1966).

Charles, *Apocrypha*   R.H. Charles (ed.), *The Apocrypha and
                          Pseudepigrapha of the OT* (Oxford 1913).

Cross, *ALQ*   F.M. Cross, Jr., *The Ancient Library of
                          Qumran and Modern Biblical Studies* (New
                          York 1961).

Cross, "Biblical   *Id.*, "The History of the Biblical Text in
  Text"   the Light of Discoveries in the Judaean
                          Desert", *HThR* 57 (1964) 281-299.

Duval, "Jer."   E. Duval, "Le texte grec de Jérémie
                          d'après une étude récente", *RB* 12 (1903)
                          394-403 (review of Thackeray, "Gr.Tr.
                          Jer.").

Eissfeldt, *Introduction*	O. Eissfeldt, *The OT, An Introduction,* etc., translated by P.R. Ackroyd (N.Y. and Evanston 1965).
Field, *Hexapla*	F. Field, *Origenis Hexaplorum quae Supersunt* (Oxonii 1875).
Frankl, "Studien"	P.F. Frankl, "Studien über die Septuaginta und Peschito zu Jeremia", *MGWJ* 21 (1872) 444-456; 497-509.
Fritsch, *Pentateuch*	C.T. Fritsch, *The Anti-anthropomorphisms of the Greek Pentateuch* (Princeton 1943).
Ghisler, *Catenae*	M. Ghislerii Romani, *In Ieremiam Prophetam Commentarii* (Lugduni 1623).
Giesebrecht, *Jeremia*	F. Giesebrecht, *Das Buch Jeremia*[2], *HK* (Göttingen 1907).
Gooding, *Recensions*	D.W. Gooding, *Recensions of the Septuagint - Pentateuch, Tyndale Lecture 1954* (London 1955).
Gooding, *Tabernacle*	*Id.*, *The Account of the Tabernacle, Translation and Textual Problems of the Greek Exodus, Texts and Studies* NS VI (Cambridge 1959).
	G.B. Gray, "The Greek Version of Isaiah: Is It the Work of a Single Translator?", *JThSt* 12 (1911) 286-293.
Harwell, *Baruch*	R.R. Harwell, *The Principal Versions of Baruch*, diss. Yale Univ. (New Haven, Conn. 1915).
	A. Hastoupis, *The Septuagint Text of the Book of Jeremiah (Chs. 1 to 25)*, unpubl. diss., Northwestern Univ. (Chicago 1950).
HR	E. Hatch and H.A. Redpath, *A Concordance to the Septuagint* (Oxford 1897).
Hatch, *Essays*	E. Hatch, *Essays in Biblical Greek* (Oxford 1889).
Helbing, *Grammatik*	R. Helbing, *Grammatik der Septuaginta, Laut und Wortlehre* (Göttingen 1907).
Helbing, *Kasussyntax*	*Id.*, *Die Kasussyntax der Verba bei den Septuaginta* (Göttingen 1928).
Herrmann-Baumgärtel, *Beiträge*	J. Herrmann and F. Baumgärtel, *Beiträge zur Entstehungsgeschichte der Septuaginta* (Berlin 1923).
Hoberg, *Baruch*	G. Hoberg, *Die älteste Lateinische Übersetzung des Buches Baruch* (Freiburg 1902).

G. Howard, "Some Notes on the Septuagint of Amos", *VT* 20 (1970) 108-112.

X. Jacques, *List of Septuagint Words Sharing Common Elements* (Rome 1972).

Janzen, *Jeremiah*   J.G. Janzen, *Studies in the Text of Jeremiah*, Harvard Semitic Monographs 6 (Cambridge, Mass. 1973).

Id., "Double Readings in the Text of Jeremiah", *HThR* 60 (1967) 433-447.

Jastrow   M. Jastrow, *A Dictionary of the Targumim, the Talmud Babli and Yerushalmi, etc.* (N.Y. 1903).

Jellicoe, *SMS*   S. Jellicoe, *The Septuagint and Modern Study* (Oxford 1968).

Johannessohn, *Kasus*   M. Johannessohn, *Der Gebrauch der Kasus und der Präpositionen in der Septuaginta. I: Gebrauch der Kasus* (Berlin 1910).

Johannessohn, *Präpositionen*   *Id.*, *Der Gebrauch der Präpositionen in der Septuaginta*, NAWG, Phil.-Hist. Kl. *1925, Beiheft* (Berlin 1926).

Johnson, *Scheide*   A.C. Johnson, H.S. Gehman and E.H. Kase (edd.), *The John H. Scheide Biblical Papyri. Ezekiel* (Princeton 1938).

Johnson, *Samuel*   B. Johnson, *Die Hexaplarische Rezension des 1. Samuelbuches der Septuaginta, Studia Theologica Lundensia* 22 (Lund 1963).

S.E. Johnson, *The Septuagint Translators of Amos*, diss. Univ. of Chicago (Chicago 1938).

Kaminka, *Studien*   A. Kaminka, *Studien zur Septuaginta an der Hand der zwölf kleinen Prophetenbücher* (Frankfurt a. M. 1928).

Katz, "Rezensionen"   P. Katz, "Frühe hebraisierende Rezensionen der Septuaginta und die Hexapla", *ZAW* 69 (1957) 77-84.

Katz-Ziegler, "Aquila-Index"   *Id.* und J. Ziegler, "Ein Aquila-Index in Vorbereitung", *VT* 8 (1958) 264-285.

Kneucker, *Baruch*   J.J. Kneucker, *Das Buch Baruch* (Leipzig 1879).

Köhler, "Beobachtungen"   L. Köhler, "Beobachtungen am hebräischen und griechischen Text von Jeremia Kap. 1-9", *ZAW* 29 (1909) 1-39.

R. A. Kraft, *Gnomon* 37 (1965) 474-483 (review of Barthélemy, *Devanciers*).

E. Kühl, *Das Verhältniss der Massora zur Septuaginta in Jeremia* (Halle 1882).

Levy — J. Levy, *Wörterbuch über die Talmudim und Midraschim* (Berlin und Wien 1924).

LSJ — H.G. Liddell and R. Scott, *A Greek-English Lexicon*[9], revised by H.S. Jones (Oxford 1940).

LSJ, *Suppl.* — E.A. Barber, *A Greek-English Lexicon, A Supplement* (Oxford 1968).

Martin, *Syntax* — R.A. Martin, *The Syntax of the Greek of Jeremiah, Part I: The Noun, Pronouns and Prepositions in their Case Constructions*, unpubl. diss. Princeton Theol. Sem. (Princeton, N.J. 1957).

Id., "Some Syntactical Criteria of Translation - Greek", *VT* 10 (1960) 295-310.

J.D. Michaelis, *Observationes in Jeremiae Vaticinia*, ed. J.F. Schleusner (Goettingae 1793).

F.C. Movers, *De Utriusque Recensionis Vaticiniorum Ieremiae...Commentatio Critica* (Hamburgi 1837).

T. Muraoka, "Is the Septuagint Amos VIII 12 - IX 10 a Separate Unit?", *VT* 20 (1970) 496-500.

O'Connell, *Theodotion* — K.G. O'Connell, S.J., *The Theodotionic Revision of the Book of Exodus*, Harvard Semitic Monographs 3 (Cambridge, Mass. 1972).

Penna, *Baruch* — A. Penna, *Baruch, La Sacra Bibbia* (Roma-Torino 1956).

Preisigke — F. Preisigke, *Wörterbuch der griechischen Papyrusurkunden* (Berlin 1925-31).

Rahlfs-Lütkemann — A. Rahlfs and L. Lütkemann, *Hexaplarische Randnoten zu Isaias 1-16*, *NAWG, Phil.-Hist. Kl. 1915* (Berlin 1916).

Reider, *Prolegomena* — J. Reider, *Prolegomena to a Greek-Hebrew and Hebrew-Greek Index to Aquila* (Philadelphia 1916).

Reider, *Index Aquila* — *Id.*, *An Index to Aquila*, completed and revised by N. Turner, *Suppl. to VT* 12 (Leiden 1966).

Roberts, *Text and Versions* B. J. Roberts, *The OT Text and Versions* (Cardiff 1951).

W. Rudolph, "Zum Text des Jeremia, I: Zum griechischen Text", *ZAW* NF 7 (1930) 272-281.

Rudolph, *Jeremia* *Id.*, *Jeremia*^{2}, *HAT* (Tübingen 1958).

Schleusner J. F. Schleusner, *Novus Thesaurus Philologico-Criticus sive Lexicon in LXX* (Lipsiae 1820-21).

M. Schmidt, "The Book of Jeremiah", *The New World* (1900) 655-675.

Schmitt, *Theodotion* A. Schmitt, *Stammt der sogenannte "ϑ'" - Text bei Daniel wirklich von Theodotion?*, *MSU* IX (Göttingen 1966).

A. Scholz, *Der Masorethische Text und die LXX. Übersetzung des Buches Jeremias* (Regensburg 1875).

Schulz, *De Ieremiae Textus Hebraici Masorethici et Graeci Alexandrini Discrepantia* (Treptow a.d. R. 1861).

Seeligmann, *Isaiah* I. L. Seeligmann, *The Septuagint Version of Isaiah, A Discussion of its Problems* (Leiden 1948).

Shenkel, *Kings* J. D. Shenkel, *Chronology and Recensional Development in the Greek Text of Kings* (Cambridge, Mass. 1968).

Sois.-Soin., *Richter* I. Soisalon-Soininen, *Die Textformen der Septuaginta-Übersetzung des Richterbuches*, *AASF B* 72,1 (Helsinki 1951).

Sois.-Soin., *Zusätze* *Id.*, *Der Charakter der asterisierten Zusätze in der Septuaginta*, *AASF B* 114 (Helsinki 1959).

Sois.-Soin., *Infinitive* *Id.*, *Die Infinitive in der Septuaginta*, *AASF B* 132 (Helsinki 1965).

Spohn, *Ieremias Vates* M.G.L. Spohn, *Ieremias Vates e Versione Iudaeorum Alexandrinorum, etc.* (Lipsiae 1794-1824).

Streane, *Jeremiah* A. W. Streane, *The Double Text of Jeremiah (Massoretic and Alexandrian) Compared etc.* (Cambridge 1896).

Swete, *Introduction* H. B. Swete, *An Introduction to the OT in Greek*^{2} (Cambridge 1914).

184

S. Talmon, "Synonymous Readings in the Textual Traditions of the OT", *Scripta Hierosolymitana* 8 (1961) 335-383.

Thackeray, "Gr.Tr.Jer."
H.St.J. Thackeray, "The Greek Translators of Jeremiah", *JThSt* 4 (1902-03) 245-266.

Thackeray, "Ezekiel"
Id., "The Greek Translators of Ezekiel", *ib.*, 398-411.

Thackeray, "Proph."
Id., "The Greek Translators of the Prophetical Books", *ib.*, 578-585.

Thackeray, "Kings"
Id., "The Greek Translators of the Four Books of Kings", *JThSt* 8 (1906-07) 262-278.

Id., "The Bisection of Books in Primitive Septuagint MSS", *JThSt* 9 (1907-08) 88-98.

Thackeray, *Grammar*
Id., *A Grammar of the OT in Greek according to the Septuagint* (Cambridge 1909).

Thackeray, *Septuagint*
Id., *The Septuagint and Jewish Worship, Schweich Lectures 1920* (London 1921).

Thesaurus
A. Stephanus, *Thesaurus Graecae Linguae* (Parisiis 1842-47).

ThWNT
G. Kittel und G. Friedrich (edd.), *Theologisches Wörterbuch zum NT* (Stuttgart 1933 -).

Tov, *Diss. Jeremiah*
E. Tov, *The Septuagint Translation of Jeremiah and Baruch - A Discussion of an Early Revision of Jeremiah 29-52 and Baruch 1:1-3:8*, unpubl. diss. Hebrew University (Jerusalem 1973).

Id., "L'incidence de la critique textuelle sur la critique littéraire dans le livre de Jérémie", *RB* 79 (1972) 189-199.

Id., "The Relation between the Greek Versions of Baruch and Daniel", in: M.E. Stone (ed.), *Studies in the Bible and Armenian Philology* (Jerusalem 1975).

Tov, *Baruch*
Id., *The Book of Baruch (Greek and Hebrew), Texts and Translations, Pseudepigrapha Series* 6, *SBL* (1975).

Turner, "Ezekiel"
N. Turner, "The Greek Translators of Ezekiel", *JThSt* NS 7 (1956) 12-24.

Turner, *Syntax*
Id., *apud* J.H. Moulton, *A Grammar of NT Greek*, vol. III *Syntax* (Edinburgh 1963).

Walters, *Text*   P. Walters, *The Text of the Septuagint,*
                           Its Corruptions and their Emendation
                           (Cambridge 1973).

                           B. M. Wambacq, "Les prières de Baruch
                           (1,15 - 2,19) et de Daniel (9,5-19)",
                           Biblica 40 (1959) 463-475.

                           Id., "1'Unité littéraire de Bar., I-III,
                           8", in: J. Coppens (ed.), *Sacra Pagina*
                           I = Bibl. Ephem. Theol. Lovar. XII-XIII
                           (Paris 1959) 455-460.

Wevers,   J. Wevers, "Septuaginta Forschungen seit
  "Forschungen"   1954", *ThR* 33 (1968) 18-76.

                           I. Wichelhaus, *De Jeremiae Versione*
                           Alexandrina (Hallis 1847).

Workman, *Jeremiah*   G. C. Workman, *The Text of Jeremiah*
                           (Edinburgh 1889).

Ziegler, *Isaias*   J. Ziegler, *Untersuchungen zur Septua-*
                           ginta des Buches Isaias, Alttestament-
                           liche Abhandlungen XII,3 (Münster i.W.
                           1934).

Ziegler, "Pap. 967"   *Id.*, "Die Bedeutung des Chester-Beatty
                           Scheide Pap. 967 für die Textüberliefer-
                           ung der Ezekiel-Sept.", *ZAW* 61 (1945-48)
                           76-94 = *Sylloge* (1971), 321-339.

                           Id., "Die Septuaginta Hieronymi im Buch
                           des Propheten Jeremias", in: B. Fischer
                           und V. Fiala (edd.), *Colligere Frag-*
                           menta, Festschrift Alban Dold, Texte und
                           Arbeiten I,2 (Beuron 1952) 13-24 =
                           Sylloge (1971) 345-356.

Ziegler, *Ier.*   *Id., Ieremias, Baruch, Threni, Epistula*
                           Ieremiae, VT Graecum, Auctoritate So-
                           cietatis Litterarum Gottingensis Editum,
                           Vol. XV (Göttingen 1957).

Ziegler,   *Id., ib.,* 7-146 ("Einleitung").
  "Einleitung"

Ziegler, *Beiträge*   *Id., Beiträge zur Ieremias-Septuaginta,*
                           NAWG, Phil.-Hist. Kl. 1958, 2 (Göttingen
                           1958).

                           Id., "Jeremias-Zitate in Väter-Schriften",
                           Historisches Jahrbuch 77 (1958) 347-357
                           = *Sylloge* (1971) 439-449.

GREEK AND HEBREW INDEXES

The Greek and Hebrew indexes list all the Hebrew words and
their main Greek renditions which are discussed in the numbered
items of chapters II-VII.

The Hebrew index is arranged according to the alphabet.

ἄβατος	III 1	V 5,11	VII 3
ἀβατόω	III 1		
ἄκρον	IV 13		
ἀλαλάζω	II 6		
ἀλγηρός	II 39		
ἀληθῶς	III 3		
ἀλίσκομαι	IV 11		
ἀλλότριος	III 19	VI 2	
ἄλσος	VI 36		
ἅμα	III 37		
ἁμαρτάνω	III 27		
ἀμελέω	II 43		
ἄμφοδον	II 32		
ἀνάγω	III 34		
ἀναξηραίνω	VI 24		
ἀναπαύομαι	III 9		
ἀνάπτω	IV 14		
ἀνασῴζω	IV 16		
ἀνθίστημι	II 30		
ἀνθ'ὦν	IV 5		
ἀνορθόω	II 20		
ἀντέχω	VI 10		
ἅπας	II 19		
ἀπό	III 28	V 16	
ἀποδοκιμάζω	II 10		
ἀποικισμός	II 42	V 30	
ἀπόλλυμι	III 2		
ἀπολογέομαι	II 40		
ἀπορρίπτω	II 2	VI 32	
ἀποστολή	V 3		

188

ἀποσφράγισμα	V 56			
ἀπώλεια	III 16	VI 60		
ἄρχων	III 47			
ἀσεβεία	VI 62			
ἀσεβέω	IV 8	VI 62		
ἀτιμία	VI 45			
ἀφανίζω	III 1	VI 61		
ἀφανισμός	III 1	V 15	VI 61	VII 3
ἀφίστημι	IV 8	VI 39		
βελόστασις	VI 50			
βόλις	VI 66			
βομβ-	V 19			
βομβέω	IV 24			
βραχίων	III 4			
γένοιτο	III 3			
γένος	III 46			
γιγνώσκω	III 38			
δέ	III 31			
δεσμώτης	II 27	V 28		
δέχομαι	III 23			
διασκορπίζω	III 12			
διασκορπισμός	VI 49			
διασπείρω	III 50	V 13	VII 2	
διὰ τὸ μή	III 28			
διεκβολή	VI 81			
διοδεύω	VI 67			
διόρυγμα	VI 31			
διότι	III 30	VI 70		
δουλεύω	III 8			
δοῦλος	III 42	V 12		
δυνατός	III 51	V 23		
ἐγχειρέω	II 31			
ἐγχείρημα	II 31			
εἰ	III 17			
εἶπε κύριος	III 18			
εἶπον	IV 4			
εἰσδέχομαι	VI 74			
ἐκδιώκω	II 29			
ἐκλαμβάνω	III 23			

ἐκλείπω	II 17	V 9	VI 35,44
ἐκλεκτός	II 3	VI 34	
ἐκταμένος	IV 19		
ἐκφέρω	III 34		
ἐμοῦ	III 50		
ἐμπυρίζω	IV 14		
ἐναντίον	III 21,22	V 17	
ἐνθύμημα	VI 79		
ἐνοικέω	V 27		
ἐντέλλομαι	IV 22		
ἐν τῷ αυτῷ	III 36		
ἐνώπιον	III 21,22	V 17	
ἐξάγω	III 34		
ἐξακολουθέω	VI 17		
ἐξίστημι	VI 38		
ἔξωθεν	II 14	V 29	
ἐξωθέω	III 50	V 13	VII 2
ἐπειδή	IV 5		
ἐπιγιγνώσκω	III 38		
ἐπίσταμαι	III 38		
ἐπιστάτης	IV 9		
ἐπὶ τὸ αὐτό	III 36		
ἐπίχειρον	III 4		
ἐραστής	VI 76		
ἐργάζομαι	III 8	V 12	
ἐρῶ	IV 4		
ἔσχατον	IV 10		
ἕτερος	III 19	V 21	VI 2
εὕρεμα	III 49		
ἔχω	III 24		
ἡγεμών	III 47		
ἥκω	II 28		
ἡμέρα	III 33		
ἤχω	IV 24		
θεός	III 37		
θεοὶ ἕτεροι	III 19	V 21	
θνησιμαῖον	IV 18		
ἰάομαι	IV 12		
ἰατρεύω	IV 12		

κυμαίνω	IV 24		
κυριεύω	V 4		
κύριος	III 37		
λαλέω	III 44		
λαλέω μετὰ κρίσεως	II 16		
λαμβάνω	III 23	IV 8	VII 6
λέγει κύριος	III 43	VII 1	
λέγω	IV 4		
λῆμμα	VI 6		
λῃστής	VI 72		
λίαν	II 23		
λοιμός	VI 46		
μαιμάσσω	IV 24		
μαίνομαι	III 14		
μάχαιρα	IV 21		
μαχήτης	III 51	IV 7	
μεγιστάν	II 11	VI 9	
μέρος	IV 13		
μετά	III 5	VII 4	
μεταμέλομαι	III 9		
μετανοέω	III 9	VI 3	
Ναγεβ	III 15		
νεκρός	IV 18		
νομή	III 48	VI 63	
νόμιμα	VI 71		
νότος	III 15		
νύμφη	VI 18		
οἶδα	III 38		
οἴχομαι	II 25		
ὄλεθρος	II 8	III 3	
ὄλλυμι	III 3		
ὁμοθυμαδόν	III 36		
ὁμορέω	VI 42		
ὅπως	III 7		
ὄρθρου	II 7		
ὅτι	III 30		
οὐ	III 40		
οὕτως εἶπε κύριος	III 18	V 14	
οὐχι	III 41		

Σορ	VI 41	
σπείρω	III 5	
σπέρμα	III 46	
σπεύδω	IV 24	
στάζω	IV 20	
στερέω	II 4	
στηρίζω	III 11	VI 68
στρουθός	II 13	
συγκόπτω	III 12	
συλλαμβάνω	IV 11	
σύλληψις	II 44	VI 36
σύμμ(ε)ικτος	II 24	
συμψάω	II 37	
συνέρχομαι	VI 14	
συνοχή	VI 15	
συντάσσω	IV 22	V 25
συντριβή	III 35	
σύντριμμα	III 35	
συντριμμός	III 35	VI 29
συστρέφω	VI 64	
συστροφή	VI 64	
σχοῖνος	VI 23	
σῴζω	IV 16	
τάδε λέγει κύριος	III 18	V 14
ταλαιπωρέω	III 2	V 11
ταλαιπωρία	III 2	VI 1
τεκνοποιέω	II 21	
τέσσαρα	VI 77	
τὸ παράπαν	VI 80	
τόπος	III 48	
τοῦ μή	III 6	
τρυμαλία	II 41	
ὑγρασία	VI 59	
ὑπάρχω	III 29	
ὑποκαίω	VI 78	
ὑποχείριος	V 1	
ὕστερον	III 5	VII 4
ὑψηλός	IV 19	
φαρέτρα	VI 43	

194